# GROWING UP
# ON ORIOLE STREET

# GROWING UP
# ON ORIOLE STREET

*A Rochester Boyhood*
*. . . and Beyond*

---

## Bob Gibbons

*Full Court Press*
*Englewood Cliffs, New Jersey*

*First Edition*

Copyright © 2022 by Robert J. Gibbons

Published in the United States of America
by Full Court Press, 601 Palisade Avenue,
Englewood Cliffs, NJ 07632
*fullcourtpress.com*

ISBN 978-1-953728-02-9
Library of Congress Control No. 2021924357

*All pictures courtesy of the author*

*Author photo by Jeanne Gibbons*

*Picture preparation by Doug Pileri*

*Cover picture: Jeanne and Bob Gibbons, soon after they were married,
reflected in a mirror of his boyhood home on Oriole Street.*

*Editing and book design by Barry Sheinkopf*

# Chapters In A Life

# An Introduction: Telling Stories

FOR AS LONG AS I CAN REMEMBER, I've loved telling stories. Back when our kids were very young, I often told those stories around the kitchen table, to let my family know what happened at work that day. Jennifer, our eldest, was also our most skeptical child. "Dad," she asked one day, "how come when you tell a story, you're always the hero?"

The heroes in this book are mostly not me; they're some of the many unforgettable people who made a difference in my life along the way. They helped make my life as regret-free as any life I can possibly imagine. If I were able to do everything all again, I'd do it the same way—and be equally grateful.

So much of my gratitude—and my stories—can be traced back to Jeanne, our kids, and grandkids, as well as to the home I grew up in and the parents and siblings I had. The Kodak family I was so much a part of also played a vital role. Jeanne and I came from a blue-collar neighborhood during the 1950s, a time and a place when few around us had more than they needed to get by—and, when we married, she and I never expected to have much more. But we do. And we still ask ourselves: How could we be so lucky?

A boyhood in the '50s and beyond was a good time, a safe time, a happy time, a time I want always to remember—and so at some point, I decided to put it down in writing. I wanted our grandkids to know, someday, where at least one of their grandparents came from, how it was back then. And I thought others might also be interested.

As I got into the writing, I found that memories were triggering others, making new connections, taking me in new directions. Once I got my *way-back gy-*

*roscope* spinning, I followed along. What started as one long story became a series of shorter, often overlapping, chapters; I've also included a picture or two of some who made a difference on the journey.

But this book is not a strictly sequential telling; like my life, it's about people and stories and moments; chronology just helps to make connections, to provide some context, to keep everything from happening at once. In the process, I've left out more than I've put in.

There will always be a lot of small-town neighborhood boy in me—and I'm proud of that. I grew up with good values—and if they're not the ones that are included on a resume, I hope they find their way into my eulogy, because they were the foundation for a rewarding life. It's enjoyable—even comforting—to go back there for another look, to wander around again in the days of my youth and beyond.

And so, if you want to join an improbable adventure, I invite you to come along on the journey back through my yesterdays. These are some of the stories of a Rochester boyhood and beyond; this is how I remember it, once upon a time, starting with the days I spent growing up on Oriole Street.

# I

# THE $8,000.00 HOUSE
# ON THE CORNER

O N A COOL AND CLOUDY DAY in October 1954, we moved into the house where I'd spend the rest of my youth. My father and uncles handled the move and after they had loaded the rented truck, they let me ride in the open back with the appliances, hanging on. My mother would have been apoplectic if she had seen that. I was seven-and-a-half years old, but I was feeling very grown-up that day.

We were moving into a duplex, a two-family home built in 1910, the same timeframe as most other homes in the neighborhood. Because it was a corner house, it had two very different addresses: 234 Oriole Street where we'd live— and 429 Driving Park Avenue, the side we'd rent to tenants.

My parents paid $8,000.00 for the house, but the rent they'd charge would cover the payments. My mother told me, "it's like living for free"; but before that could happen, my father needed to completely refinish that other side of the house. Since he did most of the work himself, that took about a year.

When the job was done, a family named the Clappers moved in and perhaps because the rent was only eighty-five dollars a month for a half-a-house, they stayed for fifteen years. They were quiet and never complained.

The house was brown and white when we moved in. My father hired three

Black men to repaint it—green on top, yellow on the bottom. He worked on ladders alongside them doing the painting; it was the first time I had seen Black people up close.

Our porch on the front faced west, so it could get warm in the evenings, but by the time I got to high school, I used to sit on a glider out there after dinner, reading the evening newspaper.

That's where I read, in September of 1962, that a high school freshman, Pamela Moss, had been strangled, raped, killed, and her body left in a ditch—and it all happened in a Rochester suburb. It took a whole year to convict a gardener, James Moore, who confessed to the crime. It was the first I read of a murder so close to home. Plus, Pamela was my age; it was scary stuff.

Behind that porch on Oriole Street was a room we called a front hall, with our only phone hanging on the wall. We had a party line—where several other families had the same number—so we had to take turns making calls. Sometimes we'd pick up the phone to find one of those other families talking. And, in the beginning, we made all calls by telling the operator what number we were calling—and asking her to "connect us." There was no dial—or keypad.

Every year, in late December, we used to put up our Christmas tree in that same room. We always had a live tree that my father got at the very last minute—and most likely for the lowest possible price. It was hard to camouflage—with ornaments and tinsel—how misshapen those trees sometimes were. And the lights we had were the kind that when one went out, the whole string died—so it often took forever to figure out which one was bad.

Off the front hall, a small passage led to the kitchen in the back of the house. Dad remodeled and enlarged that kitchen extensively three years after we moved in. He installed modern appliances and a pink-speckled Formica countertop—and hired an old German carpenter to refinish the cabinets with several coats of a light gray stain.

Next to the kitchen—via a big wide archway Dad built—was the dining room and in front of that, a living room of about the same size. The last time I was in the dining room was the night before I left to join the army and my parents had us over for dinner. When Jeanne and I got ready to leave, my father wished me good luck; there were tears in my mother's eyes.

On the second floor of our house, we had three bedrooms and a bath. In the beginning, my brother and I slept in the room at the top of the stairs, my two sisters slept in the room straight ahead, and my parents slept in the front bedroom facing Oriole Street. The bathroom was down a short hall, right next to the attic door. I spent a lot of nights with a *Hardy Boys* book on the floor next to my bed, reading by the light in the hall.

By day, I sometimes ventured into the attic. It was a place where treasures were stored.

There were a couple of heavy dressers up there with miscellaneous stuff in their drawers, but the good stuff seemed to be hidden in old suitcases and other cases under the eaves. I found a metal helmet from World War I, a red Nazi armband with a black swastika from World War II, and all my dad's army clothing from that same war. Also, in some cases, I found the components of a drum set that would one day be mine.

The attic was boiling hot in the summer and freezing cold in the Rochester winters, but it was always a place of solitude, a place to get away. I sometimes brought my drums up there—and with a record player plugged via an extension cord, I played along to records of the big bands of Mom's generation. And in eighth grade, on spring mornings before school when the attic was cool, I did my homework up there.

But the full basement was probably our home's most functional space. There was no air conditioning in those days and the basement was the coolest place in summer heat, so Dad had installed a stove down there where my mom could cook; we also had a small refrigerator, and in the center of the biggest area at the bottom of the stairs, we sometimes ate at a heavy white wooden table with six heavy wooden chairs.

Originally the house was heated with coal—I remember it being dumped down a chute into a large wooden bin—but Dad eventually converted the furnace to oil. Still, the furnace was huge and dominated the basement space.

Next to it, we'd often have a very large open box of potato chips. One of my aunt's relatives worked at the local Schuler Potato Chip factory, and when they burned a large batch of chips, he'd put them in a box and bring them to us. Burned potato chips are still my favorite.

Also in the basement, we had a toilet in a small room beneath the stairs and, in the far corner, a fruit cellar—a small space that we often used as a dressing room when my brother and I put on plays down there, mostly using Dad's old army clothing, with jokes we stole from a favorite TV show, *Sgt. Bilko.*

In front of the fruit cellar, near the wall that separated our basement from the Clappers', was a groove that ended in a capped pipe sunk into the cement. It was a drain into the street sewer—and when it rained hard, and the outside sewers flooded, filthy water poured into the basement. It could rise as much as a foot high during a bad storm; when the water dissipated, I remember my parents washing everything down with Clorox.

Outside, at the end of a short driveway was a two-car garage that never held cars. Instead, it held bikes and baseball gear and whatever my brother and I happened to be building at the time. Along one wall was Dad's very long, incredibly sturdy, obviously homemade workbench with world's heaviest vice bolted to one end. Underneath were half-filled paint cans of every color. And everywhere there were my father's "projects"—broken washing machines and dryers he had in some state of repair.

Sometime during the early 1970s, my parents moved out. According to family lore, Dad forged Mom's signature on the sales agreement; when he told her that the house where she raised her family had been sold, she was heartbroken. The selling price was somewhere around $50,000.00; Mom split part of her share among us kids.

It was the end of having a home in a neighborhood close to everything, a home where people didn't lock their doors, didn't call before they came over; they just dropped by. It was a place of comfort and warmth and I credit a lot of that to our mom; she did everything she could—sometimes against what must have felt like insurmountable odds—to keep our family together; we were lucky to have a mother who always wanted to be a mom.

# 2

# SHE WANTED TO BE A MOM

MOM WANTED TO GET MARRIED as soon as possible; by the 1940s she had passed her mid-twenties, and she worried that time was running out for her to start a family.

But those were the days of World War II and Dad was stationed on the island of New Guinea, where Japanese fighting was intense, so there were no long leaves before he was discharged in December 1945. Sixty-four days later, at 8:00 a.m. on March 3, 1946, they were married by Dad's brother, Father Paul, a catholic priest, in Holy Apostles Church on Lyell Avenue in Rochester. Mom wore a navy-blue suit. Dad wore gray.

Exactly thirteen months later, I was born. Mom and Dad were living with his widowed father in the home where he had grown up. Even then, he was around only occasionally; he worked during the day, was often out drinking alone at night. Mom was doing the best she could, without training and without much support; but she loved her role as a mom. "Enjoy the days when they're small," she told Jeanne and me when we had children, "because they grow up so quickly."

She had a tough childhood of her own. She was born Theresa Catherine Koch (at Confirmation, she would add the name Agnes, after an older sister) in Rochester on July 23, 1918. Her mother, Theresa Uhl Koch, was thirty-eight and would die of kidney failure four years later. Her dad, Francis Joseph Koch, was forty years old when Mom was born; fourteen years later, he passed away from a heart attack.

Mom was the youngest of the seven children in a family that never had much money. She was closest to her brother Al, who was just a year older than she was. When their mother passed away, Mom and Al were sent together to St. Joseph's Villa, an orphanage in Rochester, until their older siblings could care for them.

Although most of Mom's siblings never went beyond grammar school, she graduated from Holy Family School in June of 1932 and from Nazareth Academy High School five years later. It took her an extra year because the family ran out of money when her dad died, and she had to transfer briefly to a public school.

Ten years after that, she had already been married for a year and I was born. I was a healthy kid, but when something went wrong, Mom had a home remedy. Twisted ankles could be treated by soaking in hot water with Epsom salts. A cup of chamomile tea—from leaves she boiled in water—treated upset stomachs. To prevent constipation, she gave us kids enemas—using soapy water. And if we had wax in our ears, she cleaned it out with a bobby pin. In most cases, her advice was: "Just lie down. You'll feel better soon."

Mom was good at simple things, the basics. As my brother Mike said one day, "Ma could iron shirts like nobody irons shirts anymore." And we kids loved those nights when she would get a big pot of oil boiling on the stove and make hot fried cakes. We loved filling a paper bag with confectionary sugar, shaking the just-made donuts in it until they were covered all over, and eating them warm with a glass of milk.

She loved to cook, but she really liked the way Burger King made a fish sandwich—and the way McDonalds brewed a cup of coffee. She never learned to ride a real bicycle, but, every day, she pedaled a stationary bicycle fifteen miles; she never learned to drive a car, but she was world-class at talking others into taking her out for a ride. And she was deathly afraid of water, but she made sure every one of us kids learned to swim.

Thursday night was usually shopping night at Wegmans; she'd take her little two-wheeled cart and head over to Finch Street, where Wegmans was open until 9:00 p.m. On nights when she had an extra dollar, Mom would send us up to

Christoff's Market to get a pound of bologna freshly sliced, for sixty-nine cents. I grew up loving fried bologna—blackened—on bread with hot mustard.

Once a week, for dinner, Mom also usually cooked either Spam—because it was cheap—or liver and onions—because "they're so good for you." I can't eat either of them to this day. But whatever she was serving, Dad had a rule: no milk until we ate everything on our plate. "I don't want you filling up on milk," he'd say. We couldn't afford to waste food.

Of everything Mom cooked, her most beloved recipe was for German potato salad. She brought it to every family gathering, and it was the first to disappear. I swear that several people came to my father's wake who had never met my dad; they'd heard that Mom was making German potato salad, and they wanted some.

She shared her recipe with anyone who asked. "You cook up some potatoes," she'd say, "about as many as you would want—and add in the number of onions that look like they should go in. You put in some sugar and some bacon, but not too much, and then some vinegar until it tastes right." She said, "I don't know why people think it's difficult; there's nothing to making a salad like that."

Mom had opinions about everything—and her own unique expressions. *"Don't go away mad—just go away and don't let the door hit you on the way out,"* she would say. Or, *"who died and left you the boss?" "What makes you think you're God's gift to creation?" "I'm going to brain you." "He doesn't know his rear end from third base."* And the one I've always tried to live up to: *"The best thing a father can do for his children is to love their mother."*

From my earliest school days, she checked my homework; she encouraged me to read, to go to the library—and she bought me books; she told a story—endlessly—of the time she caught me reading in the bathtub, doing my best to keep the book from getting wet. And in those early days of rock and roll, Mom bought us records she also could barely afford—because she loved music, all kinds of music—the newest hits and the old songs, too.

She sang to us endlessly. My siblings and I may be the only ones from our generation who can lapse into "Moonlight Bay," or "Bye Bye Blackbird" and get most of the words right. Some nights our uncles would come over to sing and play the harmonica—mostly songs from World War II—and Mom would join in, sometimes playing the ukulele. She only knew the chords to one song, "Walking My Baby Back Home," and she didn't know that one very well. "Always sing louder than you play," she told me once, "because that way it's harder for people to tell you're not very good."

Although Dad was seldom around, Mom and he never physically fought, but they were always bickering—usually about the money he spent on alcohol. From time to time, she would take a part-time job to get a little money of her own. Her most unusual job was working undercover for Wegmans, the large grocery chain, helping catch crooked cashiers who undercharged their friends at checkout. We finally encouraged her to quit because she worked in a bad part of town and had to come home by bus, alone, late at night.

When Mom and Dad separated in the 1970s—they never divorced—she moved into a small apartment on her own, and we tried to broaden her horizons. We took her, once, to see a movie. She had loved movies growing up but hadn't been in a very long time. We picked *Godspell* because it had religious overtones and Mom was religious. "So this is what movies are like today," she said when it finished. "Well, I guess I won't need to see any more of them."

And we took her on her first airplane flight. Her sister, our aunt Mag, was living in Florida, and I had a business trip there. It took us several months to talk her into going, but it helped that Jeanne and our young kids were coming along. The flight was smooth until we hit a bit of choppiness on the landing. I told Mom what was happening, so she wouldn't be afraid. "Turbulence?" she asked. "Hmmm. This is the first part of the flight I've actually enjoyed; *this* feels like flying." It was her only trip in an airplane, her only trip to Florida, and the farthest from home she had ever been in her life. She never flew again.

Mom's last job, maybe her happiest one, was working as an occupational therapist helping residents with crafts at St. Ann's Home. She worked there during the short time my grandfather lived there—and during the long time her sister, my aunt Loretta, lived there. She was at their bedside when each of them passed away; she retired in 1985.

Although Mom and Dad lived separate lives, they kept in touch. On one trip when she visited him as he was dying in the hospital in Buffalo, my sister Judy heard her say to him: "You know, Bob, I've always loved you." He said he loved her also. It may have been the first time they told each other that in many years.

Although they'd been apart for years, after Dad died in December of 1997, Mom missed him. "Who will take me to my hair appointment?" she asked Judy one day.

"I already take you," Judy told her, "and I'll keep on taking you." But, of course, Mom's question really had nothing to do with a ride to a hair appointment; Dad's passing had left a hole in her life that no one else could fill.

And then, just seven months later, Mom was sewing at Judy's house on a Saturday night in early July 1998. Later that night, she had a massive stroke and slipped into a coma. It was at least her third aneurism, the third time that a weak spot in an artery had burst in her brain. She had always had high blood pressure but never paid careful attention to it because she was afraid of doctors.

Her first aneurism had been about fifteen years before, when she was living alone but fortunately on the phone with my sister Pat. When Pat heard the phone hit the floor—and couldn't get Mom back on the line—she called 911. Mom was rushed to the hospital in a coma, but two days later she was sitting up in bed, laughing and talking. And then, that night, she slipped into a worse coma than before. The doctors wanted to do an angiogram—to thread a tube up through her circulation system into her brain. Dad absolved himself from being involved; as the eldest child, I had to give permission. The doctor said she could die.

The operation went smoothly; the angiogram proved it was just what the doctors had diagnosed, and they decided to let everything heal while they watched and waited. One possible repercussion they told us: your mom might become more rigid in her ways, more opinionated. We told the doctors that we didn't think that was possible.

A few years later, after Mom's life seemed to have returned to normal, I was sitting with her at a party—and although she'd not been drinking, she began slurring her words. "Mom," I said, "squeeze my hand." She did—and had no strength. My uncle Al drove us to the hospital. Again the doctors decided to wait and see—and things turned out well. Again, she seemed to fully recover.

But then came the 1998 phone call to me in California on that early Sunday morning in July. It was my sister Pat. Mom had had another aneurism; the EMTs had missed the "do not resuscitate" card she carried; they'd put her on life support. Doctors were recommending she be taken off—but they needed a family member to approve that. "What," Pat asked me, "do you want to do?"

I wanted *all of us*—*not just me*—to make the decision; she was mother to us all; we were the family she had created, the only family she had left. We needed to decide together.

I flew to Rochester, and we met at the hospital with the doctor, who explained: "You are not deciding whether to kill your mother. Your mom is already dead. If she stays on the ventilator, she'll keep breathing, but everything that made her your mom is gone and we can't bring her back. You are simply deciding whether to take her off life support."

The doctor left—and together Pat, Mike, Judy, and I made the decision to take her off the machines; we asked to have it done at a time when there was a full staff of nurses on duty, so if she were in any discomfort, they could deal with it immediately. Then I went into Mom's room by myself and thanked her for everything she had ever done for me and for all of us. I promised her that I would try to take care of others when they needed me, just as she had always done. And, with my eyes flooded with tears, I said a final good-bye to the first person who had ever believed in me.

The doctor called the next day; they had removed her breathing tube, and she never took another breath. She was at peace. Theresa Catherine Agnes Koch Gibbons was gone. Two days later, I sent out this note to my friends at Kodak:

> *On July 8, my mother, Theresa, passed away following a massive stroke. After a lifetime of worrying and praying—mostly about others—she had the kind of death anyone would pray for: quick and without pain. Throughout her life, she was a champion of the underdog. So, rather than send cards or flowers, if you know someone who is struggling with a burden, and you can offer a helping hand or a few words of encouragement—she'll be looking down on you . . . and smiling.*

A friend wrote me back:

> *We'll do our part to make her smile.*

So, a few weeks shy of her eightieth birthday on July 23, Mom had passed away. She was cremated, and her ashes and Dad's sre in a crypt at the Church of the Assumption in Fairport, New York. Al and Aunt Rose are in the adjacent crypt. She is forever close to the husband and brother she always loved.

She had lived almost twice as long as her own mother. She had been the last of her siblings to be born and was the last to die. She had been alive for the birth of all her grandchildren, who would ever call her "Nana"; she had been to the college graduations of several of them. Sitting in a wheelchair, she had watched her grandson Tim graduate from her beloved Notre Dame, the school she had picked for me so long before.

She had a clear and remarkable memory until the end. Since she passed, I've often wished that I could go back and ask her about those early years she and Dad spent together. She had been too young to even remember her parents; she was marrying someone who had come from a shaky marriage of his own. What did either of them know about marriage? What did she expect on that March day long ago when she walked out of that church on Dad's arm with dreams in her eyes and rice in her hair?

I doubt that they ever discussed the future; we really weren't a family who talked things over, made plans. But I've always hoped she knew that she had created a wonderful life for us kids. And that she left behind lots and lots of people who loved and admired her.

For Mike and Pat, for Judy and me, she showed us what the love of a mother felt like. She had no example to follow, but she did her best, often on her own; even on those days when she was barely hanging on, we were always her priority.

Whenever and wherever we needed her, she showed up. With bags of groceries; a present for one of the kids. With more good food—and almost always German potato salad—than anyone could possibly eat. And always bringing love.

Any family member who doesn't think that Mom loved them fully and completely and always would was simply not paying attention. And she never made it seem like it was any big deal. But it was to us—because she was married to our Dad, and until he finally turned his life around, he was often unreliable and unavailable.

# 3

# A MOSTLY ABSENT DAD

D AD WAS A TINKERER, A PUTTERER, SOMEONE who could repair any-thing mechanical; but for all my growing-up years, he was also largely unavailable because he was out drinking.

Since before I was born, my father was an alcoholic. He was not a mean, dangerous, embarrassing, or slurring-his-words kind of drunk. In fact, he had so much practice, we seldom knew he was inebriated. We just knew that, whether he was home or we were out, he liked to sit by himself, smoke his unfiltered Pall Malls, and drink.

And he did—until that day when he had the courage to change his life. Mom and he were separated; he was living with my sister Judy, who called to tell me that his drinking was becoming disruptive; she wanted me to know that she was throwing him out. I said I'd come over and talk to him.

"Dad," I said when I got there, "you and I need to have a talk today that we should have had a long time ago—and I'm not sure if the talk is for me or for you. But I believe your drinking will kill you. If it does—and I've never made any effort to help you stop—I don't think I could live with myself. But if I try to help—and it doesn't work—and you do die from too much alcohol, I think I'll be OK with that. So I'm going to try. Today."

What followed was a long conversation filled with excuses and denials—but fortunately ended with me offering to take him wherever he wanted to go to get the help he needed to quit. Dad suggested the Veterans Administration—he knew of no place else—so that afternoon I drove him down to their offices a few miles away

We were taken to a room, and in a walked an middle-age guy wearing a rumpled shirt and blue jeans. He looked untrained, unprepared. He sat down, seemed to be trying to figure out what to say. Finally, he asked: "So, Bob, how much are you drinking?"

Dad told him he had maybe a few beers a day. "With liquor?" the guy asked. "Oh, no," Dad told him.

The guy listened, nodded. "Yeah," he said. "I know what you're saying because back when I was drinking like you're drinking, when people would ask me the same questions, I'd tell them exactly what you're telling me. And you know what, Bob?" he said, "I got to the point where *I actually believed that what I was saying was true.*" Then he smiled a helpless smile. "But," he said, "I knew it wasn't true for me, and you know it isn't true for you, and most people we've told our story to know it isn't true, so the only people we're really trying to fool are ourselves, aren't we?"

Then he just stopped and shrugged. But you could see it in Dad's eyes; here was somebody who knew what it was like to drink and to pretend—someone who had lived his story. Maybe here was someone who could help.

And so, for maybe the first time ever, Dad told the truth about his drinking. The guy just sat there and listened and nodded. And then he told him there was a detox program in a VA clinic in Buffalo to help him. He'd be in a hospital-like environment for several weeks with other alcoholics. If Dad wanted to go, fine. If not, the guy didn't care. It was Dad's problem; Dad had to decide.

"If I go," he asked me, "will you take me?" I said I would.

I did, and when we said good-bye, I think he was scared, but I think he was also proud of himself. He was the oldest member of the program—he was in his early seventies—and the younger guys looked up to him, called him "Gramps." I think that made things marginally easier for him, that others were depending on him. Still, it must have been incredibly difficult; he had to face demons he'd always denied he had before.

But he did it. He never drank again.

And not only did he need to stay aware of his alcoholic history, so did we. When our kids were very small and their pediatrician was taking a family history, their doctor said: "When your kids are old enough, they need to know that story. It's important. They have to be careful, because addiction runs in their genes." And it probably will—forever.

But for Dad, it was a new beginning. He had been born on November 19, 1917, a middle child, the second son of John W. and Mae C. Gibbons, in Rochester. Dad's brother, Paul, who became a priest, was two years older; his sister Rosemary, who had nine children—some of them adopted—was four years younger. He was never close to either of them.

His mother, whose maiden name was Lane and who was usually called Mary, had died of diabetes on January 17, 1936, at forty-nine. When she and Pappy were married—on April 23, 1913, in Rochester—she had listed her occupation as "shoemaker." Neither Grandpa nor Dad ever spoke about her, but I know that Dad loved her and believed his father's drinking had contributed to her death.

The name on Dad's original birth certificate and his baptismal record from Holy Rosary was John Robert Gibbons. Sometime later, he changed his name—although never officially—to Robert John. He graduated from Holy Rosary School (as all his children would) and attended Edison Technical, a high school that emphasized mechanical trades rather than academics, although he would quit after three years, sometime before his mother died—perhaps to care for her. A few years before, he had gotten a paper route to help pay for her medicine.

He was most likely dabbling with car repair—he was always interested in motors of all types, trying to find a direction in life—when, in 1941, eight months before Pearl Harbor, he enlisted in the army. The military considered him a semi-skilled mechanic and repairman of motor vehicles. He was a given the rank of private, sent for basic training, and ended up in the Signal Corps.

By April 1944, he was Staff Sergeant Robert J. Gibbons, ordered to ship out for the island of New Guinea, where he was a driver for a senior officer who, Mom later believed, "had eyes on Dad" as a potential husband for his daughter. But Dad came home to Mom; on December 29, 1945, Robert J. Gibbons, Serial Number 32 039 835, Staff Sergeant of the 4025th Signal Service Company, was honorably discharged at Fort Dix, New Jersey, where, almost twenty-five years later, I would take my Basic Training. According to his discharge papers, he was 5-feet 10-inches tall, weighed 180 pounds, and had blue eyes and brown hair; his Military Occupational Specialty (MOS) had been Motor Transportation Specialist; he listed his civilian occupation as "truck mechanic."

I have no idea if he saw any direct action on New Guinea, where the fighting was intense, but for the rest of his life he refused to eat rice. And when he died, he was probably the same weight he was on the day he left the army.

Dad was easy-going in many ways, but he knew what he liked, and, in some things, he refused to compromise. He would never, for example, wear button-down shirts—until he removed the buttons that held the collar in place. And one year for Christmas, when Tim was at Notre Dame, we bought him a mono-grammed sweater with the ND logo. The next time I saw him, he was wearing the sweater—without the logo. "It took me a while to cut that off," he said, "but after I did, it's a nice sweater." He didn't want anyone to think that he personally had graduated from Notre Dame.

I've often said that Dad was a person of impeccable taste because, once upon a time, he'd chosen Mom and together, they'd chosen us. But I don't remember my parents being particularly close; I only once saw them dance and never saw them kiss. They mostly argued over money. Dad never brought home more than a hundred and twenty-five dollars a week; on that, they had to raise four kids. But they never dragged us into their arguments—or gave us any reason to believe that we were, somehow, to blame for their troubles.

Since Dad was seldom around during my growing-up years, my memories of him are sporadic. When I was about three years old, he took me to my first movie, an Audie Murphy war film; we sat in the balcony of the Cameo, a now long-closed theatre on Clinton Avenue. Around the same age, he put me on the gas tank of his green BSA motorcycle and took me for my first motorcycle ride. Several years later, one night, we drove to the Rundell Library downtown, to check out books on the electrical system of refrigerators. He had some to repair.

Dad could fix almost anything. We always had a garage filled with broken-down washing machines, refrigerators, and clothes dryers he had rescued from the side of the road and brought home to repair. And everything he fixed, he seemed to be able to sell—for more money than most people believed anyone would pay. My mother kept a yellowed picture of my father from the Kodak newspaper. The picture showed Dad repairing a truck.

He and I shoveled snow together—I was about six years old—on the November morning my sister Judy was born. Sometime after I began taking drum lessons in fifth grade, he went up in our attic and found where he had stored the components to his drum set from long before. He brought them down and gave them to me.

When I was about to take my road test to get my license, his old Chevrolet had an unreliable ignition; sometimes the key worked, sometimes not. When I mentioned the problem to him, Dad removed all the innards from the ignition; I could have started the car with a stick. And when he knew I'd be embarrassed if I had to drive that rusted old car to our senior prom, he went out and bought a new Dodge convertible with bucket seats.

Through the years, Dad had a succession of jobs; he owned and managed a gas station on East Ridge Road—and then later he managed another one, a Citgo station on Chili Avenue. In between, he worked for Allstate Insurance, appraising cars that had been damaged in accidents—and he worked in the body shop of several car dealerships, repairing those cars that had been damaged. Several different times he worked at Kodak Park, first fixing vehicles and later repairing the film-making machines.

He was probably fired for unreliability from fewer jobs than he walked away from. When something wasn't to his liking, he didn't point it out or ask for changes, he simply left. If he had a motto he lived by, it was this: *Never complain, never explain.* He believed he was right—and moved on.

Even when he was drinking, Dad was an attentive driver. One snowy night, he was driving us home from a band job I had; we were stopped at a light, behind another car, when he saw, in his rear-view mirror, a car approaching from behind—driving way too fast for conditions. He quickly maneuvered our car onto the sidewalk—as the other car came out of the darkness and slammed into the one in front of us. As we drove around the wreck, he said, "I thought we should get out of his way."

In his quiet way, Dad taught me a lot; he was an introvert, someone who mostly worked by himself; from him I learned to be comfortable on my own, to figure things out, not to ask for help unless I really needed it, and not to be disappointed when others let me down.

And while those lessons have made me much less of a team player, they do make me more willing to take a chance, to try something different, to set my own standards and judge my own work. I dislike games because I have to compete against others; I prefer to compete against myself.

But I also learned from Dad what *not* to do. When he didn't show up where he said he would—or he didn't deliver on his promises—he treated it like it was no big deal. For me, it's *always* a big deal. If I say I'll do something, I will do it. It's why I don't panic at deadlines; if I promised to write something, I will. And it's why, when our children were younger, we never threatened them with something we didn't intend to do. If we said it, we meant it. If people could say one thing about me, I'd like them to say I'm reliable. "Don't make promises," my trusted Kodak assistant Linda Mahoney once told me, "you can't keep."

Dad was always a person of few words; he said what he wanted to say and stopped talking. He was shaving when I told him, "Dad, I'm going to ask Jeanne to marry me. What do you think about that?"

"Well," he said, "if you still feel the same way about her that you felt when you first started going out, I think it's a good idea."

Then he went back to shaving.

He felt no need to ask questions or express his opinion on every subject. "I don't think Grandpa ever said anything stupid," Tim told me once. But when any of us got riled up about something, Dad would listen and calmly ask, ". . . Have you ever thought about it another way. . . ?"

Although he avoided difficult discussions, he seemed unfazed by the unexpected. "When you figure out what you want to do," he said one day, "figure out what could happen if everything goes wrong. If it does, you won't be surprised— and you'll know how to deal with it."

And another bit of his wisdom: "If you hang around the barber shop long enough," he used to say, "sooner or later you'll get a haircut." In other words, whether you put yourself in a good or bad situation, you usually end up getting what you deserve.

Although he always avoided funerals—including his own father's—his end came quickly. One day, in September 1997, his buddy Wally told him: "Bob, if you're going to keep driving that car, you really need to get your eyes checked. I don't think you can see where you're going."

When they went together for an eye exam at the Veteran's Administration, Dad was asked when he had last had a complete physical. He thought it might have been in April 1941, when he enlisted in the army. When they gave him a full exam, they found cancer everywhere. Within a month or so, he had checked in to the Veteran's Hospital in Buffalo. He went downhill very quickly.

In November, I was in Rochester on a business trip and drove up to see him. I didn't realize how sick he was, and Mom was with us, so we talked mostly of inconsequential things—although at one point, he gave me his thoughts on death. "It's like," he said, "when you move to a new apartment. Naturally, you don't want to go because you like it where you are, and you don't know what the new one will be. But then you move, and it turns out OK."

Dad moved into that "new apartment" just a few weeks later. He was always a heavy smoker, never gave it up; he died of carcinoma of the lungs on December 1, 1997, twelve days after his eightieth birthday. He was cremated, and his ashes are stored in a crypt in a church in The Church of the Assumption in Fairport, New York; my mother's ashes are there also. They're closer for eternity than I ever remember them in life.

I wish Dad and I could have been alone for what became our last conversation. But we were never ones to express our feelings or our lives openly; where would we have begun? There was so much about each other we didn't know.

Still, I wish I could have said something to help him forgive himself for whatever needed forgiving, to know that I'd come to realize it's not easy being a dad and we each need to do it in our own way, and that I'll always value his clear thinking and non-judgmental approach to my life. I wish I could have helped him go gently into his new apartment with fewer regrets, realizing that I'd come to understand he had spent most of his life fighting demons more powerful than he was willing or able to admit.

And when it came time to say our final goodbye, I wish I also had had the courage to kiss him goodnight, to once again feel his scruffy cheeks that I remembered from childhood, and to finally tell him what I didn't remember saying in a very long time: "I love you, Dad."

Because I always did—and I wonder if he ever said it to his own father, the grandfather I called Pappy.

# 4

# I CALLED HIM PAPPY

H E WAS MY FATHER'S FATHER and the only grandparent I ever knew. I called him Pappy—and, when I was born, we moved in with him; he was sixty-seven years old. For the next two decades, until he passed away at eighty-nine, he provided more guidance and support to me at critical points than maybe my own dad. In his own quiet way, Pappy seemed to be there when I needed him.

The first enduring memory I have of him was when I was six years old and had to have my tonsils out. He knew I was worried, so the day before, he took me to the Seneca Park Zoo with its small amusement park—and rode the rides with me. I can still see him and me, sitting in these "airships" about six feet off the ground, going around in circles, happily "shooting" at each other. The next day, he drove Mom and me to the hospital.

Pappy was a small man, thin and bald, almost always wearing a fedora, often with a blue suit. He was born John William Gibbons on February 28, 1881, in a little town called Byron, New York, the first child of John R. Gibbons and the former Ellen Riggs, who were married in 1880. His dad was a blacksmith, born in Fowlersville, New York, in January 1850; he died of heart disease in his seventies. His mother was born in Pavilion, New York, in February 1858; she died of palsy in 1941. Both of their parents were born in Ireland.

There were five siblings in Pappy's family—two younger boys (Edward, 1894, and, Vince 1899) and two younger girls (Mabel, 1888, and Genevieve, 1891). On April 23, 1913, at thirty-two years of age, Pappy married twenty-six-year-old Mae C. Lane (usually called Mary) of 102 Jones Street in Rochester. He said he worked at Kodak Park; she listed her occupation as a shoemaker.

Mae C. Lane was born in August 1885, one of seven children; she died of kidney failure on January 17, 1936. I never met her brothers, but when we lived on Oriole Street, once a year around Christmas, her sisters—my great-aunts Nellie, Anna, and Florence—would come over to our house and sit in our living room while my mother waited on them. I don't recall them having anything to say. I wish I'd asked, "Tell me about my grandmother."

Pappy told Mom that, when he was a young man, he was the assistant for a country doctor, Doctor Belknap, in Wyoming, New York. He also said he was a Jell-O salesman in western New York, traveling by train between cities; he gave her pictures of a serious train wreck he was involved with. He may have done all that, but census records and city directories tell a different story.

In the 1900 Census, he claimed to be a "typesetter"; when he registered with the U.S. Selective Service, he said he was a "mail carrier." And he had an almost decade-long career working for liquor distributors—both as a clerk and a salesman. That may have started his lifelong addiction to alcohol because, like my dad, Pappy was an alcoholic.

But by 1913, he had a steady job. He was working at Kodak Park—the big film-manufacturing facility in Rochester—and he got the job on a ruse.

Grandpa had been born the same year—1881—that George Eastman, the former young bank clerk, started Kodak—and in those early years, Eastman was often desperate for funding. Word was, he found financing in Canada; as a result, he looked favorably on Canadians—and Pappy knew that.

On the weekend before applying for a job, Pappy took the train to Canada. When he walked into the Rochester Kodak employment on Monday morning, they asked him where he was from—and Pappy decided to interpret that literally: He was from Canada. When he didn't mention his stay was only two days, he was hired and began his career at Kodak.

Over the next thirty-three years, until he retired in 1946, he held jobs as a steel worker, film worker, and foreman. In 1939, he was paid thirty-three dollars a week.

Pappy and I were both avid readers—he only read paperback westerns—and on Saturdays in my grammar school years, Pappy would wander over sometime early in the morning, and he and I would take the bus downtown together. After an hour or so in Loew's Theatre, where we watched a whole string of cartoons, we went next door to the Clinton Book Shop.

Down in their basement, on sagging shelves and in musty cartons on the floor, they had their children's books, westerns, and others that were not only used but just plain old. Few people went down there, so, on many afternoons, Pappy and I sat there, on piles of books, or the floor, or stacked cartons, and read— often while it rained or snowed outside.

When summer came in my fourth- and fifth-grade years, I started playing organized baseball—slow-pitch softball in mornings and afternoons—and Pappy came to all my games. He was no longer driving by then, so he had to take a bus and maybe a short walk, but he was always there. I was never very good as an athlete, but he neither criticized nor provided any instructive help. And the year that we won the championship and played at night under the lights, Pappy took us all out for ice cream afterwards.

Sometimes, especially on weekends, he'd treat me to a milkshake at Critic's or at Schultz's—two neighborhood diners—or buy me a comic book or two at Sy's drug store. One night, I discovered an old Philco black-and-white TV down in our basement; it was broken, and my parents had never had it fixed. When I asked Pappy about it, he called a Mr. Ed Mooney, who "knew how to fix those things," and paid him to fix ours. That's the TV that introduced me to the Lone Ranger, Sgt. Preston, and so many of my childhood heroes.

A few years later, when I got an afternoon paper route, Pappy would sit outside waiting for the papers before I got home from school—and often have them rolled and in my bag when I arrived. He stayed every night to eat with us. He'd always be dressed for dinner—dark suit with a tie, though often with a plaid flannel shirt. It was a bit of a mismatch, but he was comfortable and confident and ready to eat. I found out later that Dad had borrowed money from him when he needed to buy materials to fix up the "other side" of the house. Rather than repay him in cash, every week, Mom took five dollars off their bill.

After dinner, when he was ready to leave, he'd wonder aloud, "One of you want to walk me home?" He lived a mile or so away, where he was renting an upstairs apartment—just a couple of rooms—in a home owned by an older woman named Mrs. Cleveland who lived downstairs with her developmentally challenged son, Vern, who wore thick glasses, moved slowly, and talked with a stutter. Pappy never talked to them—or anyone else. I never knew him to have friends.

I usually walked him home, and as we got close, Pappy would say, "Well, that's far enough. What do I owe you?" And he would take out his change purse—he always carried his coins in a change purse—and hand me a nickel or dime. We'd say good night and head in different directions.

If Pappy ever gave us presents, I don't remember them, but when I graduated from eighth grade, he gave me a card with Rudyard Kipling's poem "If" inside. It was signed in his then-shaky signature, *Grandpa*. I have the card still, have kept it for such a long time because I thought there was real wisdom there, the kind you might hear from a grandfather.

We did have some problems with Grandpa at a few points when his lifetime of hard drinking caught up with him. Plus, he was old and, occasionally, he got his days confused with his nights; instead of showing up at three o'clock in the afternoon, he'd be banging on our door at three in the morning. Dad would get up and drive him home. After a couple of nights, he straightened himself out—until he went on his annual bender. That involved serious and prolonged drinking—and included him disappearing. "Grandpa's gone," my mom would tell us, "and your father and I need to find him." They always did; he was usually checked into some sleazy local hotel under an assumed name that was some combination of his own: William Gibbons, John Williams, and William Johns were his favorites.

Mom and Dad would pick him up and drive him to a sanitarium in Clifton Springs to dry out. A week or so later, they'd bring him home, and all would be back to normal, usually for another year.

Our wedding pictures from July 19, 1969, include the last picture I have of Pappy—coming out of church, smiling in his fedora and his blue suit. A month or so after that, he took sick and was moved into the assisted-care facility called St. Ann's Home.

On a Sunday in late September, I got a call. The woman on the phone said: "If you want to say good-bye to your grandfather, come by today. He's very sick." I went immediately, to find him sleeping peacefully. I hung around, waited, decided not to wake him. I'd return after work the next day.

In those days, my mother worked as an occupational therapist at St. Ann's, and early the next day, Monday, September 29, 1969, when she got to work, she was told, "John is asking for you. . . ." She went to his room. He had his eyes closed. She decided to let him sleep. "But then," she told me, "it was the strangest thing. He opened his eyes and looked directly at me. 'So long, Theresa,' he said. And he passed away."

Pappy—the only grandparent I ever knew—was gone. He had been with me through all the major milestones in my life, including when I was just starting out.

# 5

# STARTING OUT

I N 1952, MY MOTHER PAID A GIRL named Sharon Koch—who lived a few houses away—to walk me to St. Michael's School. I was in kindergarten, the morning session, and we lived in a small house on Carl Street in Rochester. I had been born five years before in nearby St. Mary's Hospital on Holy Thursday, April 3, 1947—at 4:28 in the afternoon. I weighed eight pounds, five ounces and was twenty-one inches long. Seventeen days later—on Sunday, April 20—Dad's brother, Father Paul, christened me Robert John at 3:15 in the afternoon in Holy Rosary Church.

We lived with my widowed grandfather—Pappy—in a two-story home on Finch Street, a couple of blocks away from where I'd spend most of my growing-up years. A month after my sister Pat was born, in January 1949, my parents paid sixty-five hundred dollars for that first home of their own, across the Genesee River on Carl Street.

On June 5, 1950, my brother Mike joined the family, and on November 4, 1953, Judy became the last of my siblings.

The house on Carl Street was long, narrow, painted white—and small. It has since been torn down, the land now a parking lot for a corner drugstore; but over the five years we lived there, it left me with good memories.

For my third birthday, my aunt Mag—who was a professional baker—made me a cake in the shape of a tugboat with colorful designs and frostings. When I got up during the night to have an additional piece of it, I threw up in technicolor, all over the kitchen floor.

The home had a side porch where I recovered—with popsicles and ice cream—from having my tonsils removed. It was a three-day hospital stay back then, and I still remember the sweet smell of ether when they anesthetized me. The full operation only cost forty dollars. I have a copy of the hand-written bill.

We used to get the newspaper—the *Rochester Democrat and Chronicle*—and it had a regular column where anyone could "Ask Andy" about anything. My mother said she always wondered: "Where does the wind go when it doesn't blow?" So she asked him. Andy answered only "selective questions"; he didn't select hers.

Around that time, my younger brother Mike suddenly started having convulsions one Sunday night, and my parents were afraid he was going to swallow his tongue. My mother held him in her arms—and a white cloth out the window to signal an emergency—as my dad drove as fast as he could to the Emergency Room at St. Mary's Hospital. Mike was OK—and I don't think that the convulsions ever reoccurred.

Even before I started school, I made several friends in the neighborhood including Jimmy Bowman, who lived two streets away. When he invited me to his birthday party, it was the first non-family party I'd attended, and my mom wanted to be sure that I "knew how to act."

Jimmy's mother served us hot dogs and baked beans—and unfortunately, I got a forkful of fatty bacon. My mother had always cut the fat off anything she gave me, so as I bit into it, I didn't know what it was. I gagged. And the last thing I remember about that party was Jimmy's mother leading me into the bathroom where I threw up in their toilet. My mother was, as she put it, "mortified."

But Carl Street was in a typical neighborhood back then, where many things were done at a personal level. There was a large grocery story a few blocks away, but bread, fruits, and vegetables—even meat—were also sold from trucks that drove slowly up and down the streets. Many people had milk delivered in glass bottles to their door. A few times a year, a man drove around in his truck with a grinder, to sharpen scissors and knives. And once a week, I used to listen for the garbage collectors who would enter our backyard, put our cans on a small hand dolly, and take them to their truck to be unloaded—and then put the cans back in our yard.

And that was before recycling; everything except furnace ashes went into the same garbage cans.

It was a small neighborhood, and school was only a few blocks from our home, but Mom wasn't sure I knew the way—and she had three other younger children at home, so she couldn't take me. For the first few weeks, I walked with Sharon, the older girl from down the street.

My teacher was Sister Mary Jane, a member of the Sisters of Notre Dame. They had a reputation as being a cut above. "If you learn from them," my mother believed, "you really get an education." She may have been right; when I transferred to Holy Rosary School—staffed by the Sisters of St. Joseph—in second grade, I was beyond what the kids there were learning.

For first grade, my teacher was another Notre Dame nun, Sister Annicia, who especially valued neatness. I discovered that one day when I had erased something and made a mess of it. When I denied the erasing, I discovered that the only thing Sister Annicia hated worse that sloppy erasures were obvious lies. Not only did she feel the need to discuss it that day, she talked to me further about it after Mass on Sunday. Later in life, I'd learn that when some women have a situation in which you are wrong and they are right, they like to take endless opportunities to discuss it with you.

I still have my report card from that year in which I've since noted that Sr. Annicia made several sloppy erasures of her own. She initially misspelled my name Robert—and she corrected several grades. I did not point that out.

I also still have a holy card—nuns always had an endless supply of those to use as "prizes"—she had given me, showing the Christ child as a young boy sitting on the front of a boat on a clear blue day. It possessed both a sense of serenity and a sense of adventure—a great combination for me. And I still recall her sharing her milk with me at an end-of-year picnic when my thermos broke and I ended up having shattered glass in mine.

All these years later, through the Notre Dame Motherhouse, I was able to reconnect with those two influential women.

Sister Mary Jane Buhrman, my kindergarten teacher, told me that she was the thirteenth of sixteen children; three had become nuns. She entered the convent right out of high school, but her first real assignment was at St. Michael's school, where she taught me. At some point during almost half a century of teaching, she got her master's degree from Loyola University and then retired in 1995. She was living in the Notre Dame Motherhouse in Maryland and painting watercolors.

When I sent Sister Mary Jane a brief note about her art and told her I was including her in a little book I was writing, she closed her reply in a delightful way: *"May God bless you real good."*

Which leads me to a small digression: One night a few weeks later, our daughter Emily called. She was driving from the Coast Guard Academy in Connecticut, where she had been teaching law, to her new assignment in New Orleans. Somewhere in Pennsylvania, alone in the dark, she had just hit a bear. "Daddy," she asked, "what should I do?" I told her to call 911. She did, and everything got sorted out; her car was damaged but drivable, and she was able to complete her journey.

The next day she called again. "Every time I replay that accident in my mind," she told me, "I have no idea why I wasn't killed." I told her of the note I'd received from Sister Mary Jane. "Maybe," I suggested, "at the instant of impact, God looked down, realized you were my daughter, and decided to bless us real good."

Neither she nor I had a better explanation.

Meanwhile, my first-grade teacher, Sister Annicia, had left the order in the 1960s. She had married, and her name was now Mrs. Betty Linz Gilbert. She and her husband Walter were living in Maryland. In our correspondence, she sent me stories of her early days as a young nun and her early days of teaching.

At one point, her husband Walt thanked me for asking her for those stories; she had never told them to anyone before. Betty also sent pictures from the days she taught me; somehow, I didn't remember her being such a small woman—I thought all nuns were ten feet tall.

During first grade, at least once a week after school, I walked down Clinton Avenue to a YMCA-type gymnasium called a *turnverein*—which is German for "athletic club." They offered programs on gym equipment—floor mats, climbing ropes, and so forth. In their basement pool, I eventually learned to swim, but I had to be rescued by a lifeguard one day when I wandered too far into the deep end and couldn't make it to the side of the pool.

As I look back, the thing that strikes me as most amazing is not what I did while I was there, but how I got there—and back home: *I walked by myself down a major busy street, about a mile or so, often in the dark, across several major streets, with no way to contact my parents if anything went wrong. I was not yet seven years old.*

Times, though, were much safer back then—and I was enjoying school. In September 1954, I returned to St. Michael's to begin second grade, where Sister Mary Pia was my new teacher. But I was only there for a month or so. We were about to move back to the other side of the city where I began, into the home on Oriole Street where I'd spend all the rest of my growing up years—as the oldest brother of Pat and Mike and Judy.

# 6

# THE FOUR GIBBONS KIDS

ROM THE BEGINNING, PEOPLE SAID we didn't even look alike. Me. Patricia Marie. Thomas Michael. Judy Charlene. In that order, oldest to youngest; my parents had four kids in six and a half years. Although we were close in age, there were always some things fundamentally different about the choices we made, the paths we took, the places we ended up. But, in other ways, we were also fundamentally Gibbonses.

We all got a bit of independent spirit from our dad, a sense of core values from our mom. We all grew up in a middle-class home, had a Catholic school education, and celebrated holidays with aunts and uncles and cousins and other members of the family. None of us expected we'd ever live anywhere but Rochester.

We each picked a spouse from the local area, some of us from right there in our neighborhood. We each had children—Judy had one, Pat and Mike two, and Jeanne and I three—and tried to give them a home where they felt safe and protected. For us, it was a small world.

We were never rich but had everything we needed and were expected to take care of each other. But Mom and Dad's dysfunctional, often shaky relationship did have an impact on us—less on me but increasingly more on my brother and sisters. Judy, the youngest, later told me, "I never really felt safe growing up." She'd spent the longest living at home.

There are some noticeable differences among the Gibbons kids. I'm the only one who seemed to have a serious interest in school—and to finish college. Mike has mechanical skills I can only envy; I was the first to leave Rochester and the only one to have a long-term job with any company. Pat and I are the only ones whose marriage has stayed together over the long haul; Judy and I are the only ones who keep in regular contact with each other.

## Thomas Michael

Mike and I shared a bedroom on Oriole Street, where he remembers me as a great audience for the funny things he'd say or do—and I remember he could talk his way out of anything. When I was drafted, Mike talked to our local parish priest, who, in turn, talked to the draft board. At the time, Mike was the only one living home and not working, and yet—thanks to his talking and Fr. Wheeland's—Mike was able to get a deferment as "sole support of the family."

When he was in high school, he worked after school and on Saturdays cleaning the classrooms at Holy Rosary School; he'd inherited that job from me when I left for college—but in his case, it wasn't unusual, especially on Saturdays, for one of the priests or nuns to be wandering through the school and find Mike sitting in some classroom, with his feet up on a desk, listening to a football game on the radio and enjoying a glass or two of "altar wine" he had pilfered from the priest's refrigerator in the rectory. I loved to hear the stories of the fast talking that kept him from getting fired.

Mike was a likeable kid, but he hated school. After Holy Rosary grammar school, he went to Edison Technical, just like Dad—and, just like Dad, he dropped out before graduation. That was unfortunate because Mom always hoped he would qualify to go to General Motors Institute, a prestigious "feeder school" in Detroit for the automotive industry. He would have shone in that career because

Mike was into mechanical things from an early age; he could fix anything, figure anything out. He was much smarter than I was in practical, mechanical ways.

Although he was three years younger than me, his friends were also my friends; we collected and swapped baseball cards and army patches—and took the bus together downtown. We built soap box derby racers from discarded wooden crates in our garage, collected grass snakes from a nearby woods, fished together on vacation, and put on skits to entertain each other in our Oriole Street basement.

I played softball for Kodak Park and was never very good; Mike played Little League and a good first baseman. When he went to Canada to play an away game, at one point he became frustrated with some of the Canadian ballplayers: "I wish those foreigners would go home," he said. I reminded him we were in Canada; they *were* home.

Diving with Mike off a small dock in Fair Haven Bay, one day on vacation, I got a piece of shell caught in my eye and Dad had to go from bar to bar, looking for Dr. Bayard Hanford, the local general practitioner in Fair Haven, to dig it out. In the end, I'm surprised he was sober enough to do that without harming my eye.

But I suspect that what Mike would remember from those vacations would be the year that Dad built a go-kart, painted it gold and brought it on a trailer up to Fair Haven. He knew there was so little traffic up there, we could ride in the road—and Mike, I, and mostly our dad, did.

Every fall, when the new car models were released, Mike and I would ride our bicycles to the major Rochester dealers—Heinrich Chevrolet, Judge Ford, Ralph Pontiac, Bonenblust and Buckman Oldsmobile—to see the cars before they were shown to the public.

Mike loved cars. When he was about fourteen, before he could legally drive, he would go through my father's pockets when Dad was asleep, find the car keys, and take the car out for a late-night drive. From the first, he was a good driver; the first time I drove at night, I took Mike along with me, so he could be my "extra set of eyes."

Mike got a car as soon as he could afford one—and he was always buying older cars, fixing them up and reselling them. Eventually, he opened his own collision shop in Rochester where I suggested he name it *California Collision*—and he did. "That has a nice sound," he told me, "because people in California take good care of their cars." The shop quickly developed a great reputation; Mike was restoring very expensive cars for people who could afford them. He had lots of work; he had people working for him; he was making money. But then, just like Dad would do, he got tired of it and walked away.

He had, at some point along the way, married Joanie Bach, a great girl from our old neighborhood, with whom he would have two children, Shauna (born January 1980) and Brandon (born August 1981). Eventually their marriage broke up and although Joanie married again—to Bruce Powell—Mike never did. Joanie continues to believe in him.

Mike would end up losing his business, his home, and his marriage but he never lost his talent. He was still the best there was at seamlessly repairing cars—and when Judy needed to have new hardwood floors installed in her home in Spencerport, Mike came in and did a terrific job. He's a good guy whose heart is always in the right place, who would do anything for someone in need. Once, I was that someone. When I was in the Army, stationed in the middle of Kansas, I had an opportunity to make extra money by playing in a band with a fellow soldier, Patrick O'Dell, but I needed my drums brought out from Rochester and I wasn't sure I could afford to do that.

I called my mother and she said she'd figure it out. A day or so later, Mike showed up with my drums. He and his friend Jim had driven non-stop, more than twelve hundred miles; they stayed for a day or so—where Mike talked his way out of having his camera confiscated when the MPs caught him taking pictures in the motor pool—and then headed for Miami. A hurricane was expected there, and Mike figured he could make a bit of money getting cars unstuck after drivers had lost control in the heavy rain.

Today, Mike continues to struggle with alcohol—as, like Dad, he's done for most of his life; but he has a talent for craftsmanship that he can always rely on. When he needs money, he picks up work helping someone who builds, refurbishes, or restores houses. He stays close to Shauna and her family, and to his son

Brad and his family. His former wife, Joanie, also tries to watch out for him. He's still a good guy—and he's still my only brother.

## Patricia Marie

Pat is only about twenty months younger than I am; she followed me to St. Michael's for her kindergarten, and to Holy Rosary for the rest of her grammar school education. Because Aquinas at the time was an all-male school, Pat graduated from Nazareth High School, just like our mom.

In her early grammar school years, Pat—and Judy—took tap dance lessons at *Bob Kuchman's School of Dance* in a storefront a mile or two from where we lived—and once a year, the school would have a special recital at some other location we'd have to drive to. I still remember someone calling out, "shuffle, ball, change. . ." or something like that. I have no idea what any of it means.

Pat was a year behind me in high school, much more interested in boys than I was in girls—but she was always looking out for me. When "tapered pants" came in style, she had a sewing machine and tapered mine. Also, she was the one who taught me to dance; we used to practice in our basement with the record player plugged in and sitting on Mom's ironing board. She was always encouraging me to introduce her to my friends. . .and she ended up going out with one or two of them; we sometimes double-dated—and she once came out to Notre Dame for a football game.

I had my license by the time Pat took Drivers Ed in school and, on the night before her road test, she asked me to take her out for some additional practice. I tried to do that, but it took her so many tries to figure out how to back the car out of our short driveway that I finally gave up. She said that, in Drivers Ed, they never covered backing out. But the next day, when she took her driver's test— which included backing up—she passed on the first try. Go figure.

Unlike me, Pat never seemed to have any interest in college and instead, she went to work as a receptionist for Case Hoyt, one of the premier printing companies in Rochester. When she got tired of that, she joined Hertz and worked out of their office in the Rochester airport where, for a while, she was dating the airport manager.

Pat always seemed to be dating someone different every time I checked, but she fell in love with Ted Edgecombe and married him on May 8, 1971, while I was in the Army. Ted has always been in the excavating business, digging foundations, handling projects that mostly involve moving large volumes of dirt and gravel. He's a plain-speaking guy, a hard-working guy, but being in the business he's in, he's also "hooked up" with guys who help those who are out of other options.

Ted's parents—Bill and Ruth—were older, quiet people who lived on a small street and got along well with their neighbors until some punks moved in and played their music at the highest possible volume, at all hours of the day or night. When Ruth asked them nicely to turn it down—and they ignored her, she mentioned it to her son, "Teddy."

As Ted told me the story: "So," he said, "I call my friend, Eddie the hat. Eddie pays the punks a visit, carrying a baseball bat. He raps on their door a couple of times; nobody answers, but the music is still loud. Eddie figures maybe they can't hear him, so he smashes every window on the first floor of their house—just so they can hear him better. And when they come running out he says: 'You should turn the music down, so I don't have to get started on the windows in your car.'" And this time they did.

Pat and Ted would have two boys—Todd Michael (born January 15, 1975) and Toby Patrick (born January 3, 1977). Todd graduated from Alfred State University; Toby from the University of Buffalo. Todd and his wife Stacey—she's retired from the Navy after a twenty-year career as a senior chief—have two boys, Chase and Smythe. Todd is in the excavating business like his dad.

Toby's degree is in architecture, but he has a very successful business in landscape design, doing a lot of high-end work in the Rochester area. He and his wife Jennifer have two boys, Connor and Andrew. In between, they had a girl, Sydney, who just before her second birthday, passed away from pediatric cancer. In the wintertime, Toby and Todd and their dad all plow snow in Rochester.

Pat is retired from Park Ridge Hospital where she managed their senior center. Ted is older than her, but he'll probably never retire. He still owns heavy equipment, picks up work here and there, wonders whether the cost of all the insurance he needs to carry is worth the money he makes from the jobs he gets. But he likes staying connected with the guys and the business he's known all his life. Pat and Ted own a condominium in Fort Myers Florida. They spend part of the year down there—Pat more than Ted; he misses his business and friends in Rochester.


## Judy Charlene

Judy is the furthest from me in age, but maybe closest in temperament.

Mom originally wanted to name her Judy Marlene, but she was born on November 4, the feast of St. Charles, so Marlene morphed onto Charlene. But my mother still wanted Judy—*not Judith*—and that was going to be problematical: Judith was a saint's name, Judy was not. Uncle Paul, the priest, came up with the solution: since her middle name was Charlene—a feminine form of Charles and thus a saint's name—her first name didn't matter. She was baptized Judy Charlene Gibbons.

Since my father was not home at bedtime most nights, I was the one who often read stories to her—or made them up. Mine often starred a character named "Bam Bam" who was always getting into some situation that I borrowed from the television cartoons I was watching. Whenever Bam Bam got into a situation where he seemed to have no escape, I had him run into something— usually a tree. A lot of what I tried out on her as a big brother, I ended up using as a dad when our kids were very young.

Judy liked to watch TV and we had a big old set where the television cabinet went all the way to a few inches above the floor. When she was misbehaving, I'd warn: "If you don't stop, I'll fix the television, so it won't work." At the time, I had a small clip-on light so I could read at night—and I noticed that its brown electrical cord was the same as the cord that came out from underneath the cabinet to plug the TV set into the wall. I hid my light under the cabinet, unplugged the TV cord, plugged in my small light, and turned my light off. Unless someone looked closely under the set, it looked like the TV was plugged in.

When she misbehaved, Judy would turn on the TV—and I'd point out: "It must not be working because you've been bad." When her behavior changed—and she was off doing something else—I'd remove my light, plug the TV back in, and it would work just fine.

One summer during her high school years when I was home from college, she was learning to drive and asked me to take her out for some practice. I did—to a large empty parking lot…where I'd only allow her to drive in reverse. I told her it was as important to know how to handle a car going backwards as it was driving one forward. In a note Judy sent to our son Tim many years later she said, "I didn't agree with his logic then, but I do now."

Judy graduated from Nazareth Academy high school in 1971 and took several courses at Monroe Community College; sometime in 1974, when she was twenty years old, she decided to marry Gary Korn. I always believed that Judy and I were so close in temperament that I'd be enthusiastic about her choice of a husband—and I didn't think Gary was the right one for her. When she told me of her plans, I tried to talk her out of it. My arguments didn't work; Judy and Gary were married on August 30, 1974. Their only child, Kymberly Terez was born two years later—and four years after that, Judy and Gary divorced.

Gary remarried and never provided any support or guidance for Kymberly during her growing up years, but Judy did a remarkable job as a single mom on her own and the fact that Kymberly became a successful nurse is largely traceable to Judy's steady influence. At different times my mother or father—but never both at once—lived with them. Theirs was the last home Dad lived in before he passed away; it was in Judy's hallway that Mom—who was visiting—would have the stroke that led directly to her death.

Judy's daughter Kymberly married Gerald Fenton Weaver on May 2, 1998; their daughter, Marigrace, was born in December 1999—just months ahead of their divorce. Kymberly found herself in the same situation her mother had—raising a daughter as a single parent—but she did a great job. Judy provided help along the way.

In March 2021, Marigrace married Justin Brumley in Leesburg, Florida where she, Kym, and Judy had been living for the past decade. She's a hair stylist, he's a chef.

For many years, Judy had a very successful residential and commercial cleaning business in Rochester until that day it was—in her words— "snowing sideways" and she resolved never to spend another winter in snow. She considered living in California—and moved in with us for several months—until she decided that Florida would be the place where she, Kym and Marigrace could all afford to live. In June of 2011, we packed her car with everything she owned—and she and I drove from California to her new home in Florida. It took four days and we had great fun along the way.

After living with her cousin Mary Anne and her husband Nick for several months, Judy, Kym and Marigrace moved into a shared room in the Samaritan Inn, a transitional housing unit that helps parents with small families get their lives in order. Judy began volunteering for them and after working for them for several years, she developed a strong attraction to the power of religion and a real passion for helping others in need. "I had a business helping people clean up their homes," she said, "but it's more gratifying to help them clean up their lives."

Since then, Judy, Kym, and Marigrace have moved on. Kym is a successful nurse; Judy continues to have a succession of part-time jobs to help pay the bills while she establishes LIFESTEPS, an organization to help women build a healthy and stable future for themselves and their families. She and Kym live in Judy's home where, on trips to Florida, I've tried to help with a bit of painting and other light work. And, as she gets ideas for jobs she'd like to pursue, I've written cover letters and updated her resume. It's what big brothers do.

SO, MORE THAN SIXTY YEARS AFTER the October day, we all moved into the Oriole side of the duplex on the corner, the Gibbons kids are scattered all over the country, living in places our mom and dad never could have imagined, doing things we never expected.

A lot of people helped us along the way, but looking back, there is one remarkable woman who—especially in the early years—gave us the support we needed to believe in ourselves. She was like a second mother to us.

We called her Auntie.

# 7

# AUTIE

**S**HE SHOWED UP EVERY MORNING, carrying everything she needed for the day in an old shopping bag; she was as close to being a selfless person as a person could be.

We had lots of aunts, but she was our only "Auntie." She was a wonderful but worrying lady. In the early years, when Uncle George drove her, she worried if he drove faster than twenty miles an hour. During the years when she took the bus, she worried when it crossed the Driving Park Bridge; she was afraid of heights and falling into the water below. But she came every day so Mom could take a part-time job and we'd have someone home to fix us lunch and to be there after school. She never had kids of her own; we would always be her family.

She was born Laura Louise Koch—although, for a reason that was never explained, she was mostly called Loretta—in 1904, maybe in a hospital, but more likely in the family home, in the section of Rochester called "Dutchtown" because of all the German families who settled there. She was Mom's oldest sister; Auntie's mother, Theresa Uhl Koch was twenty-four, her dad, Frank was twenty-six and a driver for a brewery.

In Auntie's grammar school years, classes were taught in German, and she could always speak a bit of it in a hard, guttural way. "*Dumbkopf,*" she would say—literally "dumb head"—or "*Halt's Maul*" "close your mouth"—using the term for an animal's mouth, rather than a human one. Her family also spoke German at home; she graduated from Holy Family School in 1918; she never went beyond eighth grade. But in 1926, when she was twenty-two and working in a box factory, she married thirty-two-year-old George Tremer, a plumber living on Flower Street in a home where they'd live together for the rest of their lives

Uncle George would eventually go into business with another plumber named Joe Badhorn and when he drove their truck to our home, we kids would find big black hunks of tar on the back floor. Plumbers used tar to fill holes—but we'd bite off a piece and chew it like gum. There's no reason why we didn't become "deathly sick" from germs.

Uncle George was a quiet, thoughtful, good man who was in love with Auntie—not with public displays of affection but in ways in which people show they care for each other, where they're always ready to give more than they expect to get. He called Auntie, "Loll," and never seemed in a bad mood. In his younger days, he'd been an avid hunter. I have a vague recollection of him bringing over some rabbits he had killed and cleaned—and maybe even some deer meat—but when my mother cooked them, none of us liked them and he never brought them again. But he did give us vegetables and fruit; they grew cherry tomatoes alongside their house and had apple and pear trees out back.

Auntie was a heavy woman, always having trouble with her legs, but when we came home for lunch, she was always standing there, frying us up some bologna—burning it because she knew I liked it blackened and crispy, for fried bologna sandwiches—or cutting thick slices of sweet onions, adding salt and pepper and hot mustard—because she knew that we liked "onion sandwiches with mustard on."

Auntie's world was a small world, and one where religion played a large role; she had a great and special devotion to Mary, the mother of God, and to St. Anthony. When she was very nervous or concerned over something, she'd sit, close her eyes, and pray the rosary. She prayed often but she also lived a life of sacrificing for others. She was always giving from what little she had, never expecting any-thing in return. She was a great supporter of the Catholic missions, especially those in Alabama. "Alabama," she told me one evening, "is a very poor state. The people there really need our help."

"Auntie," I asked her, "What's the farthest you have ever traveled from your home here in Rochester?" Her answer: "once, back when George was alive, we went on a trip to Binghamton." Binghamton is about ninety miles from Roch-ester; Auntie was in her late eighties at the time and in her whole life, she'd never been farther than a couple of hours' drive from where she grew up.

But, despite her lack of travel, she never acted as if she had missed out on anything. She always seemed satisfied with what she had—and perfectly content when others had more. She was always a good listener, eager to hear what us kids were doing both when we were young and going to school—as well as when we had children of our own and had moved on.

At some point, Auntie could no longer care for the home where she and Uncle George lived for so long, the only home she had ever really known; it was sold to a distant relative and Auntie moved to St. Ann's Home. My mother worked there, so she could visit Auntie often. And, to break up her week, and give her someone else to talk to, I'd drive over for an hour or so every Sunday night.

In the beginning, it was fun. She was happy for the company, always had a treat, maybe a bag of popcorn someone had given her and now she wanted to give to me "to take home for the kids." We'd laugh and talk about our yesterdays; she always wanted to know what our kids were doing and saying. I told her, once about our then-very-young Emily talking about her older brother, Tim. Emily had said that "when Tim grows up, he's never going to be married; he's going to be a 'spatula'."

"Honey," I told Emily, "the word is 'bachelor', not 'spatula'. Tim is going to be a bachelor, not a spatula."

"'Bachelor, 'spatula,'" Emily said. "I knew it sounded like that."

Auntie roared over that story when I first told it—and every Sunday night when I'd come back, she always asked to hear it again. "Tell me the spatula story," she'd say—and I would. She seemed to enjoy it as much every time she heard it.

Back in the late 1970's, when Jeanne and I bought our first home, we picked up Auntie and brought her over for a visit. Her legs were giving her trouble and she moved slowly, but she liked to get out "for fresh air." She could still do that back then—and for a few years after that, she also liked us to bring the kids to her for a visit. One of my last pictures of her is with our kids and Mike's at St. Ann's on Mother's Day. It was appropriate; she really was a second mother to Mike and me.

But slowly at first—and then more rapidly—she started to slip away; she stopped watching TV, reading the newspaper. She had always been so aware of what was going on; she lost interest in all that now. She stopped going to group activities—including Bingo, a game she always loved to play. She seldom left her room and sometimes, she didn't even leave her bed.

The medical staff at St. Ann's wanted to put her through a series of tests to prove conclusively if she had some form of dementia. When they asked permission, they suggested the tests would be thorough, but maybe a bit tough on her. My brother Mike asked the best question: "If Auntie does have dementia, what will you do differently for her than you would do otherwise?" The staff admitted that, although they'd know more, none of her daily care would change. In that case, we decided, we weren't going to let Auntie be subjected to any tests. They would be difficult and maybe demeaning and we loved her too much to put her through that.

And so she never was. I would still stop by to talk to her on Sunday evenings, but oftentimes, I felt like I was just talking to myself. I'd sit by her bed, tell her stories to no reaction; she stopped asking for the spatula story, stopped laughing when I told it anyway. I was never sure she heard me, but that was OK; it was the least I could do to be there for her, in return for all the times she'd been there for me.

I remember one night when I was in the Army, alone, living in the barracks out in Junction City Kansas. My take-home pay was sixty-eight dollars a month and I tried to send some of that home to Jeanne—and to save even the smallest amount so I could afford to bring Jeanne out to live with me. I was flat broke all the time, couldn't even afford to go to the movies on base, where a ticket cost twenty-five cents. I never told anyone because I didn't think they needed to know.

But then, one evening I got a letter from Auntie—and inside was a twenty-dollar bill. She didn't make a big deal out of it, she just sent it along with a note that said she hoped I was doing well. For me, it felt like all the money in the world, more than a week's pay, enough to cut through the loneliness and brighten what were then dark Army days. That twenty-dollar bill was so important that more than forty years later I can still see myself on that evening sitting out on the second-floor porch of the barracks, opening the envelope, finding the money— and crying. I still tear up thinking about it. I hadn't asked, but Auntie "just knew" that I needed someone to "help out," just as she had always known—and always come through along the way.

The last time I went to visit her at St. Ann's Home, she was lying in bed, eyes completely closed; she was sleeping and didn't seem inclined to want to wake up. I stayed for a little while—and when I left, I knew the Auntie I loved—and who loved us—for so long, was gone.

Loretta Tremer died on the first of April 1993, two days before my birthday. She was eighty-eight years old, and when she died, she took a piece of our yesterdays with her. Because Auntie belonged to us Gibbons kids of Oriole Street. She had been with us from the beginning and always seemed to show up exactly when we needed her, beginning when we needed her most—during our grammar school days.

# 8

# GRAMMAR SCHOOL DAYS

TWENTY YEARS AFTER I GRADUATED, Holy Rosary grammar school burned to the ground. On Saturday, December 19, 1981, Al Goff was walking to his early morning job at Wegmans, when he smelled smoke and saw flames in a basement window. He rushed to the rectory just across the driveway. *"Father,"* he told the priest who answered the door, *"the school's on fire."*

Twelve fire companies answered the three-alarm blaze that morning; it would be more than two hours before they had the fire under control. Only two things had been spared: a stained-glass window showing Christ teaching young children—and a crucifix hanging on a melted nail in a third-grade classroom. Some said they were miracles, signs that Holy Rosary School was meant to go on.

Within a month after the fire, a committee was formed and four months later, they recommended to the bishop that the school be rebuilt. It would incorporate the stained-glass window saved from the original building; and the spared crucifix would hang on one of the walls. In September 1984, two hundred and seventy-two students started their new school year in that building.

It was very different from the original red brick building that for seven years had been a center in my life—and would forever influence who I would become.

Classes had already begun when we moved into Holy Rosary parish in October of 1954; our home on Oriole Street was three houses from the school. No student had a shorter walk, could get up later in the morning or get home earlier in the afternoon; no one had more time for lunch.

There was a public school—School 34—just a block or so away on Holmes Street, but there was never any question about where my brother and sisters and I would go to school. We were Catholic and Catholics went to Catholic school— which was very affordable back then. In those days, we were taught by nuns and most of their expenses were covered by the Sunday church collection. School tuition *per family*—for as many children as a family had in the school—was *two dollars a month*, sent into the teacher in a small white envelope. And, for that, we were given an education that gave us a grounding in the fundamentals that provided values for a lifetime.

We came to school every day ready to learn—with assignments completed on time—because the consequences of not doing that included all the ways that kids were disciplined back then: a rap on the knuckles, a whack on the seat of the pants, searing criticism in front of our peers, being kept after school—or being sent to the Principal's Office. We had a fear of—and respect for—authority back then.

My father had gone to this school from kindergarten in 1923 through graduation in 1931—exactly thirty years before I would graduate. But when I transferred here, I was in second grade, a month or so into the school year; my new teacher was Sister Barbara Joan, a young nun who had grown up in Canandaigua, a lake-town about thirty miles east of Rochester. Our classroom was one of four in the school basement—two first grades at the front of the school and one other second grade classroom around the corner. For most grades, there were at least two classes, sometimes three; Holy Rosary had twenty-two classrooms for nine grades. Often, there were more than thirty kids in a class.

Second grade was the time when we made both our "First Confession" and "First Holy Communion" and I did both in May of 1955; both required wearing a white shirt and tie and being in a procession from the school to the church.

Catholic schools were seriously into kids lining up silently before they did any-thing—mostly according to height. Since I was tall from a young age, I was usually the last one in line.

Standing someplace in front of me would be John Houle, distinctive for his red hair; he'd be my friend, co-worker, and at one point that year, he'd be the kid who threw me backwards on a metal railing—we were wrestling in the school parking lot—causing a small hole in the back of my scalp that my doctor had to clean with peroxide. When John later—also accidentally—nicked my brother's head with a baseball bat in a pick-up game, my mother decided we had to "stop playing with John. . . ."

Mary Gruttadaria, a second-grade classmate, died during that year and al-though I didn't know her very well, it was my first realization that it was possible for someone my own age to pass away.

In the summer after second grade, I went away to Camp Stella Maris, a Cath-olic camp staffed by young seminarians on nearby Conesus Lake. It cost fifty dollars per camper, included a full week of crafts and swimming, and ended with a "contest:" *Prizes for those who could pick up the most pieces of paper littering the camp compound.* It was, of course, just a ruse for us to clean up the area; but I was later appalled to learn that the older campers had a system for winning: they ripped everything they picked up into several small pieces. I never stood a chance.

When camp finished, my parents took me to Lollypop Farm, the animal res-cue center where Dad paid five dollars for a little black and tan mongrel I called "Winky." She lasted only a few weeks before getting distemper and had to be put down. A couple of years later, I got another mongrel called "Muggsy" who lasted only a few weeks longer. My mom had warned me: *"If you don't take care of her, you'll have to give her away."* I didn't—and my mother made good on her threat. When the people came to pick her up, my mom insisted that I be the one to hand her over.

My third-grade teacher was Sister Celina. Those were the years before Cath-olic school kids had to wear a uniform, so I often wore my favorite shirt to class—a bright red flannel shirt in honor and emulation of my TV hero: *Sergeant Preston of the Yukon.* For a kid who had never been more than fifty or sixty miles from home, the program opened my eyes and my imagination to a place of even more ice and snow that we'd get in a typical Rochester winter. Years later, I'd discover that most episodes were shot in California, close to where we would later live. Richard Simmons who played Sgt. Preston died in Oceanside, California, in 2003; we'd move there eight years later.

One Saturday when I was in third grade, Uncle Al Marriott picked up my brother Mike, my sister Pat, and me, drove us to the Lexington Avenue station, and took us for a ride on the subway. "The subway system is going away," he told us; "I thought you should ride on it before it's gone." The idea for a subway began in Rochester in 1918 when the Erie Canal was rerouted to bypass downtown Rochester and the abandoned portion of the canal was bought to serve as the core. It was discontinued in 1956; today, more than half a century later, Rochester officials are still arguing over what to do with the land.

By fourth grade, I was spending more time with books than television—a habit my fourth-grade teacher, Mrs. Mueller, encouraged. If we finished our classwork early, she'd let us read. She even had a few serial books in the small library she created—two shelves against the wall, between the radiators. That was the year I was introduced briefly to *Dan Carter—Cub Scout, Rick Blaine, Ken Holt, Chip Hilton,* and others. I read all the serial books she had, but before all those, I had discovered the Hardy Boys.

My adventures with them started when my mom was shopping downtown at Sibley's department store—as she did every Wednesday—and arbitrarily picked up a book whose cover art caught her attention: it showed two young guys swimming away from a boat on fire. She always encouraged me to read, so she bought the book and brought it home. Its title was *The Hardy Boys: The Hidden Harbor Mystery*—and, with it, my lifelong love of reading began.

I followed them to secret cabins and cliffs and caves where they found clues in footprints and feathers and flickering torches and solved mysteries in an old mill, a lost tunnel, a wildcat swamp. I read the books as quickly as Mom could bring them home—or I could get others by swapping mine with friends who had other titles I wanted to read.

There was a lot of suspense in their adventures and every chapter ended in a cliffhanger, but there was a lot of humor in those books also and the violence was toned down. There was the occasional fistfight, but evil men were more likely to *cackle and snarl,* or even *roar;* in one book, a pirate spoke to the boys *sardonically.* I don't recall anyone ever being actually killed.

Although the books were written by several authors under the pseudonym, Franklin W. Dixon, most of my favorites were the work of Les McFarlane whose autobiography was called *Ghost of the Hardy Boys.* I read all twenty books he wrote—including his last one, *The Phantom Freighter,* published in 1947, the year I was born—plus nineteen others. I still have copies of each one I've read.

I went through a growth spurt during fifth grade and ended up with lots of stomach problems the previous and following summers. And in the fall of the year, I had so many ear infections that, at one point, I was laying on the couch in my parents' living room with a serious earache, wondering if I'd recover in time to make my Confirmation. It turned out that I did, just barely—and on a rainy evening in October, I took the name "Francis" in honor of my mom's dad. I was now Robert John Francis; I had my father's name, as well as that of both grandfathers. For a gift from my sponsor—my Uncle Anthony—I got a new fishing tackle box with lots of his old rusty tackle inside.

And fifth grade was also a "musical year." It was the year when Sister Anna Louise, the nun who gave singing lessons once a week to all classes, told me she couldn't decide if I was an alto, soprano, or something else; she just knew I couldn't carry a tune. But that was the year I also began taking lessons to play the drums; if my instructor Frank Melville were still alive, I'd love to thank him for all the fun I had with my drums over the next fifteen years.

My sixth-grade teacher was Sister Josita and because she was one of my most influential teachers, I later asked the archivist at the Saint Joseph's Motherhouse for more information about her. Her name, they said, had been Elizabeth Granville and she was born in Ireland in 1899; she came to Rochester with her dad after her mother died and ended up in St. Patrick's orphanage, run by the Sisters of St. Joseph. Elizabeth worked there for a few years before she entered the convent in 1919. She taught for forty-five years in several schools of the Rochester Diocese including twice at Holy Rosary. At the time of her death in 1980, her fellow sisters said that she "was always generous with her time and had a keen sense of humor."

*A sense of humor?* You couldn't have proved it by me. I would have said, *an unflinching focus on the basics.* But she did call all us boys 'master'—and we used to have a bit of fun behind her back when she called on a boy named Timothy Bates, *"Master Bates…"*

But she drilled us endlessly on grammar, making us diagram sentences until I thought my eyes would go blind and my brain would go numb. *"What is the part of speech and how is it being used in the sentence?"* she would ask repeatedly as she drew straight lines on the blackboard to separate the subject from the verb—with diagonal lines for adverbs and then dependent clauses on lines above and dependent phrases below and on and on.… .

In the end, her teaching was incredibly effective with me. She greatly heightened my awareness of writing and how everything fit together. I've spent the greater part of my forty-plus years in business as a corporate writer and I've often said proudly: "most of what I know about grammar came from my time with Sister Josita in the sixth grade." As I once told my boss at Kodak: "Your inability to use adverbs correctly in your presentation really annoys those of us who understand gerunds, past participles, and parallel construction."

In seventh grade, I had Sister Gemma Marie and she had been teaching for twenty-five years before I came into her classroom. I have only a few recollections from that year with her: one embarrassed her, the second one gave me an idea I'd use often in my writing throughout my life.

One day—and Sister really should have known better with kids our age—she invited each of us to come up to the front of class and tell our favorite joke. I still remember the one my classmate Bobby Baker told.

"A man is standing on a street corner," Bobby said, "and he's stretching something in his hands. Somebody comes up to him and looks at what he's stretching. 'Gee,' says the other person, 'it looks like rubber. It feels like rubber. It even smells like rubber. Where did you get it?' 'I got it,' the man says, 'out of my nose.'" "Mr. Baker," Sister said without so much as a smile, "that is *not* funny. Sit down." The rest of us? We were screaming with laughter.

Earlier that year, when we returned to the classroom in September, Sister asked us to write about our summer vacation. Around that time, I had been doing a bit of writing, but my heroes were usually young boys in a band—I wrote what I knew—and named Ted and Tom and Al—short names because I was writing everything longhand. I found that I enjoyed writing but wasn't serious about it. Still, from my reading, I liked a good story and wanted to tell one in the essay she asked us to write.

My story took place on a past summer day as I was diving off our rented boat on Fair Haven Bay. My brother Mike had loaned me his pocket-knife to use for some project I'd been working on back at the cottage; and, for some reason, I had it in the pocket of my swimming trunks when I dove in the water, went down deeper than I normally did. . .and got caught in dense seaweed below the surface.

And so there I was in my story, down about fifty feet, caught and struggling unbeknownst to everyone else in the boat above, unable to hold my breath much longer. *What would Frank and Joe Hardy do?* Suddenly, I remembered my brother's pocket-knife and with my lungs nearly bursting, I cut myself loose, kicked my way to surface, and exhaustedly swam over to the boat. Only to find—I added as a little 'kicker'—*my brother was angry because, in my struggles to save my life, I had dropped his knife.*

Part of that story was, of course, true; I often dove in Fair Haven Bay. The rest, not so much. But the fun came from blurring the lines between fact and fiction. But Sister Gemma Marie seemed not to care. She read it to the class. It was the first thing I remember writing that someone wanted to read out loud.

There were two eighth grade teachers at Holy Rosary in 1960—Sister Lucida and Sister Cyril. In a comment on how women were viewed at the time, neither nun was shown in our class graduation picture—although all five parish priests were. But I was lucky I got Sister Cyril because she was by far the better teacher.

She was in her mid-forties when she taught me, but her attitude was younger, fresher, and she was a straight shooter—you played fair with her, she played fair with you. She reminded us often: *"I know all your tricks because once upon a time, I tried them myself. But,"* she said, *"if you're honest and I believe you, I'll defend you against anyone. Even Sister Mary George.*" Sister Mary George was the Principal of Holy Rosary School, our female version of the Pope. I couldn't imagine anyone being willing to tell Sister Mary George: "*You're wrong. Bob is right.*"

Sister Cyril never had to defend me against anyone, but she was one who always spoke her mind—and in simple language. "Your future is behind you" she'd tell the slackers in the class; and that year, when the class took a graduation trip to Roseland Park, an amusement park in nearby Canandaigua, she warned the boys against spending money on girls. "You don't have to be playboys", she said. I wondered if she had read that magazine. I had not.

And she seemed fearless. "Last night we had a mouse running around the convent," she told the class one day. "It was so fascinating to watch, I forgot that I was supposed to be scared." Many years later, I was talking to another nun I always respected, Sister Jean Louise, who was the convent cook in those days. I mentioned how much I liked Sister Cyril. "Cyril was great," Sr. Jean Louise said, "she and I used to have so much fun together. One time we were fooling around, and I think she fell down a flight of stairs."

The most significant world event of my eighth-grade year was the inauguration of John F. Kennedy. There were no TVs in classrooms back then, but somehow, Sister Cyril got one, and on that cold January day in Washington, we sat in our warm classroom in Rochester, watching the first Catholic president take office in black and white. Since she died in 1993, Sister Cyril lived long enough to learn the truth about Kennedy's philandering, but I don't think that would have phased her or made her regret showing us the event. She was a woman in touch with her times. And she was a wonderful teacher who knew how to bring out the best in us. She gave me a great foundation for my high school education.

And so that was Holy Rosary during my grammar school years. It was kind of a "bare bones approach" to education; we didn't have a lot of the extras that schools consider necessities today. There was no gym and no classes in art or physical education. There was a very small Nurse's Office, but we had a nurse in it only a few days a week. If kids had problems that required a school psychologist or other similar support, they weren't available at Holy Rosary. We never heard of "teacher's aides" or a school librarian. Classes always had more than thirty—often more than forty—students in one room, but the teacher never had any problem being fully in control.

The only language taught was English; those who misbehaved were removed from the classroom—or sometimes, the school. If you didn't want to learn, you weren't allowed to interfere with others who did.

But what the school offered was an excellent education taught by dedicated teachers who maintained a sense of discipline and created in us a sense of fairness and a belief in a higher power. They held everyone—including themselves—accountable. They expected the best from us, every day and, in the process, they taught us to expect the best from ourselves.

And after it was all finished, there I was, the tallest kid in the graduation picture, standing in the center of the top row with the other ninety-five members of my class (forty-five boys, fifty-one girls—including Jeanne Stein, the girl I'd marry); we were the Class of 1961, Holy Rosary School, right there in the old tenth ward.

# 9

# THE OLD TENTH WARD

From the October day in 1954 when we moved into the neighborhood—until the day I walked up the street to Holy Rosary Church to get married on July 19, 1969 and left the area forever—the tenth ward was home.

Once, Rochester had twenty-four wards—extended neighborhoods—of which the tenth was arguably the largest; in the center of it were "the bird streets" —Finch and Canary, Starling, Wren, Lark and Dove; we lived on Oriole. It was a nice middle-class neighborhood back then, a place of family-size homes, mostly built in the 1890s through the 1920s—as part a large growth in the area after the Rochester Driving Park Racetrack closed.

My grandfather remembered the track from the days of his youth; the home we lived in would have been across the street from its southern boundary; Jeanne grew up along what would have been its northern edge.

The mile-long track opened in 1875 and doubled as a baseball park for the 'Rochesters' during its first two seasons. It had a bandstand, luxury boxes, restaurants, wine rooms and a hotel. Over the years, "The Driving Park" would book a variety of events—including Buffalo Bill's Wild West Show, and Barnum & Bailey Ringling Brothers Circus—before the wooden grandstands burned in an 1899 fire and the massive grounds—easily sixty city blocks—went into foreclosure four years later. Some say that those living in the neighborhood are still able to dig up a horseshoe or a bit of harness iron from their flower gardens. We never found any of that.

But when the track left, the builders created a mixed-use neighborhood, with homes and shops often in the same building. Albert's Coffee Shop was one example. Joe and Ann Albert—and their son Joey, who played the clarinet and became a friend—had converted their lower floor into a restaurant where they once treated my brother and me to a free meal. They lived upstairs.

Albert's Coffee Shop was one of many shops in the area—mostly along Driving Park, Dewey, and Lexington avenues. It was a commercial block dominated by Wegmans, a then-medium-sized supermarket that would go on to become a giant in the grocery business—and a celebrated leader in its field, wildly successful in Rochester and beyond. It had two entrances and exits, one on Finch Street between a collision shop and residential homes; there were checkout cashiers at each end. Its parking lot bordered Winteroth's Shoe Store.

Ed Winteroth lived a couple of blocks away, across the street from where I had lived with Pappy in the early years of my life. In summer, we lived in the sneakers we bought from him; they were black high top Keds and cost three dollars a pair.

We bought a new pair at the beginning of summer and wore them mercilessly; baseball on asphalt is especially tough on the soles of sneakers. Within a month, we'd have a hole worn in the bottom and we'd put several layers of baseball cards into the sneaker to keep our socks from being torn. But as the cards wore through, I'd show the now-sizeable hole to my mom, and she'd tell me: "Take the shoes back to Mr. Winteroth and see what he wants to do." What he did was replace them, free, with a brand-new pair. At least once a summer. Every summer. Small shopkeepers were like that back then.

Next to the shoe store was the local post office and an alleyway that led to the apartment where my friend Mickey Farrell lived upstairs. Mickey once brought a small alligator back from Florida and kept it in an aquarium in his garage. When it outgrew that tank, he let it go in Lake Ontario.

There were other, mostly family-run, stores in the neighborhood. DiJunes market sold fresh produce; from their discarded orange crates, we carved tomahawks and built soap-box derby racers. Old Ben Grayley at Grayley's Pharmacy often had an empty cigar box he'd give us to keep baseball cards; and next door, in Haller and Jones Music, the two young owners in white shirts and ties always had the latest records—and would let us listen before we bought.

Just down the street, Ledlie's Jewelers was run by Jim Ledlie who had a lending library of books on jewelry in the back of his store—and advertised the new books in his collection weekly in the *Tenth Ward Courier*. Christoff's Market sold packs of six Topps baseball cards—with a fat piece of bubble gum—for a nickel, and when we'd ask "to see your penny candy," they'd take a large cardboard box from a back shelf and put it on the counter. There was always a good selection.

Sy's Drugs had a big machine I used to test the tubes in our TV whenever we lost the picture—and he sold replacements. He also always had the best selection of comic books and every year, when school began, he gave out a free lollipop to any kid who stopped by to say, "hi Sy." In a former bank building on the corner of Dewey and Driving Park Avenues, Duke Spinner ran a huge music store and I always found reasons to visit. My friend Dave Smering taught music there and sometimes Jack White would stop by. Jack was the drummer for the Duke Spinner Orchestra, one of the better-known big bands in the city. He never had a lot to say, but I liked being around another drummer. But one day, right there on Driving Park Avenue, Jack accidentally ran over and killed a young boy; and Jack never seemed right after that.

There were a couple of diners in the area, including Critics and Shultz's where Pappy would take me for milkshakes. Sometimes, when Pappy was up for a walk, he and I would head up to Edgerton Park where we'd go to the library (it was the only one around in those days) —and maybe across the street to Al's Stand for a five-cent sno-cone. A few years later, Al was accused of selling horsemeat mixed with the beef for hamburgers and I stopped in with my friend, Mike Fenton. We each ordered a burger and when the cook put them on the grill,

Mike said, "and they're off." When the cook flipped them over, Mike said, "and they're coming to the clubhouse turn." Before they finished cooking, Al chased Mike and me out of the restaurant.

Perhaps the most unique vendor of food in the neighborhood was one room on the side of a house on Dewey Avenue. It was only open for a few hours on Friday—and sold only fried fish, cole slaw, and french fries—all by the pound, and only "to go." There was always a line of people down the block, waiting to buy. One day, I stopped over and bought a bag of fries for a snack. I put so much salt on them, before I could eat them, I had to wash them off—at our side outdoor faucet.

Fish fries were very popular in Rochester—and still are—along with white hot dogs, ground rounds, Genesee beer, and a thing called a 'garbage plate,' which includes two hot dogs (or cheeseburgers), baked beans, and macaroni salad on a paper plate, all covered with hot sauce. That's what we grew up eating—and somehow, we survived.

Although we kids never had much spending money, you could often find me at Herman's Hobby Shop—where I bought a lot of plastic boondoggle for two-cents a yard to braid into lanyards, or balsa wood to carve into airplanes. Herman's was run by a man and his wife. His name was Herman Pfund and although I never knew her name, my friend Mike Fenton called her "Mrs. Herman's Hobby Shop"—and she seemed OK with that.

Next door to Herman's was the Liberty Theatre. It was very convenient, but it was a third-run house; it played movies only after they finished playing in larger first-run theatres downtown. Still, on Saturday afternoons we often stood in long lines wrapped around the building, waiting to see *Davy Crockett* or *A Light in the Forest* or *Forbidden Planet*. It was a single screen theatre with twelve hundred seats. Tickets were twenty-five cents. It finally closed in December 1959, when I was in seventh grade and the building was demolished.

By that time, when I was looking for something to do, I often took the bus downtown with my brother and our friends. We mostly ended up at Army surplus stores around South Avenue or in one of the music stores—Relins, which was always well-stocked with used instruments or Levis, a large store on Main Street with booths where we could listen to records. Sibleys, McCurdy's, and Edwards were the three main department store and they dominated downtown. Sibleys occupied an entire block with nine stories of merchandise and a twelve-story tower; at one point, it was the largest department store between New York City and Chicago and on its top floor it had an elegant executive dining room. At Christmas time, after breakfast with Santa, Sibleys offered a free train ride through a holiday wonderland. A block away, at Neisners, a slice of pizza cost a dime; for nineteen cents, I often bought a hot dog on a steamed roll with mustard and onions.

Although the bus also only cost a dime—the #10 Dewey Avenue dropped me off two blocks from my home—there were days when I didn't have enough money to get something to eat and to ride the bus—and so I ended up walking the several miles from downtown to home. The day I'd gone downtown to see the Disney movie, *Toby Tyler*, it was dark and snowing heavily when the movie finished. The bus I was on got stuck in the snow about halfway home—and I decided to get out and walk the rest of the way. I arrived home cold and wet—with snow in my boots—but the city was much safer back then and my mother never seemed to be worried about where I was.

Rochester in general—and our neighborhood in particular—was filled mostly with good people who seldom left. In a 1967 contest to identify the longest residents in the tenth ward, the winner was Barbara Ludwig of Emerson Street; she lived in the same house for eighty-five years.

Since we all did our own chores, cut our own grass, often sat out on our porch, we tended to know our neighbors. Next to us on Oriole Street was Ed Wincup, an older man who had a drill press in his basement where he once drilled out the axles so we could use cotter pins to keep the wheels on our soap-box derby racers. And next to him lived Eddie and Fun Generieux, from Canada, whose garage window I once broke when I was playing baseball in the adjacent Holy Rosary parking lot

Our neighbors on Driving Park Avenue were Louis and Rosalie Paone; Rosalie and Mom sometimes split the cost of a two-dollar daily double ticket at the local racetrack on a tip from Rosalie's husband Louis who spent endless hours sitting in his Chevrolet Impala, checking his racing forms. Down the street lived my friend Craig Lay—we called him Butch—whose mother sometimes drove us kids to Seneca Park Pool on hot summer evenings. There, for twenty-five cents, we got the use of a locker, showers, and—for an hour-and-a-half—the often-freezing-cold pool.

Next to Butch Lay's house was a big green four-story apartment house; two of the apartments were rented to Hungarian families—the Czmadias and the Jankowiczs—who settled in Rochester after escaping Hungary during the 1956 revolution. Their experiences with the Russians must have been harrowing, but Eugene Czmadia—a small, quiet boy who was a year or two younger than me—was laughing when he told me of pouring boiling water on Russian soldiers who tried to break down their doors during the night. I was interested in their culture, so when Eugene and his cousin Steve Jankowicz asked me to teach them to play baseball, I asked them to teach me to count in Hungarian. They did—and to this day, I can still count from one to ten.

I'd eventually become friends with other kids in the neighborhood—John Houle with whom I later worked, Charley Myers who would follow me to Notre Dame, Dave Smering who has his own story in this book, and Gary Cook who lived right across from us on Driving Park Avenue. Gary and his parents, Norm and Jean, rented a half-double from the Capuanos, whose son Frank—with whom I graduated from Holy Rosary—died in Vietnam when he threw himself on a live grenade to save his other Marine Corps buddies.

I'm not sure how I met Gary because we never went to school together but at some point, his ability to play the accordion and mine to play the drums brought us together and we played for several years as members of a band called *The Quintones*. When Gary was about sixteen years old, he was hit crossing Driving Park Avenue—and was thrown into a telephone pole. He was hit so hard, his sneaker was left in the crosswalk; I'm not sure he ever made a full recovery although within the next four years, he'd enrolled in and dropped out of a small college where he was studying music—and then joined and was released by the Navy.

He called me one day when I was home from college—and bragged a bit about his military situation. "When you get out of college, you'll be drafted," he told me. "But I don't have to worry about that. I hated basic training so much that I convinced them I have a bad back—and now I'm classified 4F. I can't be drafted. I'm done—and you still have military service ahead of you." That was the story he told back then, but I think he oversimplified the truth; his old injuries may have played a role. And although he didn't have military service ahead, he also didn't have a college degree for a professional job—and had a record of being physically limited for handling manual labor. Put all of that together and his job prospects were a bit slim.

For a long time, the last I had heard of Gary, he was working as a debt collector for Household Finance—which had to be a dangerous job—and had left Rochester. And although I always had others like Gary to hang around with, my parents didn't have many non-family friends in the neighborhood, but the Schneiders were one. They lived only a block away from us and their son Billy, who was a few months older than me, became a friend of mine.

Billy's mother Catherine seemed to be sick for most of the time I knew her, lying on the living room couch, covered with a blanket. She was very religious and hoped to see her son as an altar server; he and I were both in training, but he wasn't making much progress.

One day she asked me to come into the living room. Alone. In her hand was the little Latin card we had to memorize to be a server—and attached to it with a paper clip was a five-dollar bill. She told me that she didn't have much time left. She said: "If you can help Billy learn this whole card, there is a five-dollar bill for you." I said that I wasn't yet a full altar boy and didn't know when I would be one. *I'll do what I can*, I said, but mostly I wondered: *What did she mean that she didn't have much time left?* I do remember that she had tears in her eyes when she put the card back on her blanket; the five-dollar bill was still attached. Catherine Schneider passed away in early July 1957, when I was about to go into fifth grade. Her husband Bill carried on as a single parent.

We called him Big Bill because he was a solidly built man; he often wore sleeveless undershirts and took pride in being rugged. He came from Germany and never completely lost his accent. Although he claimed to have been in the

US Army during World War II, my mother told me that the Army wouldn't accept him because they thought he might be a spy. My mother might have made that up.

Big Bill's house was always a mess; wall panels were missing, the glass on his kitchen table was cracked. He didn't seem to care. "Billy doesn't have a mother," he said one time; "if people don't like the way our house looks, they don't have to come over." But we did love to come over because Big Bill was an artist and, on Saturday mornings, he gave us lessons, teaching us to draw pastels in chalk. Mike and Billy and I would sit happily at tray tables in their living room drawing and watching *Mr. Winky Dink* or *Sky King* on their small television set.

In addition to being an artist, Bill was, he said, a restorer of damaged goods. He had several damaged pianos in his garage at the end of his long tree-lined driveway—and one day, he decided to paint an extension of that driveway on the outside of his big garage doors. It was impressive until the day one of his clients drove down that driveway and kept on going—until he found himself and his car inside the garage, all tangled up in restored pianos. The next day, Big Bill painted his garage door white.

Working from home, he always seemed to have time available to spend on us kids. He built a tree fort in the largest tree along the driveway and held hot dog and marshmallow roasts beneath it; he made a wading pool out of four ladders and a heavy piece of canvas and one April he held an Easter egg hunt in his yard. In summer, he'd pile us into his rusted white Desoto with the back seat removed and take us to the Kodak dump for old lumber or to the Bausch and Lomb glass pile on the banks of the Genesee River; some afternoons we'd end up at the end of Island Cottage Road where, between two houses, and over a fence that had been knocked down, he'd take us swimming in Lake Ontario.

For a long time, Bill Bill came over every Friday night, bringing fish that he'd cook using "his special recipe." I enjoyed it until my mom told me that "I think he likes me; he wants to replace your dad"—and she didn't want that to happen. To help discourage him, I pretended not to like fish, to suggest I wanted something else to eat on Friday night. The ruse took time to work, but eventually he stopped coming over so often. And meanwhile, his health began to deteriorate—

but unfortunately, he tried to treat himself. When a back molar began to bother him, he went into his toolbox out in the garage and found a rusty pair of pliers. He washed them off in the sink, put those pliers in his mouth—and as he sat at his kitchen table with us kids watching—he pulled that tooth out of his mouth. But, even worse, he was always a heavy smoker and when he began having throat problems, for some unknown reason he treated himself by eating a combination of sugar and iodine. When he perforated his larynx, doctors performed a tracheotomy and installed a tube in his throat through which he talked in a very raspy voice. Big Bill died in May 1968; I later heard that Billy eventually married, got involved with drugs, and died young.

By that time, the old tenth ward was changing—and those changes would accelerate. There were two big changes that provided clear reminders that my yesterdays there were gone forever.

In 2008, citing declining attendance at city parishes, Holy Rosary closed its church and school that had served the Catholic community from that one location for well over one hundred years. It was small consolation—to me at least—that Holy Rosary had achieved landmark status and a listing on the National Register of Historic Places, so the church campus had been preserved. It's since been converted into apartments and housing for low-income families.

And the second indication that my yesterdays were irreparably gone: a year before—in 2007—claiming it now had the smallest footprint in their Rochester chain and was experiencing declining sales, Wegmans shuttered their Dewey-Driving Park store. I mourned its loss because that's where Mom always shopped, but perhaps equally important, it was in that Wegmans parking lot where I had learned to play blacktop baseball.

# 10

## BLACKTOP BASEBALL

I LEARNED TO PLAY SPORTS ON ASPHALT. My grammar school, just up the street, didn't have a playground or gym. The local public school, which was just a block away, had basketball hoops and a small baseball diamond, but they were surrounded by a chain-link fence with a gate that was always kept locked. There were no open fields in our area; and so, we played catch in the street in front of our home; we played basketball in Gary Cook's driveway because he had a net on his garage; and when we held football games in Holy Rosary parking lot, they were always 'touch,' because you can really get hurt being tackled on asphalt. Although I was never particularly good at any of that, what I really enjoyed was heading over to play a pickup game of baseball in the early evening at Wegman's parking lot.

Monday through Thursday, the store closed at six o'clock and so, every evening by about six thirty, we'd be over in that lot, getting a game together. No formal invitation was ever sent; the number of kids on each team depended on who showed up; one of the kids brought a ball—sometimes painted red or blue; several brought bats—and it wasn't unusual to have a few of those cracked and held together with screws; we each had our own gloves. There were no batting helmets or batters' gloves or any sort of protective gear.

It was always slow-pitch softball, but when you play on blacktop, you do some real damage to the ball. As it goes skimming along the rough asphalt, the laces get torn, the covering begins to fall off, the string inside begins to unravel. We always had masking tape around and sometimes it was so fully wrapped that I wasn't sure if we were playing with a real ball or just a wad of tape. For bases, we'd use Wegman's discarded cardboard, spread around the parking lot in roughly a diamond shape, at whatever distances seemed appropriate that evening; sometimes, in a wind, second base would end up deep in center field.

There were no umpires to call balls and strikes—and only a few simple rules: four foul balls and you were out; the game was over when anyone broke a window—or the ball became unusable.

Although I was never much good at the game, I did like to play it and one day, just before fourth grade let out for the summer, Mickey Farrell invited me to join a real team. Back then, Kodak, the company that dominated Rochester, sponsored free summer baseball leagues for grammar school kids. It was slow-pitch softball, and Kodak provided t-shirts, baseballs, bats, and the umpire; games were played mornings and afternoons on five or six full-sized baseball diamonds, mostly on Kodak property. And Mickey was captain of one of the teams. When I eagerly accepted his invitation, I thought he valued my athletic skills; looking back, I realize he needed to find enough players so he could be captain of the team.

I usually played a position called "rover," which is the tenth person on a nine-person team and seems to have been invented to give more kids a chance to play baseball. The rover plays just beyond second base—and it's a valuable position to have if your team has a slow shortstop or a lazy center fielder. We had a great shortstop—Danny Farrell, Mickey's cousin—and a very fast center fielder, my friend Doug Coleman. We didn't need a rover.

When only nine players showed up, I played right field, which was a place where balls were seldom hit. At one of the fields there was a large evergreen tree in the middle of right field. I played directly in front of that tree—and only once was the ball hit to me there. I misjudged it, it bounced behind me, and rolled under the tree. The umpire gave the batter a double.

And so, for me, there were four years of Kodak baseball, always on Mickey's team, always (I suspect) because he couldn't get enough other kids who wanted to play. Every year, I'd ask if I could play a different position; Mickey didn't have the courage to tell me I didn't have the ability—until the day our catcher didn't show up. "Today," Mickey said, "you'll be our catcher."

In Kodak softball, a flimsy mask was the only protection the catcher had against the batter, so I was scared. I put on the mask and crouched down about ten feet behind home plate. Mickey was the pitcher and he motioned me closer. I moved forward about three inches. He motioned again—and again—and again.

Finally, when I was in the right location, I stuck out my glove, Mickey pitched, the batter swung—*and took the glove right off my hand.* The batter walked to first base, our right fielder came in to catch and I trotted out to keep the tree company in right field. We played without a rover that day. And so it went; I showed up for every game, always played but knew I wasn't really helping us win . . . until that day when we played the only all-black team in the league.

Their pitcher was a tall lanky kid named Henry and he was legendary. The day we played his team, I wore sneakers on which, as a joke, I had written "left" and "right" on each toe—and Henry came over to point out to his friends, "this dummy doesn't know his left foot from his right." Actually, I had my feet figured out; the thing I didn't know that day was how I was going to get a hit off Henry. I wasn't much better at bat than I was in the field, but I knew that Henry was deceptive. He dressed raggedy, looked tired, seemed to do everything slowly— except pitch. He'd stand out there on the mound, reach into his big floppy glove and grip the softball. He'd crouch a bit, go into a bit of a windup, and release the ball. . .*at a thousand miles an hour.* How could I ever hit that?

The two teams were tied when I came up to bat late in the game—and Mickey had a suggestion. "Bob," he said, "you swing too slowly. You need to swing your bat as fast as you can—*as soon as Henry goes into his windup.*" It seemed to make no sense, but Mickey knew lots about baseball—and so when Henry reached his big right hand into that well-worn glove and began that slow process of delivering the baseball, I swung as hard as I could. *And I got a hit!* It was one of my very few hits that year—and I started a rally. Everyone else on our team figured that if I could hit Henry, *anyone* could hit Henry. We won that game and, that year, we won the league championship and we got to play our final game at night under the lights at the field with the big evergreen tree in right field. I played right field that night, but no balls were hit my way.

That was the last summer I played organized baseball, although I did stay interested in the game. The Red Wings, Rochester's AAA team played at a stadium that was a long, but possible, walk from my home and—in a few games from a seat in the outfield bleachers—I watched Luke Easter, Satchel Paige, Boog Powell and others who went on to great careers. One day, Pappy took me to that stadium to see a game by an amazing softball pitcher, Eddie Feigner, who traveled with a team of three other guys—first baseman, shortstop, and catcher; they were called, "The King and His Court" and regularly defeated a full team of nine players. In 1967, in a charity game, Feigner struck out Willie Mays, Willie McCovey, Brooks Robinson, Roberto Clemente, Maury Wills, and Harmon Killebrew—all in a row. They were kind of a white baseball version of the Harlem Globetrotters—entertaining, skillful, with a bit of comedy. When someone asked him why the team had four members, Feigner said that they couldn't play with three: If all three got on base, there would be no one available to come to bat. I still remember walking back home with Pappy on that cloudy afternoon; it had been a wonderful treat. I never played organized baseball—or even played in a game—after those years

But even then, perhaps because I wasn't very athletic, I wasn't much interested in sports; when I learned to play the drums, I found something I loved.

# II

# KEEPING THE BEAT

I N FIFTH GRADE, I SIGNED UP TO TAKE DRUM LESSONS. The instructor was
Frank Melville, a traveling "music man" who gave band lessons at five Catholic grammar schools, one each day of the week. When I asked him once
how he learned to play all the instruments, he told me it was a long story. I think
the short version was—he knew the basics; he made up everything else. He
taught in small group sessions; every Thursday, three or four would-be musicians
trying to learn to play the same instrument would gather for a half-hour lesson
upstairs in an unheated room over the priests' garage. It cost a buck a lesson—
the same price as a music book, or a pair of drumsticks. We drummers each sat
on a folding chair—and played on the wooden seat of another chair in front of
us; Mr. Melville would be playing along, tapping his sticks on the chair's metal
backrest.

After lunch on the same day, he'd get all his students together in that same
small room and have band practice. There were about twenty-five kids in the
band, and whenever anyone would make a mistake, Mr. Melville would stop the
band and point it out in a loud voice. One day he bawled out the bass drummer,

John Walsh, but John seemed unfazed. "You know," he said in return, "they don't make Frank Melvilles like they used to make Frank Melvilles." I wasn't sure why we practiced so often because in the four years I took lessons, we had only one public performance; he brought a few of us from different schools together to play at a local football game. Apparently, he taught the same music to everyone.

A long time ago, Dad had been a drummer. He had played with his friend, Mervin DeVilbus. "We had a three-piece band," Dad once said. "Mervin played piano, I played the drums, and we had a friend who tapped his feet." They stopped playing when Mervin had a motorcycle accident and his serious head injury caused him to lose his ability to play piano—or do much else. But I knew that somewhere up in the attic, tucked away in packing cases, Dad had the components of his old drum set.

About a year after I started taking lessons, when he figured I was serious, Dad brought down the set and gave it to me. The bass drum was huge, the floor tom-tom looked like a large kettle, the small tom-toms were cracked wood with Polynesian figures painted on their varnished calfskin heads. The larger drums were black, the smaller ones a creamy off white. Dad took them all to a car body shop where he worked and painted them 1960 Ford metallic green.

He also gave me a couple of cymbals, one of which had been dropped and had a dent in its rim. Most drummers at the time were using a "rivet cymbal" that was drilled out with rivets that bounced around and made a softer "splashing" sound. I found that I could get approximately the same effect by attaching a penny or two—loosely—to the cymbal with masking tape. I had other home-made solutions. I made a platform out of two-by-fours to put on a regular chair so I could sit up high, like drummers did; and to keep my bass drum from creeping forward when I kept the beat, I tied it to my chair with rope.

And...originally, Dad had given me an old suitcase to carry my sticks, stands, cymbals and so forth—but I had replaced the handle so often with old coat hangers that I finally decided to use a carboard box. Over at Wegman's, in their discard bin, I found one big enough to carry everything—and that's what I used through my grammar school years. Only when I replaced it with a real case did my mother point out the lettering on both sides of the box. In big red letters, it said—*Kotex*. "I loved the fact that you were so innocent," she said.

I was interested in all things related to drums. Down in our basement, I set up my drums in the fruit cellar and wrote simple march music for drums; whenever I was downtown, I went into music stores to admire new drum sets; several times at the Edgerton library I checked out *Jasper, the Drumming Boy*, by Margaret Taylor Burroughs, the story of a young black boy who wanted to be a famous drummer like his grandfather.

Although Dad seldom took us anywhere, one Saturday night when I was eleven years old, he took my brother Mike and me to a drum corps competition—and I was hooked. I can still see the black and white uniforms and red sashes of the winning corps, the Skokie Indians, from Skokie, Illinois—and every year for several years after that when the corps came to town, my brother and I and our friends would ride our bikes down to Aquinas Stadium, to listen to them practice in small groups as they warmed up for their show. And then, because we often didn't have a dollar to pay for a ticket, we'd park our bikes outside the chain link fence and enjoy the music, despite being unable to see what was going on.

Those were the years when I knew all the legendary corps—the Hawthorne Caballeros, the New York City Skyliners, the Reading Buccaneers, the Yankee Rebels from Baltimore, the Brigadiers from Syracuse, the Musketeers from Upper Darby Pennsylvania, the Jolly Jesters from Toronto Canada. Rochester had two corps of its own—the Grey Knights of Rochester and the Crusaders from the western suburb of Hilton. I played very briefly with both of their junior corps— the Dutchtown Lancers and the Ridge Culver Statesmen—but I quickly found that listening to the music was much more enjoyable than playing it.

When I got to Aquinas, I tried joining their marching band—as a tenor drummer—but that didn't stick either. Although it took me a while to realize it, I didn't want organization and regimentation; I wanted to play in a small group, to be the only drummer keeping the beat. And luckily from the time I was in sixth grade, I was able to do that, but musicians came and went; only my friend Dave Smering on sax stuck around—but then I met Gary Cook. He played the accordion, which was hardly an instrument that was widely used for the rock and roll music that was then beginning, but Gary lived close, could come over easily with his accordion case and we too could play together. Before long, Dave also joined in.

Gary took lessons from Wally Batog, a gregarious, red-headed, professional accordionist who had a lot of students and on Saturday afternoons would get them all together for band practice in the basement of a nearby shopping center. One Saturday, Dave and I went down to listen. It was an all-accordion band—except for a guitarist named Allen Fitzpatrick, and a very young kid playing drums.

The drummer wasn't very good and when the band took a break, I asked him if I might sit in. One of the more advanced students took out her accordion and asked if I could play a boogie beat. I could. Dave had his sax and joined in, and we got Wally's attention. At the end of the session, she invited Dave to join the band—and asked me to replace the drummer. Wally was a big woman with a wonderful heart, and she took us around Rochester to entertain others—to hospitals, nursing homes, and picnics held by charities. At some events, Dave, Gary, Allen, and I—and sometimes Wally's daughter Judy—would play a song by ourselves.

By the time we got to high school, we considered ourselves a band. We called ourselves The Quintones; to prove we were serious, we had business cards printed—"Dance music for all occasions"—and when I was a sophomore, I bought a new set of drums. Unlike the sets many drummers used at the time, mine was not white mother of pearl, it was burgundy sparkle; they were Gretsch drums—a great name even now—and they cost nearly five hundred dollars. With savings I had from working after school—and a small loan from Mom—she and I figured out how I could afford it. I paid cash—which was how we always did business back then. And using black contact paper—and copying the lettering style of my favorite band, The Ventures, I pasted our band name to the front of my bass drum head. I added cymbals which, at that time, cost a dollar an inch—and today may be more valuable than the whole set.

We played a lot of dances—including various "sock hops" at my high school, Aquinas, the local girl's school, Nazareth, and others. We were never paid more than twenty-five bucks—five bucks each—for a night's work, but we weren't playing for the money, we were playing for the fun. We wore red sport coats, white shirts, black ties, and black slacks—and at the end of the evening, it wasn't unusual for us to be so soaked with sweat that our shirts turned red from the suit coat dye. One night we plugged all instruments into one amplifier and melted all the soldered connections inside. Dave Smering took to occasionally changing into Madras shorts, climbing up on a nearby chair and jumping off, landing on his knees, while playing a solo. We were young then, invincible, and sometimes crazy.

I loved the energy of rock and roll, but I also enjoyed dance music from my parents' generation; I used to set up my drums in the attic and play along with records from that era. One Sunday, I got a chance to play it for real. Dave Smering had also been playing older music with a serious accordionist named Joe Miltsch, who was in my class at Aquinas. Dave called to tell me that they had an audition that afternoon and their drummer was sick; could I fill in? I said I would. Although we didn't get the job—we were too young to play the bar gig we were auditioning for—Joe's dad, who drove us to the audition, liked the way we sounded together, and Joe invited me to join his band.

And so, for the next two years—during my junior and senior years of high school—Joe, Dave, and I played a lot of Friday and Saturday nights, sometimes with Jeff Reznik on trumpet and Joe's brother Harold on guitar. We played at different restaurants and party houses for private parties, weddings, celebrations; we were the house band at the Green Lantern Inn. I was missing high school events—games, dances, parties—but I was earning money for college, playing music I loved with a band that got people up and dancing close.

When high school was over, we went our separate ways. Dave went to the Berkeley School of Music in Boston; then went into the Army band playing at Fort Hood in Texas. Joe stayed in Rochester, went to St. John Fisher College, and put together a new band and kept playing the kind of music he did. At Notre Dame, I played in a short-lived rock band called The Dirt Merchants my freshman year, and then put the drums away for a while. Since Jeanne and I were married right out of college, it didn't seem fair to have Jeanne stay at home by herself on weekends while I went out playing. In the nine months I was in Rochester before being drafted into the Army, I didn't try to reconnect with Joe or anyone else. I figured my playing days might be over.

Kansas—and a kid named Patrick O'Dell—changed that. I met him as a fellow soldier at Fort Riley, sometime in the summer of 1970. He had been playing piano by himself at the Ft. Riley Officer's Club and invited me to join him. I did—and when that gig ended, he found steady weekend work for our little duo—at the Ramada Inn in Manhattan Kansas, right near Kansas State University. When it came to drawing up a contract for that job, they asked for the name of our little two-piece band and somehow the "Pat O'Dell Duo" sounded—even to him—too simple. Since we lived in Junction City and often joked about the number of pawn shops nearby, I suggested *The Junction City Philharmonic Orchestra and Pawn Shop*—JCPOPS for short. Patrick wrote that into our contract.

The only clear memory I have of those nights is the one when, somewhere in the middle of one of our songs, the light fixture above my bass drum began to leak water. It turned out, the person in the room over our little bandstand had returned to his room drunk, turned on the water in the tub, and passed out while the tub overflowed. They stopped the water; I dried my drum set—and we went back to playing.

When that job finished, we played only once more—at an Elk's Club before I was transferred to Fort Bragg and Patrick was discharged from the Army. The last song we played was the Burt Bachrach tune "Knowing When to Leave." It would be the last time I'd play with Patrick and the last time I'd play the drums. Since then, they've been packed away in the garage. I may not ever play them again, but I can't bring myself to sell them because they bring back memories of my yesterdays—but those yesterdays have changed.

In November 1988, Wally Batog passed away; Patrick O'Dell died in 1995; Dave Smering passed in 2018. I had wondered what happened to Gary Cook until he contacted me one night via the internet. He had gone to college at Tulane University, gone into advertising, and spent several years in the police force in Louisiana. When an injury prevented him from continuing in that work, he went back to Rochester, met his wife Marjorie and they ended up having two boys who are now off on their own. Gary is an ordained minister and sometimes plays the pipe organ in the local Anglican church where he serves.

On my sporadic trips to Rochester, I occasionally see Joe Miltsch who's still actively playing music, mostly the old songs for nursing homes and other gatherings of people who appreciate songs of that bye-gone era. Joe's wife, Karin with whom we used to double-date in high school, passed away a few years ago. Allen Fitzpatrick is still around; he lives in Rochester and in Florida (part time) where he's had a successful career in real estate. At our fiftieth Aquinas reunion in 2015, I sat with him and his wife and swapped stories. Allen and I still trade emails on a semi-regular basis. I have no idea what happened to Judy Batog, or any of the guitarists—Jim Johnson, Phil St. George, or others—who filled in along the way.

But in those early years, when I first picked up the drumsticks to keep time, the person I was most often playing with was Dave Smering. More than a solid musician, he was a good friend and back in 2011, I reconnected with him where he told his long—and ultimately sad—story.

# 12

# DUVID'S SOLO

WHENEVER I LOOKED UP FROM MY DRUMMER'S SEAT, the one musician I most often saw playing in front of me was Dave Smering. I met him in fifth grade at Holy Rosary School. We both took lessons from the same music teacher, decided we liked to play together—and so we did—at first, just in our garage, but eventually in a rock band and then a dance band. We went to different high schools, had different interests and a different group of friends, but if Dave was in a band, so was I. He got a few musicians together and played for our wedding in 1969 but, for more than forty years, that was the last time I saw him.

But then, in the summer of 2011, I was on a road trip by myself driving from Florida to Rochester, and I decided to call him at his home in the southern part of New York state—and ask him if he was up to a visit, to "catch up after all this time?" He agreed—and so on this July day, I pull up at his home, and Dave comes out the door. His hair has gone gray, and he's balding, but he seems not to have put on any weight in all the time since I'd seen him so long ago. "Bob Gibbons," he says with a wide smile, and we embrace like old friends do. "Come on in."

Inside, the room where we sit is filled with saxophones in various stages of disassembly and repair. There's a workbench in the corner; along one wall several open empty instrument cases are on the floor. "I've always liked to tinker, to fix things," Dave says, "and most of these are instruments that belong to my students. As they get ready for something better, I buy what they have, refurbish it, resell it. It's part of what I do." He also teaches, plays in a band, owns several pieces of property that he is fixing up and getting ready to sell.

"By the way," he says, "I'm now known as 'Duvid'; it's Hebrew for David; I started being called that when I lived in Israel for several years and it just stuck. My friends call me that; people who aren't my friends call me something else; I don't care what people I don't like call me."

I remind him that it's been more than fifty years "since we first played to-gether, and you were always better than everyone else." He thanks me for saying that but believes that's more a comment on how bad others were. "If I had better teachers, I would have been much better," he says. "Frank Melville used to hit my fingers with a pencil when I did something wrong." He says that like it scarred him for life—and then he talks a bit about his life so far. He went to Berkeley School of Music in Boston for a year, went into the Army band for a couple of years, and then spent six years at the State University of New York at Brockport, getting his degree and teaching. He was playing saxophone and dancing profes-sionally in a show when one day, as the curtain opened and the show was ready to begin, he looked at himself and asked: "What the hell am I doing here?"

He wasn't sure. So, he ended up putting the horn aside, working for a security company in New York City, moving to Israel to teach physical therapy, and falling in and out of love—several times—along the way. He never mentions if any of those relationships ever turned serious.

In 1989, a friend invited him to come back to the Corning, New York, area, but to do what? He thought again about the saxophone, began practicing "to get my chops back" and ended up playing in—and leading—several local bands. Along the way, he began meeting young kids, and some not so young, who asked him to teach them—and he decided he wanted to do that. He now has thirty-five or forty students during the regular school year, fewer in the summer. He teaches jazz saxophone and beginning classical saxophone at a small art school in Elmira and "a lot of these kids are just brilliant. They're so dedicated. I have a little Korean girl who is better than all the rest, but some of the Chinese are really good also. I don't give out compliments easily, so when I do, the kids know they really earned what I'm saying."

Duvid has a goal for all of his students: "I tell them, I want to help them to be better than I am—and when they get to that point, they have to leave me. And some of them have."

We talk more about the saxophone, about the kind of music he plays (jazz from the fifties and sixties), about whether and how he practices (he does, mostly chord progressions because they provide the basics for everything he will play in a band), about how he gets repair business and students (he doesn't advertise, it's all referrals).

He wishes he still had his original Martin alto sax that "would be worth about five thousand dollars more than I paid for it." Today, he has two saxes—an alto and a tenor; he also plays clarinet and flute and a soprano sax on which he played *Amazing Grace* at each of his parents' funerals. With that, he looks into my eyes and non-stop, he begins talking about his parents' deaths.

His mom and dad—Rose and David—had a little home at 551 Driving Park Avenue, a few streets away from where we lived. His dad was easygoing; his mother was very high-strung, nervous. She had five major bouts of depression in her later years, he says, most of which he only found out about afterwards. One was when his younger sister, Karen, was born; one was when he went into the army. There were three others—including one that Christmas in 1998.

When he and Karen went back that year to Rochester to celebrate in the family home, his mother was on the couch the entire time; he remembers that his dad was "not himself." During their time together, his father gave him his original camera and told him and Karen "where the envelopes were." They didn't trust banks with their savings, kept their money hidden around the home. "When my father started talking about that, I knew something wasn't quite right," Duvid says.

His dad assured him that things were fine.

His father was eleven years older than his mother; she was just in her mid-seventies, and he had counted on her to help in his declining years; but now, looking back on that Christmas, Duvid could see that his father realized that wasn't going to happen. He couldn't rely on his wife and that was bothering him deeply. He was—Duvid is convinced—losing his mind, maybe his last tenuous hold on a future he counted on.

And so, at five in the morning on a day in early January—after Duvid and Karen had gone back to their homes—his father took his fifty-year-old shotgun out of the closet, loaded it with a fifty-year-old shell—and shot his mother.

She didn't die immediately. The rifle and the ammunition were so old—and the charge so weak—that she was only wounded—but mortally; she would die later in the hospital. And then, his dad reloaded and turned the gun on himself. But the rifle was long and awkward—and he missed; he ended up blowing a hole in his hall ceiling.

Duvid's dad called the police, told them what he had done. He was taken to the Rochester Psychiatric Center and then put in jail for several months—and back in the Psychiatric Center. Some wanted to convict him of malicious murder, but—Duvid believes—there was no malice in what he did, just desperation, maybe love, pity and despair. He was unable to watch someone he had loved so fully—and counted on for so long—go into such a deep state of depression that she was literally crawling up the stairs to go to bed at night.

She wasn't really living—his dad told Duvid later—she was just existing: he believed he was doing the charitable thing by putting her out of her pain and desperation. He would also later tell his son, "I still don't see myself doing it. I see it all as if I'm standing there, watching a dream." His dad lived another three years; he died when he was eighty-nine years old heavily sedated on morphine; he was scheduled that same day to be moved back to the home where he had shot his wife.

Duvid tells me that story with tears in his eyes. "I don't talk about that much anymore," he says as he reaches across the table to grasp my hand. When I called—he says—he wasn't sure we should get together, that he'd be able to go back through his memories, but he seems glad we did. "So. . ." he says. So, we leave and drive to lunch, talking all the while.

I ask him if he records. "Yeah, but not much," he says. "Everything I do is derivative of the past; I really find no need to leave anything for the future." I will later find one of his performances on YouTube. When I ask him about his plans for the future, he answers by telling me about his Uncle Al who spent his whole career working for the Rochester Parks Service. His uncle retired when he was sixty-five—and dropped dead of a heart attack two years later. "I'll be sixty-five next year. I have my health. I've got to start making plans," Duvid says.

As we pull up to the curb in front of his home and he opens the door, we shake hands one more time and we both promise to keep in touch, to not wait another forty years. In parting, I tell him to "keep practicing," because I always liked what musician Miles Davis once said about that. I quote Davis: "It takes a long time to play like yourself."

"That's a good quote," Duvid agrees, but then he repeats it, removing just one word that makes it so very different, so very personal. "It takes a long time," he says, "to like yourself."

We embrace good-bye and then, as these things go, I go back to California and lose track of him. In early 2019, I received this email:

> Hi Bob,
>> My beloved husband died on July 8th of last year. A heart attack.
> Ewa Smering

It was a shock in several ways. Duvid was gone—and although he had shared that very personal story of his parents, he never told me that he had married. I went looking for his obituary and found this:

> Elmira—Duvid Smering, a beloved musician, teacher, and husband, died unexpectedly of a heart attack on July 8th. He is survived by his wife of 22 years, Ewa, a sister Karen (Keith) Cook of Rochester, NY, and tons of grieving friends and cousins. A memorial service will be held on Sunday, September 16th, at 2PM at Community Arts of Elmira, 413 Lake St, Elmira, NY 14901.

The Ithaca newspaper had a guestbook filled with notes from friends and students who spoke of his talent and his kindness, his joy of playing, his love of music, his eagerness to develop the abilities of others. . .and the fact that he was so 'old school,' he still insisted on having cuffs on his pants.

Duvid had joined his Uncle Al before he had time to carry out his plans. I thought back on my own Uncle Als—I had two—and my other relatives who would listen as Dave and I would play together in our garage on Oriole Street where my mom would say, "The Smercase can really blow that horn." Duvid passed away exactly twenty years later—to the day—after my mother.

Mom's brothers and sisters—as well as Dad's—all my other relatives, are gone now also. But we saw most of them often, growing up.

# I3

## IT'S ALL RELATIVE

ROWING UP, I WASN'T RELATED TO ANYONE who didn't live in Rochester. My mother's parents came from Rochester and my dad's family came from not far away and they and their siblings all stayed in the area. For most of my youth, depending on whether I counted great-aunts or not (I usually didn't), I had about a dozen aunts and uncles—and maybe about a dozen cousins. Although all of them lived within a few miles of where we did back then, I've never been sure exactly how many cousins I had, what happened to them, or even their names. Here's why: Although we got along fine with my father's side of the family, we seldom saw them.

My father had one older brother and one younger sister. His brother, who was about two years older than Dad, became a priest. Uncle Paul was ordained five years before I was born and although he served for seven years as a parish priest in Rochester, for most of the time I knew him he was a professor of Latin at St. Andrew's Seminary. In those days, anyone in the greater Rochester area who had a vocation to the priesthood went to St. Andrew's for high school and then to St. Bernard's Seminary for college. Both were near where we lived, both were free, and both were generally full. The large number of Catholic schools in Rochester were a steady feeder system for the priesthood.

Uncle Paul was a highly popular teacher at St. Andrew's and when I was learning to be an altar boy, I spent a Saturday morning at the seminary where he taught me a bit about serving. He came over to our home on Oriole Street for dinner occasionally, but I never recall my father being home at the time. My mother seemed to respect him because she always respected priests.

He was a large man with a rosy complexion and a rheumy voice. He liked to drink alcohol and smoke cigars; he laughed a lot and he ended up baptizing our son Tim, but other than that, we never included him in family picnics or gatherings. After suffering from cancer for three years, he died on February 1, 1986 at St. James Mercy Hospital in Hornell, New York. An article in the local Hornell paper called him "a great Irish wit and classical scholar."

My father also had a sister Rosemary, about four years younger than him; she was a large woman and looked like her brother, Paul. She married Ray Madigan and my mother told me they had nine children—Mary Kay, Jackie, Peggy, Paul, Raymond, Rosemary, Molly, Patricia, and Mike—including some who were adopted. At one point, Aunt Rosemary had her leg amputated because of diabetes, but we seldom saw her or her family. She and Uncle Ray have passed away—she is 1996, he ten years later. Although I've tried several times to locate my cousins via social media, I've been unsuccessful.

It's a different story with Mom's family; she had three brothers and three sisters and, except for one uncle who passed away before I was born, we saw them often. All but one (Aunt Agnes) were married—some several times.

Mom's oldest brother, Lawrence Francis, was born in 1901 and was an ambulance driver for Strong Memorial Hospital in Rochester. In 1925, he married Emilie Buchanan and her name stuck with my mother. When Jeanne was pregnant with our third child, Mom asked me what we planned to name the baby. I said we liked the name, Emily. "You wouldn't call a young baby Emily," Mom said. "That's a name from my parents' generation." For us, it was time to use it again.

Uncle Larry died in 1946 of throat cancer—he may have been a heavy smoker; most of Mom's family were—and I have no idea what happened to the original Emilie Koch. They never had children, but at one point—for a year or so when she was much younger—our Emily changed the spelling of her name to Emilie—and then changed it back.

The next oldest member of my mother's family was Laura Louise—we called her Auntie—and she was the closest of all our relatives. She has her own chapter in this book.

After Loretta came Anthony Phillip, born in 1906. In 1924, he married Marie Johnson, who—according to notes from my mom—died in childbirth. I tried to verify that—but what I found is very strange.

Most of my parents' families are buried in Holy Sepulchre Cemetery in Rochester and according to their online records: on April 11, 1925, a still-born Koch baby was buried in Tier 9, Grave 35L1. Exactly seven years later—on April 11, 1932—Marie Koch was buried in Tier 9, Grave 35L. Did the cemetery get the years wrong? Or was my mother wrong? In any event, the baby was the only biological child my Uncle Anthony would ever have and, by 1932, he was a widower.

A year later, he married again – to Lillian Searth. She was thirty-five, had been married before, and would pass away just three years later—and so Uncle Anthony tried again. In 1938, he married Lorraine Enderlin; she was the aunt I would know during my growing up years.

Uncle Anthony and Aunt Lorraine owned a cottage in Fair Haven—sixty miles from Rochester—and they were very generous in letting us use it. It was on a piece of land above Fair Haven Bay, but with its view of the water fully blocked by large trees. Still, we could walk down to the water where my aunt and uncle had a small right of way to swim in the bay—or tie up a rented boat to a dock. And at night we fell asleep listening to the hum of the boats on the water.

Uncle Anthony and Aunt Lorraine were quiet people; when they stopped by, they mostly sat at our kitchen table and talked—while he smoked. The one memory I have of her is when they had an ant problem in their home; she was using small tin traps that had to be punctured with a sharp pointed instrument so the ants could come in and get the bait, which would kill them. When she was puncturing one, she slipped—and the awl went into her finger. It poisoned her and she had to have the tip of that finger amputated.

Aunt Lorraine would outlive Uncle Anthony by four years—he died in 1970, she in 1974 and at some point, they had adopted a small boy, a relative of hers named Larry—we called him Ricky—when he was two years old. Although I have no idea what happened to him, Uncle Anthony and Aunt Lorraine are buried in Fair Haven Cemetery where they spent most of the years of their retirement.

Next in line in my mother's family was Agnes Loretta; she was born in 1908 and died of cancer in 1954, so I was only seven years old when she passed away and have few memories of her. Aunt Agnes never married although when she stopped by our house, she was usually accompanied by a man named Allie White who I remember as impeccably dressed in a suit and wearing two-tone, highly polished brown and white shoes.

She had a clerical job at Kodak Office and as the only single member of Mom's side of the family, she seemed to live in a world of her own. Being without children, she had money and was a stylish dresser. And Mom said that she was also a professional card shuffler—whatever that was; according to family lore, she may have been a high-priced call girl, or at least a professional escort.

When she died, I went with my dad and uncles to help clean out her apartment. Among her furniture, she had an old windup Victrola—the early version of a record player in a large and heavy wooden cabinet—that we inherited from her and for a long time kept in our basement.

Aunt Agnes lived just across the street—in an upstairs apartment—from her sister. Mary Magdalen—who married twice and outlived both husbands—was born in 1912 and died near the end of 1996. We called her "Aunt Mag" and she was the one who baked our special birthday cakes when we were small. When we were older, she always brought fruit or vegetable Jell-O to family get-togethers. She called it a "treat"; we kids hated it.

Aunt Mag was a wonderful cook; she had worked as a baker at a company called Commercial Controls and then at Singer Company, from which she retired.

She was a blunt, plain-speaking person who had an opinion on everything—including things with which she had no experience—but if you brought up something she didn't want to discuss, she'd simply ask: "Isn't that just the craziest thing you ever heard?" And refuse to talk about it further. She was six years older than Mom—and they argued constantly.

In 1945, Mary Magdalen Koch married Alfred J. Marriott; she was thirty-two, he was fifty—and he had been married before. He claimed to be an executive from General Motors in Detroit; that may not have been true.

He was originally from Rochester, born in 1894, the third son of a tinsmith. In his draft registration for World War I, he listed himself as a sheet metal worker and although there's no record of him ever serving in the military, he'd always claim to be a veteran. By 1921, he had moved to Detroit where he married Virginia M. Shubert, who had also been born in Rochester. She was seventeen years old and a stenographer, he was twenty-seven and said he was an electrician.

There's no record of them ever having children and ten years later—when he claimed to be a laborer in an auto factory—they were divorced. By 1940, they were both back in Rochester where she was managing a dry-cleaning business and he was a machinist. At some point around then, Mary Magdalen entered his life. They spent their entire married life living in a small, rented apartment—a long narrow living room, tiny kitchen, one bedroom, a single bathroom, a few tiny closets. The kitchen was so small, you had to move a chair to open the door to the bathroom.

Uncle Al and Aunt Mag never had any children, but they were always generous with us kids. When we were young, they would take turns taking us out—two at a time—to dinner on Friday nights for a fish fry. When it snowed heavily, they would pay Mike and me to help shovel the driveway in front of a garage they rented down the street. When they'd drop over to our house in the evening for a visit with my mom, they'd always ask what we were doing and find a quarter or even a dollar to help us with what we were hoping to buy.

The only time I ever went to the circus, they took me.

On Sundays, Aunt Mag and Uncle Al would take us kids out "for a ride," often to a park where, in autumn, we'd throw sticks up into chestnut trees and gather the nuts that fell. Sometimes, we'd have a picnic in the park and roast ears of corn over an open fire. During my grammar school years Uncle Al taught me to bowl and gave me my first bowling ball—and in 1957 he brought me a basketball signed by all the members of the Rochester Royals, the only NBA team Rochester has ever had. The Royals would leave Rochester that year for Cincinnati and finally for California where they became the Sacramento Kings.

Uncle Al would usually have an unlit cigarette behind his ear—I never saw him smoke—and he had a whole gaggle of expensive 35mm Leica camera equipment. I used to joke that the amount of his photo gear was surpassed only by his inability to correctly use any of it—but that was not quite true. When he passed away in February 1967, he left behind a trunk filled with boxes and boxes of Kodachrome slides. Many were poorly cropped or incorrectly exposed, but the ones I saved are some of the few pictures I have from our childhood. He was the family photographer.

Uncle Al had a 1958 blue and white Chevrolet Impala—and he paid a huge amount of attention to that car. He took it regularly to the same small gas station where the young kid who pumped the gas—it cost about twenty-five cents a gallon—always asked: "how much do you want?" Uncle Al always said: "Give me three bucks worth. If it takes more, you can have the car." It never took more.

Aunt Mag never drove a car while my uncle was alive—neither did any of her sisters—but after he passed away, she decided to take lessons and learn. She failed her driver's test several times, but when she finally passed, she bought a Chevrolet for herself—and, after she'd been driving it for several weeks, took it to a car wash.

It was one of those washes that pulls the car through on a chain while you sit in the car just watching what's going on. Except, my aunt wasn't used to something like that and, at one point, she thought her car was being pulled in the wrong direction. So, she put the car in drive and tried to steer her way out. She tore the molding off the car—and bent several of the brushes in the car wash.

Sometime in the 1970s—a half dozen or so years after Uncle Al died from cancer—Aunt Mag married Bill Wagenhauser, who had kids from a previous marriage. It was a short marriage before they both passed away.

My mother's closest brother, Aloysius Charles, was born in 1916. He was the one she looked up to and especially loved; as the youngest siblings in the family, when their mother died and their father couldn't care for them, they spent several years together in the orphanage at St. Joseph's Villa. She was with him on the morning of May 8, 1990, the day he passed away.

Uncle Al would be the only other one of my mother's siblings to have children. He and Aunt Rose (the former Rose Kelly, a nurse from Geneva NY) had two daughters—Mary Anne and Nancy—with whom we were close growing up.

Since he was an insurance agent, Uncle Al set his own hours and sometimes, on warm summer days, he'd stop by and take my brother and me fishing at one of the local ponds. We never caught anything larger than a sunfish or small perch and we always threw them back.

Uncle Al and Aunt Rose also had a cottage on Lake Ontario, and we sometimes drove out there for a swim and dinner on hot Sunday afternoons. When their close friends, the Bechtolds, would stop by, their son Scott would bring his canoe and he and I would go out paddling together on the lake. Scott was the middle boy—he had an older and younger sister; when he was killed in Vietnam, his younger sister Peggy became an Army nurse and, in his memory, volunteered for duty on board the helicopters that flew into the jungles to rescue the wounded and dying. She survived the war.

Uncle Al was a big guy, mostly bald from the time I knew him, and told stories with a dry wit. One day—he said—he was making a sales call somewhere on some residential street. He had parked his car but left his driver's door window open because it was a warm day. "And so, I go to get out," he said, "and along comes the oldest bicycle rider in the city of Rochester. He apparently didn't notice that my door was open because he smashed into it and went over the handlebars of his bike—through my open window, and back onto the pavement. I picked him up, put him in the car, and drove him to the hospital. It turned out that he was OK."

I went one night to a party held in Uncle Al's honor. It was supposedly his retirement party but when I asked him when he was retiring, he claimed it wasn't anytime soon. The party, he said, wasn't his idea.

At some point, before he did retire, Uncle Al had a heart attack and had to be revived by paddles. "If anybody ever wants to do that to me again," he said, "try to talk them out of it. I'd rather die." Before he did pass away, he saw both his daughters married—Mary Anne to Dominic Nuciforo in 1971 and Nancy to Ed Kohlmeier in 1983—and spend time with his grandchildren: Nicky, Lisa, Megan and Michael to Mary and Nick—and Paul to Nancy and Ed.

Aunt Rose would outlive Uncle Al by several decades and was always a lady of great common sense who was not afraid to speak her mind. When my mother was coming out of the hospital after her first stoke, there was some family pressure that she move in with us. I was surprised that Aunt Rose called and advised, "Don't do it. She will never move out and it will be tough on your family. I had my father move in with us under the same circumstances; don't make the mistake I made." We didn't. In the end, Aunt Rose was so sick that when she'd wake up in the morning, the first thing she'd say would be: "Damn, I'm still here." She died at eighty-eight in 2006.

She was the last reminder of those years long ago when we were a large and close-knit family, those years when our great adventures lay ahead. Back then, my next great adventures would be in high school.

# 14

# THE AQUINAS SPIRIT

FOR MANY, HIGH SCHOOL IS STRESSFUL; not for me: I loved Aquinas. When I finished eighth grade at Holy Rosary in 1961, Aquinas was really the only choice. McQuaid, the only other all-boys Catholic school in Rochester, was several bus rides away and the local public high schools—John Marshall, a bit north, and Jefferson, a bit south—were out of the question; my mother wanted me in a Catholic school. Tuition was two hundred and twenty-five dollars a year, plus another few bucks for books and lab fees. It was a bit expensive, but the school promised a terrific education—and it was only about a twenty-minute walk away. Despite the Rochester storms and freezing winter days, I walked to school virtually every day, back then.

From the first day I felt that I fit in. I worried a bit about freshman initiation, but that never happened. I liked that Aquinas attracted mostly blue-collar kids like me, and there weren't any cliques to make things uncomfortable for a somewhat shy kid like me. In my first year, I was in the homeroom of Mr. Kenna, a young seminarian studying to be a Basilian. The Congregation of Saint Basil ran the school and although there were a few lay teachers, they were rare.

For all four years we had to wear a suit coat and tie with a collared, tucked-in shirt to every class. Our hair had to be short, combed, and parted—and our pants had to fit loosely. Irregularities were noted and offenders were given a jug (forty-minute detention period) or a whack (a smack across the seat of the pants with a solid piece of wood). Teachers were allowed to hit students and there was no way for us to appeal to our parents. If they didn't support school decisions, Aquinas didn't want us there.

Since I had done well in grammar school, I ended up on kind of a "smart track" where I had most of the same kids in all my classes; every day we had the same schedule, every class was held in a different room, and we had three minutes to change classes—which sometimes meant going up or down several floors. There were two 'up staircases' at the ends of the building—and two 'down staircases' in the center. Aquinas had three floors.

For first class, I had Father Abend for English. He was an older priest, but a good teacher and I loved reading my first Shakespeare play, *The Merchant of Venice*. For second period, I had Father Doser for Algebra. He was a small man who seemed to talk through his nose, but he was a whiz with numbers. In senior year, I'd have him again for Calculus. Occasionally, he'd try to teach us tricks to do complex computations in our heads, but we never got as excited about it as he did.

For third period, I came back to homeroom for Mr. Kenna to teach us Christian Doctrine. He was a good guy but, apparently, a heavy smoker because when he gave it up for Lent, he was a real bear. Fourth period was spent with the legendary Fr. Cross, in Biology. He was tall, thin, humorless. We dissected a worm and a frog that year and it wasn't unusual for some kids to smuggle out parts of those dissections and sneak them into other kids' sandwiches.

After Biology, we had lunch and then went to Latin with Mr. Samberg, another seminarian. He was a no-nonsense teacher who, one day, was telling us the fable about two boys, Romulus and Remus, in ancient Rome. When he said that Rome was named for Romulus, the kid sitting behind me, Joe Grussenmeyer, shouted out: "Remus became a suburb." We all laughed, but Mr. Samberg walked slowly down to Joe and took off Joe's glasses—and smacked him as hard as he could across the face. "Joe," he said, "don't do that."

Seventh period was, for me, a study hall, a time to get a head start on homework. The final period of the day was called Citizenship Education, but really, it was geography taught by a priest named Father Brown who made me sleepy. On Fridays, the last two periods were replaced by Gym with Father Spratt, a very old priest who liked to jump rope; freshman year was the only year we had to take Phys. Ed. in high school.

Although I never liked phys. Ed, I loved to watch sports and they were popular at Aquinas. Our football team played at Aquinas Stadium, a twenty-thousand-seat facility built two years after I was born, back when Aquinas was a football powerhouse, playing teams from other states. By the time I got there, Aquinas was much less dominant, not only in football but also in basketball where the home games were played in the Aquinas gym with its wooden bleacher seats along one side and the court's out-of-bounds-line about six feet from the building's wall.

In September 1962, I started my sophomore year where I ended up in the homeroom of Father Cullen, who taught art. I wanted to take art classes but was on the "academic track" and my guidance counselor advised me to take a modern language instead, so I took German from a priest named Father Klem who made learning the language fun. The first thing he taught us to say in German: *"Pinkeln stets ins Becken, weil der Naechste könnte barfuss sein."* It means: "Make sure you pee in the toilet because the next person could be barefoot." I ended up taking three years of German from Father Klem, to go with my three years of Latin that I took from three different teachers. I was well grounded in languages in high school.

Sometime during junior year, I took a typing course—we used manual typewriters with blank keys to discourage us from looking down as we typed—from Father Roy, a priest who mostly seemed befuddled—and the kids conspired to make him more so. The roller bar that held the paper in the typewriter was called a "platen;" it had knobs on each side so it could be rolled forwards or backwards and the paper could be advanced or moved back down into position. At some point, someone in our class discovered that if he twisted the knobs in opposite directions at the same time, the platen could be made loose, so it was just "floating" at the edges of the screws. And then—that person discovered—if he simultaneously smashed his palm on as many keys as possible—while calling out "Father Roy, I have a problem"—the whole class would come to a halt while father tried to disentangle the pile of keys and the platen in the bottom of the typewriter.

Junior year was also the year I worked on Randy Block's campaign for Student Council President. Randy was clearly the most popular—and one of the nicest—kids in school. Randy was a star on the football team, the captain of the basketball team, and he still holds the Aquinas record for the one-hundred-yard dash in track, almost sixty years later. He gave me access to the top athletes at school and I liked them and wanted to be like them—and so, although I was never good at sports, I decided to run track my junior year.

The track and field coach, Fr. Ware, let everyone be on the team if they just came to practice and so I started running with my friend Tom Whalen, trying to get in shape. Within a couple of weeks, I knew it wouldn't work; I hated every minute—plus, I had too much going on in my life.

Between daily practices—and then going to work doing maintenance for a couple of hours—and then doing my homework—and playing in the band on Friday and Saturday nights—I got to the point where I worried that I was having a nervous breakdown. I told my mother about it, and we decided I need to stop some activities. I'd still work on Saturdays and keep playing in the band because those paid well—but I dropped my after-school job and Mom suggested I stop running.

But when I told Father Ware that I'd be quitting the track team, he had another idea: how would I like to be a track team manager—to help take care of the equipment and the uniforms, to keep score at the events, to be a part of the team, traveling and working with them, just not running on the track? I told him that I'd like to do that very much.

And so, I became one of the four or five managers—and every night I'd go down to a small room under the gym, haul out the hurdles and the cross bars for the uprights for the high jump and pole vault, get the poles and other equipment ready. We'd also organize, pass out and collect the uniforms before and after meets, keep track of the Aquinas team sweat suits, and do any other odd jobs required.

We ate with the team, we travelled with the team, we celebrated with the team. And we had an undefeated team that year. Mike Smith, one of the Aquinas co-captains was such a fast two-miler that he often lapped other contestants during that race. When he did, he sometimes ran backwards; "I just do it to demoralize the other runners," he told me. And Dick Buerkle, who ran the two-mile after Mike Smith graduated, didn't know how fast to run his first race so he ran it as a sprint. He set a school record but passed out at the end. He eventually tried out for the Olympic team.

During junior year, Father Ware was so happy with the team's success that he decided to give every member of the team—including us managers—an *Aquinas school letter.* That meant we could buy an Aquinas maroon-and-white letter sweater—which many guys (not me) gave to the girl with whom they were "going steady." Apparently, that meant different things to different kids because one day I overhead this conversation: "Let me I understand this," one kid was saying to the other: "You're going steady with a girl, and you don't even know her last name?"

That junior year, most individual days at Aquinas are a blur, but I remember exactly where I was on the afternoon of Friday, November 22, 1963; I was backstage in the Aquinas auditorium. The school asked a few of us to play some music for the students at an assembly. We were waiting for Father Whitley to decide if we could go on because the school had just received an unconfirmed report that President Kennedy had been wounded by a gunman in Dallas. We did go on— Richie Pecora, Al Fitzpatrick, me, maybe Phil St. George—three guitars and me on drums—and we played *Memphis* by Lonnie Mack. Then, the assassination was confirmed, and we went home in stunned silence. My friend Tom Whalen had a record where comedian Vaughn Meader imitated the Kennedys. Tom's father made him throw it away.

In my senior year, in Father Wajda's English class we read *Crime and Punishment.* He assigned a chapter or so a night—and had an interesting way of checking that we were doing the reading: the next day, we'd have to turn in three or four multiple-choice questions—with answers—based on what we'd read. For the final exam, he used a selection of our questions. It was kind of a *Tom Sawyer* approach: Have others do your work for you.

When it came to assigning another novel to read, he wrote down several titles on folded slips of paper, put them in a box, and had each of us draw a slip. I drew *Rebecca* by DuMurier. I told him I wasn't sure I'd like to read a female author. He disagreed. "You read that one," he said. I did—and loved it. More than fifty years later, I read a second book by her, *Jamaica Inn*, and again really liked her characters, sense of story, and her style. She cured me of my fear of reading female authors. There are several I enjoy.

I liked English—I liked most of my courses—but by the fall of senior year, I was looking for a way to use my interest in art and design and signed up to be the layout editor for *Arete*, the Aquinas yearbook. When the editor quit, I was named editor in chief; it was an impressive title for a job where there was little to do. The publisher handled most of the details. I helped select the cover design, did some picture-cropping, and wrote a bunch of captions. Our business manager for the *Arete,* Nick DiPonzio, ended up working for me at Kodak although I was never sure what he did on the yearbook—or if I even met him at Aquinas, except for the yearbook picture we took together.

When the books came out, we signed each other's. One of my favorite notes in my yearbook came from a classmate named George Scharr. "I hope your band goes places," he wrote. "But not where I'm going."

Aquinas had an academic achievement system based on two tiers; if your average in all subjects was ninety percent or above, you were in the St. Thomas Club. You could earn that honor quarterly or, if your cumulative average for all four years met that standard, permanently. My overall average was 89.9-percent—and there was no rounding up. The same thing happened in college. To be on the Permanent Dean's List, I needed an overall average of 2.50. My average after four years was 2.49. Some have suggested that I should have argued my point, but I didn't. I believed that, on average, I was graded fairly. For me, school wasn't about grades—it was about learning how best to learn.

But finally, after four years of Aquinas, there was graduation at the Eastman

Theatre in downtown Rochester. We would all wear rented caps and gowns, of course, but—we were advised—that beneath the gown, we should wear a plain white shirt because the front of the gown was a bit low, and our shirt would show. Apparently, every other member of the graduating class heard the "white shirt" as a requirement; I heard it as a suggestion. When we got to the theatre and changed into our gowns, everyone else's shirt was white; mine was a red and white stripe. Still, I received my diploma, my parents took us down to Glen Edith to celebrate, and my high school years at Aquinas were over.

Nearly twenty thousand alumni—boys, and now also girls—have graduated from Aquinas since the school began in 1902; there were three hundred and fifty young men in the graduating class of 1965; I'm proud to have been one of them. And yet, when each class day finished, I was also going on to another school. To help pay Aquinas tuition—and set aside a little money for college—I had a part time job doing maintenance at my grammar school, Holy Rosary.

# 15

## I CAME. I SAW. I MOPPED.

WHEN I WAS IN EIGHTH AND NINTH GRADES, I had an afternoon paper route. It was a good first job because unlike other jobs, you didn't have to be sixteen to have a route; I was thirteen when I got mine. I had fifty customers, and some were very demanding; the paper had to be in their screen door or—in apartment houses—on an inside landing. It took me at least an hour, six nights a week, to deliver, and a bit longer on Thursday night to collect. If everyone paid, a rarity—I made six dollars a week. It was about the same as my Aquinas tuition, but when I finished my freshman year of high school, I was looking for something that paid a bit more. And I found it right up the street at Holy Rosary School where Paul Sayre—the grandfather of a friend from Carl Street—was a co-janitor. He worked with Walter Parks and they both were retired but picking up a few bucks watching over the property.

Mr. Sayre was a thin, quiet man whose nose seem to run all the time; he was always sniffling or clearing his throat and seldom around. Mr. Parks was barrel-chested, often wore a neck brace, sometimes used a respirator, and ran a nursery that supplied all plants for the parish. Together, they stayed out of each other's way.

The school, church, and convent were in older buildings. Classrooms and hallways needed to be swept—and in the winter, sometimes mopped—every night. On weekends, lawns needed to be cut, the grounds needed to be picked up; on vacations, the church needed to be vacuumed, school rooms needed to be painted, windows needed to be washed. And as needed, snow had to be shoveled and other tasks done to keep things in order. It was not a difficult job, but it was not a job for retirees.

It was a job for high school kids. And it paid $1.25 an hour—a total of $22.50 a week for two hours cleaning classroom every night and miscellaneous work on Saturday. It was almost four times what I earned from the paper route. Mom talked to Paul Sayre who remembered her from the old neighborhood, and he said he'd see what he could do about hiring me. Early one summer morning a kid named Tom Whalen showed up at our house; he came to tell me that he worked at Holy Rosary School and I was supposed to start work that day.

And so it began. In the beginning, it was Tom and me and Denny Fagan. Then Doug Hargather joined us and eventually John Houle came on board also, after he left the seminary before his junior year. On the third floor there was a small closet with a long unpainted board on which the mops and brooms were hung. Through the years, the different kids who had worked at the school had "signed in," leaving their names and sometimes a quote or other remark. Along the way, someone had quoted Caesar: "Veni. Vidi. Vecci." *I came. I saw. I conquered.* I wrote my own version in English: *I came. I saw. I mopped.*

And I did. Every night after school, Tom and I split up the classrooms—half to him and half to me. We swept the halls and the stairwells. And in the winter, when the kids' boots in the hallways left behind pools of water, we mopped up the pools with hot water and Jetsen, a thick red soap that came in industrial-size cans. On Saturdays, we used Vanisol, a strong disinfectant to clean sinks, drinking fountains, and toilets—sometimes all with the same sponge.

On weekdays when it had snowed overnight, Tom and I would be at the church around 6:30 in the morning, shoveling and spreading rock salt on the church steps prior to the 7:00 a.m. Mass. Eventually we put so much salt on the concrete steps that they needed to be replaced.

This was a Catholic school, so everything was usually neat and orderly, but there was one day when I found the second-grade room to be a real mess. I cleaned it and then wrote on the blackboard: *Please try to keep this room a little neater. Thank you.* I thought I was being helpful, but the next afternoon, Mr. Parks patiently explained: "Your job is to clean up the mess, not complain about it."

I'd eventually have fun leaving notes for Mr. Parks; I knew he seldom talked to the school principal, so I'd sometimes sign the notes from her. One example: "Dear Mr. Parks: Could you come over to the convent please? We're missing a nun and last saw her habit floating in one of our toilets. Please check the plumbing." I saw him smile when he threw the note away; but for me, that may have been the start of what later became my job—ghost-writing for people in authority.

Mr. Parks and Mr. Sayre shared an office in a basement room dominated by a huge boiler that heated the school. During my first summer on the job, the boiler needed some repairs and thus, some of the insulation bricks and thick canvas covering had to be removed. What I understood to be my job—from the instructions Mr. Sayre gave me before he disappeared—was to tear all the insulation off the boiler, including the canvas coating—*except* for one row of bricks around the pipes at the top.

I got some help from the other guys and all day long we tore at the insulation until we were knee-deep in a mess. We had most of the bricks removed when Mr. Parks came by...and exploded. *What were we doing?* According to him, we should have done just the opposite—removed just one row of insulation around the top pipes—and left everything else on. He told me that he'd have to talk things over with Mr. Sayre, show him the mess we had made and see what he wanted to do. It was a very expensive mistake; I was sure I was going to be fired.

But the next day, Mr. Sayre just looked at it and asked: "What have we here?" "Bob made a mistake," Mr. Parks told him. Mr. Sayre looked around. "We'll need to get this fixed," he said. And then he disappeared. Mr. Parks called someone to reinstall the insulation bricks and that was the end of it. I never heard another word—except for my friends, who never let me forget what happened.

Denny Fagan still mentions it, more than fifty years later. But, the worst came from a friend of Denny's. "Cheer up, Bob," he told me. "We all make mistakes. Once I lost a quarter."

We did a lot of painting during those years, and one day, Denny was painting the outside double doors to the school. He had set up his roller pan, and was about to begin, when Mr. Sayre walked by. Mr. Sayre watched him for a few minutes, then headed upstairs in the priest's garage. A few minutes later, he came back down carrying a couple of pieces of masking tape and a homemade sign that said, *Wet Paint.* "Here," he told Denny, "let me tape this to the window." And as he reached to do that, Mr. Sayre stepped in the roller pan.

"Oh, no," he said. "Oh, no, no, *no*. And these are my new Hush Puppies."

Denny helped him wipe off his shoes, but later, when he told us the story, he couldn't stop laughing. "They were his *brand-new* Hush Puppies," Denny said.

One winter Saturday, I was working right outside those same doors when Sister Mary George, the dreaded school principal, came by and asked me what I was doing. I was trying to bury a box of ice cream bars, to keep them cold in the snow. They had been slipped to us earlier by the convent cook, Sister Jeanne Louise, who was always looking out for us kids. "Snow won't keep them cold," Sister Mary George said. "Take that box over to the convent and give it to Sister Jeanne Louise. Ask her to put it in the convent refrigerator for you. Tell her I said it was OK for her to do that." And so, I did—and Sister Jeanne Louise put it back until she gave it to me—again.

Sister Jeanne Louise was also a friend of my mom. "Theresa," she'd sometimes call Mom to ask, "do you have any liquor in the house?" Mom would pour some of my dad's Seagrams-7 into an empty jar and put it in a small bag that I'd take it up to the convent and put it into one of their outside trash cans. Since I worked at the school, it wouldn't look unusual for me to be in the area. At some point Sister Jeanne Louise would "take out the trash," get the bottle, and make it through another tough evening.

Holy Rosary School had been converted from an original church and so it had a peaked area over its top floor. It had a large "common area" with plywood on the attic floors in the center section where unneeded desks were stored. There were makeshift walls built on either side of that area, and crude doors leading off them. We assumed there was plywood on the attic floors beyond those walls—a wrong assumption, as we found one day when we decided to go exploring.

John Houle and I went through one of the doors and moved into the space over the seventh-grade classroom where everything was coated with a thick layer of dust. Suddenly, below us, in the next room over, we could hear the school principal giving an orientation to a nun new to the school. We moved more slowly, trying to be quiet. . .*until John fell partway through the ceiling.* He caught himself on the beams before he fell completely into the classroom below, but a piece of ceiling tile had broken loose and was hanging. The question was: had the nuns heard? Apparently not. John and I lay down on the beams and moved carefully back to the center plywood section. After the nuns left the building, we got a tall ladder, stapled the tile back in place, and cleaned off the dirt. It never fit exactly, but unless you knew what you were looking for, it wasn't something anyone would notice.

But we did other damage that would be noticed. One Saturday, Doug and Denny were wrestling in the hallway, right outside the principal's office where the makeshift walls were partially made of a pressed cardboard-like material. I found Mr. Parks. "Do we have any spackle?" I asked him. Spackle was a pre-mixed compound we used to fill in small holes. "How much do you need?" he asked me.

"I don't know," I said. "Probably a lot. Enough to cover a hole the size of Denny Fagan's ass." It turned out that spackle alone wasn't enough; it took other material and paint, to get things looking good before school resumed on Monday.

Working in the rectory, we got to know several of the priests, and one, Fr. Richard Orlando was young and liked to hang around with us. He often joined us at the beach with our girlfriends. One Sunday night after a parish basketball game—Tom, Denny, Doug and I were on the team—a bunch of us, including some cheerleaders, decided it would be fun to watch TV together in the parish hall. We needed to get permission from one of the priests to go into the hall at night—and so I went to the rectory, asking for Father Orlando. He was out, but since I worked at the school, I had a key and so when I came out of the rectory, I said to the group waiting in front of the priest's garage, "Father Orlando isn't here but let's go in anyway." As I looked at the group, I realized that father had come home and had joined them. "I think that's fine," he said. And we did— and that's where we all first saw The Beatles on the Ed Sullivan show.

Tom, Denny, Doug and I all became good friends; I made the parish high school basketball team because they told the coach they wouldn't play unless I could also. Whenever our band was playing, they'd always be there. And Doug had access to his father's car—an old green Hudson Wasp—and would usually end up driving us around on Friday nights before we'd end up at Schaller's or Char-Broil where for less than a buck, we could get two burgers and a coke. Eventually, we'd be in each other's weddings.

But in August of 1965, two months after I had graduated from Aquinas and three years after Tom had come knocking on my door that summer day, I turned in my keys and said good-bye to my first long-term job—at Holy Rosary School. Tom and Denny had graduated from Aquinas the year before, and they were both at St. John Fisher, a local college. Denny would later transfer to the University of Detroit to major in something none of us had heard of—Environmental Engineering. Doug would go into the Army, become an MP working with dogs, and be sent to Vietnam. He'd tell me later that, when they caught looters, it was more humane just to shoot and kill them. He said it was tough to watch "when we let the dogs get them."

For me, Holy Rosary had been a good job. I had made a bunch of money— $22.50 a week normally, $50.00 a week during vacations—maybe as much as six thousand dollars in total, enough to pay for more than two years of college back then, if I'd saved it all. I was heading off into the next stage of my life. I was going to the University of Notre Dame.

When I left, I'd be leaving behind my first real girlfriend.

# 16

# THE VALUE OF
# A GOOD FIRST GIRLFRIEND

URING MOST OF MY HIGH SCHOOL YEARS, I wasn't serious about dating. I liked going to dances where a bunch of us could just pile in the car and go. There were several places with great bands: Wilmer Alexander and the Dukes played at Clover Lanes or out in Brockport on Sunday afternoons at the rundown DeMays Hotel; The Rogues were at Willow Point Park on Friday nights; Herb Gross and the Invictas were loud and raunchy most nights at Tiny's Bengal Inn.

Guys came by themselves; the girls came by themselves; we danced and went our separate ways. If I needed to invite a girl to a formal school dance, I took a different one each time. My priorities were on school: I didn't think I could concentrate fully on my studies—and on girls—at the same time.

That changed one evening in the summer of 1964 when I met Paula Klos. My favorite actress in those times was Doris Day and, to me, Paula looked like her younger sister. She was a natural platinum blonde, enthusiastic and outgoing, always smiling, and confident. I was a shy kid, introverted. She may have been the first real extrovert I ever met. She lived in Irondequoit, the better side of town; I wondered if she was "too good for me."

Paula came from a Polish family—their original family name had been Kloskowski—where she grew up the youngest of three girls. One of her older sisters, Rosie, had passed away previously from Lupus. Her other sister, Joanne, was married to an undertaker, Jack; they lived with their children on Long Island and seemed, the way Paula described them, to be quite well-to-do.

Her parents—Paul and Jean—were great to me. She was a housewife; he was an artist at a company making directional signs for the freeways around Rochester—and often gave me tips on making posters for which I sometimes won art contests.

All during our senior year when we dated, I was the drummer in a house band at a party house, playing most Friday and Saturday nights. My time in the band was competition for my time with Paula. She couldn't have been happy, but she always seemed to be understanding. That Christmas I gave her a poodle-knit sweater (my mother convinced me it was the latest thing) and a charm bracelet with one charm—a drum.

In the spring of the next year, we both got our licenses and since we were eighteen, we could drive at night. Sometimes she drove, sometimes I did. One night, she drove us through a very dense fog on our way to see *John Goldfarb, Please Come Home*, a terrible movie about Notre Dame playing in her neighborhood. As she was moving the car along at a good speed, I said, "Wow, I can't see anything." "I can't either; I'm scared to death," she said cheerfully. Paula was always self-assured. But she didn't slow down—and she didn't hit anything.

In downtown Rochester, back then, there was a popular restaurant called "Top of the Plaza." It was one of the highest points in Rochester and Paula and I sometimes went there for a special evening out. One night we were there, double-dating with my sister Pat and her boyfriend, when Pat asked the bandleader to announce: "This is Paula and Bob's six-month anniversary." He looked out into the audience. "Where are you?" he asked.

Paula just glowed. I shrunk in my seat, too shy to acknowledge that I was the "Bob" the bandleader was referring to. I'm sure Paula was hurt—or at least disappointed—but what was becoming obvious to me was, despite being comfortable together, we were too very different people.

"We never fight," Paula said to me once. "I don't want to fight, but making up would be so much fun." I remember saying that I didn't want to fight over small things—and if we ever found anything so big that we had to fight over it, that would probably be the end of our relationship. I had grown up in a past where my parents were always arguing; I didn't want that to be my future.

I told Paula also that I grew up in a home where my dad was unreliable—I expected to go through life without ever having a person I could really count on. She told me, "That was no way to live." I think I could have always relied on her completely.

It was a big deal back then for kids in high school to be "going steady" and since we were, I gave her my Aquinas ring—and she gave me hers from Mercy. She had small fingers, added gobs of tape to mine, and wore it happily. When I put hers' on, it got stuck on my finger and I finally had to cut it off. When I gave it back, I don't know if she ever had it repaired.

Despite going steady, we knew we'd soon be going in two different directions: she'd be staying in Rochester at Nazareth College; I had been accepted at Notre Dame.

But that September, when I headed off to South Bend, I never even said good-bye to her; I just left. She wouldn't have been surprised—she knew I was going—but she had to be disappointed, maybe even hurt. Why was I doing that? I don't know; maybe I was my father's son; Dad didn't even attend his father's funeral.

Paula and I wrote often—she more than me because she was a prolific writer with the neatest handwriting, and she always had something to say. I'm sure she wasn't dating anyone else, and neither was I. And when I came home for Christmas, we had more time to spend together than we originally expected.

We had such a heavy snowfall that year that all roads were clogged and my train back to South Bend was delayed for several days. I called Paula and decided to walk over to her house. The walk took several hours; once I got there and we spent the day together, the question was: How was I going to get home?

Paula's parents decided I should stay overnight. A "sleepover" then was very different from "spending the night together" now; we each had our own rooms—and we each slept in them, after just a kiss good night. And besides, her parents were wide awake, I'm sure, in the next room.

Eventually, the snow stopped, the tracks were cleared, and I made my way back to South Bend. I spent that Easter in Florida with friends from school, but she did fly out for our spring dance at Notre Dame, and we had a good time.

We were still going steady that summer although she had given back my ring because we were in college now and high school rings weren't symbolic of anything. But she had transferred from Nazareth to Marygrove College in Detroit, which was closer to South Bend.

But then came that Saturday night in September before sophomore year. I still don't remember what, if anything big, happened but when I said good night to Paula that evening, something fundamental for me had changed. After dating only her for two years, I began thinking about also dating others. I wasn't ready to say good-bye to her completely, but I wanted to broaden my horizons.

I should have talked to her about that; we should have figured out what was going on, see if we could work it out. I should have been honest about my feelings, but of course, I was not. Looking back, if that's the way I was going to treat her, she is lucky she didn't end up with me.

The next day was Sunday; and since I had been up late, I went to a later Mass, sliding into a mostly empty pew at the last minute, oblivious to who was already sitting there. It turned out to be Jeanne Stein, the girl from grammar school who I hadn't seen in some time.

We ended up talking after mass; I invited her to the movies before I returned to school, and I was now dating two girls.

Paula invited me to a dance at Marygrove that year and I went; I invited her to a football game at Notre Dame and she came. Paula stopped by my room in Zahm Hall at one point—she was in town with some girlfriends from Marygrove—and we talked, but it wasn't the same. When it came time for our spring dance at Notre Dame, I invited Jeanne.

Paula and I had stopped writing; in a small frame on my desk, I had replaced Paula's picture with one of Jeanne. It was, for me, a turning point.

Several years after we broke up for good, on an airplane headed somewhere, I came across an article in a *United* magazine entitled: *"The value of a good first boyfriend"* and as I read it, I brought back memories of Paula and of what she had contributed to my life. And I came to realize that while many people helped me get what I've got, only a very few helped me become who I am—and, for me, Paula was one of those very few.

She was really my first serious girlfriend, the one who taught me how to behave around girls, who gave me someone to trust and who, I later recognized, although we never really talked directly about that—really loved me.

She was always a beautiful girl with the biggest, most generous heart. She believed in me long before I ever dared to believe in myself. She was proud of me, proud of herself, proud of us; there was never a time or a situation when I wasn't proud to be with her.

Paula was unfailingly cheerful, unfailingly forgiving, unfailingly trusting. She was what so few people really are —a person with all the right values. I was lucky to have had her in my life during those pivotal years. And so why would I move on, look elsewhere, find somebody else?

A couple of years ago a movie gave me an answer—or, at least, an indication that these kinds of things also happen to others. The movie was *(500) Days of Summer* and although the story it told was more than a bit different from ours, we did go together for about five hundred days—and there was a sense of joyful innocence in both our relationship and the one on screen.

In the movie, Tom (Joseph Gordon Levitt) and Summer (Zooey Deschanel) met in a copy room, and he was a lot more adventurous than I was back then; but always the film kept cutting back to her big blue eyes that sparkled with happiness and expressed the feelings of a fully engaged heart and brain. Yeah, Paula was like that.

And yet, in the end, Tom and Summer broke up and the next time he saw her, she was married. He asked her why? "You know all the things I was not sure about with you?" she asked. "With him, I was sure."

Could it be that complicated, that inexplicable, that simple? I was unsure of what I'd do with my life; Paula always seemed confident. Maybe because she was an extrovert and I was so shy, I didn't fully understand her and worried that, in the end, because we were so different that she might be disappointed with me.

Maybe that's why I wasn't sure, why we went our separate ways. We eventually lost track of each other. But through the years, when I thought of her, I hoped she was happy, had found someone good enough for her. Had she? One day, I found out.

I was in Orlando Florida on a business trip when I got a call from my sister Pat. Pat and Ted had a condo in Fort Myers, a few hours' drive away; she had been shopping at a consignment store and got talking to the saleswoman. The woman had asked Pat where she was from and when Pat said, "Rochester," the saleswoman said she was from there also.

Pat asked where the woman had lived in Rochester. "In Irondequoit," she said, "on Barry Road."

Pat said, "My brother Bob married a girl whose parents live on Barry Road."

"Your brother married Jeanne Stein," the woman told Pat. "I'm Paula Klos. If you don't think his wife would mind, I would love to hear from him again." She gave Pat her phone number.

I called her, we talked, and I drove over the next day to visit her and her husband Fred in their home in Fort Myers. He's a retired CFO from General Motors; they have a small dog named Josie, the nickname I have for our oldest daughter. We had a lunch with good food and better memories. It was a time that seemed forty years in the making, a day when there were so many stories I forgot to tell.

Since that day in 2007, I've seen Paula and Fred on several other business trips to Florida. The last time I thought I'd see her, I finally told her something I should have said years ago: that she helped me become who I turned out to be. And I'll never forget what she meant to my life.

When I got home, she sent me a note thanking me for saying that.

*That was the nicest thing you've ever said to me. I will treasure those words always. Paula*

We always exchange Christmas cards; every year, I send a card for her birthday. Why? We're getting older, more fragile. Too many people who've been an important part of my yesterdays are now gone from my tomorrows. I want to stay in touch with those I can. They're not in my head every day, but when something important happens in their lives, I like to know—even though, I may not see some of them, including Paula, ever again.

I remain convinced that I married the right person for me; I hope that Paula would say the same about her marriage to Fred. And yet, I count myself as one of those people who has never had a lot of good friends, but the ones I've had, I want to keep. I think we all have room in our hearts and in our heads for those special people who have been such an indelible part of our lives—and I'd like to think that Paula Klos, the girl I met once upon a time on that summer night long ago, will always have a place in mine.

I'll always think back with gratitude for that year we had together before I headed off to Notre Dame.

# 17

# SOMEWHERE WEST OF BUFFALO

I WOULD BE THE FIRST MEMBER OF MY FAMILY to go to college and the first to complete four years. And I planned to go to the University of Dayton. In high school, I was good in math and so I decided to major in computer science. At the time, Dayton was one of the few places that offered that, so I had applied and been accepted. It was the only college I applied to because applications cost twenty-five dollars back then and that was a lot of money for my family; I didn't want to spend any more than I had to. I'd start there as a freshman in September 1965.

My parents hadn't been to college and let me make my own decisions, but one day my mother came home from her part-time job with a different idea. "I was talking with one of my friends and she talked about Notre Dame," Mom said, "and it sounds like it would be a good school for you. Have you ever thought about going there?" I told her that I'd be attending Dayton. But I didn't want to shut her down. I asked her more about Notre Dame.

It turned out, she didn't really know the first thing about it—how much it cost, how difficult it would be to get accepted, even where it was located. She thought "it's somewhere west of Buffalo. They have maps at gas stations," she told me. "We can figure it out." She only knew what her friend told her: I would get a great education there. "I'd be so proud if you would go to Notre Dame," she said; she dropped the subject, but I got the message. At Aquinas the next day I got a Notre Dame catalog and applied. I received my letter of acceptance on my birthday, two days after Dayton's final deadline to let them know my decision. If Notre Dame hadn't accepted me, I wasn't sure where I'd go.

But I was going to Notre Dame and so, on September 17, 1965 in the middle of the night, my parents, sister Judy and I loaded our 1965 Dodge and headed "somewhere west of Buffalo" —five hundred and twenty five miles to South Bend, Indiana. There were 1,605 of us in the class of 1969 out of a record enrollment of 7,155 that year; tuition—including room and board, laundry, even football tickets—was $2,150.00 a year; it would go up about one hundred dollars annually during the four years I was there. In total, when I graduated, I was about $4,000.00 in debt. My full four-year education had cost about $10,000.00.

We arrived by the 1 pm check-in time and I was assigned a second-floor triple in Zahm, an overflow dorm; the next day, when they found they had rooms available in Cavanaugh, the freshman hall next door, I was given a single, room 452, on the fourth floor on that dorm. I was in a small wing where I'd make friends to last a lifetime. Four (Marc Imundo, Jim Blakely, Joe Anderson, and Bob Wilhelm) became doctors; three (Roger Kiley, John Rank, and Tom Payne) became lawyers; Dave Pender, Dan Cox, Pete Nardone, and I went into business; and one, Bob Gessner, became a Brother of the Holy Cross.

Each room had the basics—sink, desk, bed and metal closet—plus daily maid service. The maids made our beds and dusted our floors, but their real purpose was to make sure we weren't doing irreparable damage to ourselves or to the dorms. Toilets and showers were down the hall.

Brother Robert, our floor prefect, was a stickler for quiet study time. *No one in the hall after 7 o'clock; no noise coming from the room after 8 p.m.; lights out at a reasonable hour.* We didn't like him. One late night, someone took an old bowling ball, heated it red hot on a small electric hot plate, and rolled it with a large thud into Brother Robert's door. He woke up, was furious, picked up the bowling ball—and scalded his hands. They never caught the kid who did it.

To enter or leave the dorm in the evening, we had to sign in or out at the back door where a guard—we called him "Herman the German"—stood watch at the bottom of the four-story stairwell. One night a couple of my dormmates came by carrying a sloshing wastebasket. "Pee in it," they said; I did and they moved on to the next room. The last I heard, they were standing at the top of the four-story stairwell, yelling down. "Hey, Herman." When Herman looked up, they dumped the bucket on him.

At one point, someone did something that wasn't just ridiculous, it was, we decided, gross—and so, using masking tape to cover an 'Era of Ara' button (Ara Parseghian was our football coach) and some marking pens, I created a MOST GROSS! award that was presented on a regular basis. Among the winners: Jim Blakely for mooning a group of passing nuns; and Marc Imundo for going into Dave Pender's room when Dave was out, turning the radiator up full, coating it with Adsorbine Jr. and urinating on it. Some remember a wrestling match ensuing when Dave returned.

John Rank brought the original award to our fiftieth reunion and presented it to Jim. When Jim later decided that Marc was its most deserving owner—and tried to send it to him—the award went missing in the mail, most likely due to the open carry gun laws of Texas. I made a copy—and accompanied by a *Certificate of Authenticity*—sent it to Marc for perpetuity. "The eagle has landed," Marc wrote me when the award arrived in the mail.

Despite the pranks, Notre Dame took education seriously. Ninety-seven percent of its students graduated within four years—and it had a few rules to help assure that: all freshman had Saturday morning classes; we were expected to study five hours a day, in addition to time in class; honors freshmen students (I was one) had to carry twenty-one credit hours—plus Phys. Ed.—per semester with three cuts per class; missing the last class before vacation—or the first class afterwards—resulted in an automatic failure of the class.

Since Notre Dame didn't offer a Computer Science major, I thought I'd major in math, but quickly found myself out of my league. My professor had such a thick Italian accent, I couldn't understand him—and one of my classmates was doing calculus for relaxation; I'd actually fail physics at the end of the year but be given a special passing grade of D-star—provided I agreed not to major in the sciences. I agreed.

One of the difficulties about Notre Dame academics was being in class on the Saturday morning when campus was filling up for football weekend; the spirt of the Fighting Irish pervaded the school—and we were immersed in that spirit from our first days on campus. Right after dinner on the Friday night of a football weekend, the band would begin high-stepping around campus playing the *Notre Dame Victory March*—and we'd pour out of the dorms to follow them, flinging rolls of toilet paper into the trees as we headed for the fieldhouse. There, as students catapulted others into the air using Army blankets they'd removed from their dorm beds, the football team would step out onto the balcony of this dirt-floored building to ear-piercing screams—and coach Ara Parseghian would promise another victory. Mostly, he delivered.

We went to all the home games of course—the six-dollar game tickets were included in tuition—but I only went to one away game: the famous 10-10 tie in 1966 at Michigan State sophomore year. Several of us drove up in Dave Pender's station wagon that was leaking so much oil we couldn't see through the blue cloud we were trailing. And then, as we drove through State's campus surrounded by crowds, Dave—who had done some championship drinking to prepare for the game—announced he was going to be sick. Peter rolled down the window and jammed Dave's head out as crowds watched him throw up all over the side of the car.

From our first days on campus, drinking was a weekend activity, thanks to Peter Nardone's ability to alter our Notre Dame IDs using press-on letters from the bookstore—but not all pranks involve alcohol. Tom Payne, a serious student who lived across the hall had a scholarship from the Ford Foundation. He had to send them "progress reports" periodically and one day, Marc Imundo offered to mail one of his reports for him. Marc had a bottle of cheap perfume from his girlfriend—and he soaked Tom's letter in it before putting it in the mail. We never heard whether Tom held on to the scholarship.

Another dormmate, Peter Nardone was a wiry kid who'd sometimes climb into a footlocker that we'd close and carry into another kid's room. "Open it," we'd say. And when he did, out would pop Peter. Peter would also climb into the laundry chute built into the wall at the end of the hall and close the door. When the next kid would open the door to throw down his bag, there was Peter. "Hi," he'd say, "got laundry?"

At some point, in the fall of freshman year, I started a band with three other kids who played guitar. We practiced in an adjacent dorm, in an empty, fully tiled shower room in the basement. The acoustics were terrible—and so, we finally admitted, were we. We played for one dance and broke up. A priest who chaperoned the dance told me, "You're not half-bad." He didn't mention the other half.

For fall semester freshman year, I had no credit card and only ninety dollars in cash—to cover books, snacks, transportation home at Thanksgiving, and all activities—so there wasn't much I could afford to do. But more than that, I was a shy kid who didn't really believe he deserved to be at Notre Dame. I figured it was just a matter of time before the school found out that I was neither smart nor—as many ND students were—athletically inclined. In Phys. Ed., we played racquetball and I was put on a doubles team with Ed Turk, a serious athlete. We were in an "elimination tournament" and, surprisingly, made it all the way to the finals. But before the final match, Ed came to me and said: "Bob, I know how we can win this. Tomorrow, you need to stay home. Let me play by myself." He did. I did. And he won.

But I began to gain confidence in myself when, in sophomore year, I transferred to the college of Liberal Arts; there, for two reasons, I eventually decided to major in modern languages: first, I began to think about a career in international marketing and wanted to be able to speak another language; but second—and perhaps more important—that was the major that allowed the broadest array of electives. When else—I reasoned—would I be able to learn a little about so many different subjects?

And so I took a course each in accounting, marketing, design, logic, statistics, transportation, psychology—even a basic course in computer programming; and although I never ended up in international marketing, the subjects I sampled were all helpful in my career. For languages, I took a course in Russian and a number of courses in German, including one from a graduate student, Walter Holzheuer, who learned English by listening to radio plays in Germany; he knew every American idiom for "murder," and assigned us crime stories to read in German, which he then acted out by running around the room, screaming and pretending to be the murderer—or the victim. The only time I ever used German was when I was on field maneuvers with the Army in Germany, and I handled the translation required to buy snacks and beer for the troops.

In sophomore year, I moved back to Zahm Hall and began rooming with Peter Nardone; he was a friend from freshman year, a finance major from Rhode Island who liked the room quiet when he studied but was always considerate of my plans. He had a small TV in the room and liked to watch Johnny Carson who came on at 10:30 in South Bend. In the morning, he'd ask: "I'm thinking of watching Johnny tonight. Would that be OK with you?" I'd room with him in different dorms for the next three years because we got along well although he was a heavy smoker who also liked to party on weekends. One night, coming back to campus, he found an abandoned bicycle and brought it up to the third floor. I heard him come riding down the hall at full speed, miss a turn and slam into a wall. He brought the bike into our room, opened the window, and threw it out. Sometimes, to prove he was sober—or maybe that he wasn't—he'd walk the railing over the St. Joe River after a night of drinking in town.

One day, Peter got an idea to paint our room. He went to Sears and bought two gallons of white paint and some tubes of blue pigment. His plan was to paint twelve-inch horizontal stripes around the room—dark blue at the top, lighter for the lower stripes—and with the help of our next-door friend, Mike Lippa, that's what he did. He ended with eight stripes in various shades of blue; the lines weren't perfectly straight, but several days later, I was asleep when I heard our door open and several maids peek in. "See," said our maid, "I told you they painted their room." At Goodwill Industries we found a very-used blue-and-white-striped couch and bought it for our room.

And that was the year Peter got me interested in scotch. His girlfriend back home sent him pints of J&B through the mail, but he was very strict about how scotch was to be drunk: either with water, soda, ice, or neat—never mixed with anything else. John Rank, a kid across the hall, once mixed his scotch with ginger ale—and Peter stopped speaking to him for the rest of the year.

On weekends, Peter, Dan Cox, and several of my other friends and I drank at a place in town called *The Original Coney Island*; it was a run-down hole in the wall we called *Billy's* where a Schlitz draft cost twenty-five cents and I seldom had more than one or two beers all night. Billy, the old Greek bartender, didn't care—and once he served you, he didn't ask to see your ID again. That was good because ours were all fake and we didn't bring them with us. The cops never stopped by.

Sophomore year, I was a member of class government—I put together a year-book supplement on our class—where our class president, Rick Rembush, had a great policy: we each got two free tickets to all the concerts on campus. And so that year, I saw the Four Tops, The Temptations, The Fifth Dimension, and my personal favorites, The Mamas and Papas. I usually had one of the guys—most often Dan Cox—go with me and Dan often was well-tuned when he got there. He was a diligent student who spent every non-class moment from Sunday through Friday in the library—but from Friday night through the end of Saturday he spent every moment drinking. His motto: "when the kid studies, the kid studies; but when the kid wails, the kid wails." He was the Philadelphia kid.

We mostly took Amtrak back and forth during freshman and sophomore year because it cost only thirty-three dollars round-trip to Rochester. We'd get on in South Bend around six in the evening—and arrive in Rochester around four or five the next morning. The problem was that South Bend was a couple of stops after the Great Lakes Naval Training Center and so there would sometimes be so many sailors already on board, we had nowhere to sit but on our suitcase. One night, I cleared a space in the overhead luggage rack, crawled up there, and tried to go to sleep. But, when the porter came through checking tickets, my friend Mike Lippa called out, "hey, Bob." "Yeah?" I answered.

The Porter stopped, looked around, turned on his flashlight. "Where you at?' he asked. "Where you at?"

"I'm up here," I said, "trying to get some sleep."

"You can't sleep up there," he said. "You got to get down; you got to get down now." He was *really excited*—and so I did.

By the end of sophomore year, I was a Modern Languages major and my GPA was improving—and since those with higher GPAs were given priority in room selection, Peter and I were able to get a fourth floor room in a prestigious dorm, Lyons Hall. The dorm was on one of the two small lakes on the campus—and in the room next to us that year lived a very serious music major who built his own klavier; that's a piano-like instrument he was inclined to play dramatically—and very late at night.

One night, his playing woke Peter, who went next door to fix the situation. "When it's late and it's very dark, and I really get into my playing," the music major told Peter, "I imagine the ghosts from centuries past coming out and joining me."

"When it's very dark and late and I'm sleeping, and you wake me up by your playing, I imagine those ghosts coming back and squeezing the living shit out of you," Peter told him. The late-night playing stopped.

The Vietnam war formed a backdrop for our entire undergraduate career, but junior year seemed to offer some hope; Martin Luther King was leading massive, peaceful, but effective rallies—and Bobby Kennedy had announced his intentions to run for president. But then. . .in an event some called electrifying, Kennedy spoke on campus the same day King was killed in a Memphis hotel—and just sixty-three days before Kennedy was gunned down in Los Angeles.

For me personally, junior year was a decision point. I was working part-time at the library to make a little spending money in a job I found disruptive and one which I kept for only a short time. I was doing well in my courses, but bored—and wondering at times what I was doing here? Did I really need a college education? Should I continue at Notre Dame? In times of trouble and confusion, I often turn inward, to take my own counsel—and that's what I did here. I reasoned there would never be a better time to complete what I started—if only because, if I stopped now, I might never have the courage to begin again. I remember the night and the place—it was a snowy evening in front of the Notre Dame bookstore—when I made the final decision: I'd complete my eduation at Notre Dame.

It was among the best decisions I ever made.

Another was to marry Jeanne; we got engaged on the evening before her birthday in August before I returned for senior year. That year, Peter and I moved down two floors in Lyons Hall. It was a much larger room, overlooking the lake and Peter liked to sleep with the windows open for fresh air. There were mornings in winter we'd wake up with snow on our floor. That year to counteract junior year's mental boredom, I decided I needed something to *physically do*, so I took a course in advertising design—where I learned to solve marketing problems by making things with my hands. One of my solutions—to sell foods in reusable Tupperware-like containers instead of cans—may have been ahead of its time— but the other was clearly wrong for the future: I suggested an elaborate design for the folder that held airline tickets; the folder would soon be a cost-cutting thing of the past.

But perhaps the most interesting aspect of the course was the professor who taught it. It wasn't unusual to come into class and find him curled up on the lower shelf of one of the long worktables in the classroom. He'd be sleeping off his latest hangover.

For another change that year, I enrolled in a German class at St. Mary's, Notre Dame's sister college a shuttle bus ride away. The teacher, Frau Grosser was a highly-intelligent, very well-educated, very proper professor who taught seminar style; six sudents would sit around the table and talk completely in German. When we walked into the room, we had to leave our English outside in the hall. I learned more German from her—including a respect for her hero, Johann Wofgang von Goethe—than I learned in any other language course during my four years.

Notre Dame had always had a number of restrictive policies ranging from disallowing students to have cars, drink alcohol in the dorms, or have females in our rooms—to restricting the speakers who could be invited to campus, requiring us to wear suit coats and ties to dining hall meals, or having to sign into our dorms after ten o'clock at night. Gradually, many of those restrictions lessened or disappeared entirely—if only because student government held events and activities to test the rules and limits. Not all were successful, including the infamous Pornography and Censorship Conference our senior year. It included controversial speakers, controversial films, and a controversial art exhibit that was described as "not well hung." But we were an all-male school; students got overexcited. Everything quickly fell apart; fights broke out, the police intervened, the conference was cancelled.

That was a year when student protests were disrupting college operations everywhere—but when they started at Notre Dame, Father Hesburgh took swift and decisive action. In a letter he sent to every student on February 17, 1969, he said clearly that he expected better of Notre Dame students—and he spelled out the consequences of not living up to his expectations. If we were so inclined to take over anything, we'd be given fifteen minutes to cease and desist, after which we'd be expelled from the University. Further protests were more peaceful.

A month or so after that letter, Linda Keymel passed away. Back in Holy Rosary grammar school, she had been the most popular girl in school, a pretty blond who, at some point, had met my Aquinas friend Randy Block and they'd gotten engaged. Now, suddenly, she'd fallen ill and died. I wasn't close to her, but her death affected me. We were too young to die. I mentioned it to Peter—and he had an idea. Peter had a car on campus. "Why don't we go to Rochester for her funeral?" he suggested. And so we did. Peter (it was his car), Tom Murphy (he was dating a girl in Rochester), Roger Kiley (he went everywhere we went) and I got into Peter's car after class one Friday afternoon—and headed east. The funeral was on Saturday; we'd drive back on Sunday.

Sometime that Friday night, we were someplace in Ohio and Tom Murphy was driving when we got pulled over for speeding. The speed limit was sixty-five; Tom was going ninety. It was late, but the cop offered to take us someplace where we could pay the fine. The fine was twenty-five dollars and we all pitched in to pay it. But Tom was curious: we were going twenty-five miles above the speed limit; did they set the fine at a dollar per mile? *No*, the cop told Tom, *the fine in their small town was twenty-five bucks flat—no matter how fast we had been going.* "Oh," Tom told him, "if I had known that, I would have been going a lot faster."

The next time I came home was to surprise Jeanne at her bridal shower—and to take her back to Notre Dame for my graduation. Our friends Mike and

Rosie Lippa had married the year before and were renting a little house in South Bend, so Jeanne could stay with them. My parents also drove out to watch the class of 1969 become the first class ever to graduate in the newly-opened Athletic and Convocation Center. Our speaker was Senator Daniel P. Moynihan, who said nothing I would ever remember.

But that was it. Nearly four years after that night when we headed "west of Buffalo," my college education was over; Notre Dame was in my rear-view mirror.

I've gone back a couple of times since then, once on a business trip for Kodak to offer some audio-visual counseling to members of Notre Dame's staff, another time when I was visiting friends in Indianapolis and drove up to wander around campus—and several times when our son Tim was a student from 1994 through 1997. But being an alumnus had benefitted me in other ways; at a pivotal point in my Kodak career, my boss and his boss were Notre Dame graduates and they provided mentorship and support. And from time to time, I even followed Fighting Irish football.

Then in 2017, John Hickey, a classmate I had never met, started the *Class of 1969* blog. His reasoning: our fiftieth reunion was fast approaching (in 2019) and we had been a large class who often hadn't known anyone out of a small circle of classmates; perhaps the reunion would be more fun if we at least met each other virtually, online. He invited class members to tell their stories and I— among many others—did. When a few of us—John, Gary Campana, Dave Sim and I—seemed to be far outpacing others with our postings, John invited us to collect the blog stories and others into a book about our class to be published before the reunion. We wrote that one to commemorate our class—and, later, another one to celebrate our reunion. Nearly all campus pictures—including the cover pictures—in both books were mine. And both books are in the Notre Dame archives and the Library of Congress. I'm proud of our efforts.

And Jeanne and I loved the reunion. We reconnected with our classmates— and their spouses—from freshman year in Cavanaugh as if no time had passed. But it did. Through the years, ten percent of our class has passed away, others were too ill to make the journey, and yet, three hundred seventy of us did come back; and thank God for name badges with large print—because some of us stared at each other's thinking: *Really?*

We came back to remember, to laugh over the long-ago craziness, to acknowledge that at Notre Dame, we earned a degree that would mean something forever. The school set high standards but recognized that we were young. It expected us to show the courage of the Four Horsemen; often, we behaved more like the Three Stooges. Most days, we were somewhere in between. After a food fight in the dining hall freshman year, the dean of students told the freshmen instigators: "You're the smartest class we've ever admitted to Notre Dame—and the least disciplined."

Notre Dame has changed through the years; the once all-male student body is now almost half female; a four-year education that cost me less than ten thousand dollars now costs a quarter of a million; the number of buildings has more than doubled—and most have technology inside that wasn't yet invented in our day. It holds a higher position on a more demanding world stage.

Still there was a familiar—and a welcoming—feel to campus. It was good to revisit old classrooms and walk the stairwells to our dorm rooms; to remember playing frisbee on the lawns and hitchhiking into town; to recall those freezing winter mornings walking to class and hot fall nights in dorm rooms; and to shake our heads over all the rest. As we swapped old stories and told new lies, it was clear that since graduation, we'd heard different drummers, moved to different beats, dealt with our own realities in our own ways. But underlying those differences was the foundation of a shared experience—we were graduates of Notre Dame and that links us forever.

Once a month, a dozen of us 'wingmen'—classmates from that little wing in Cavanaugh Hall—have a Zoom call, to stay in each other's lives, to tell our current stories and—once in a while—one from long ago. We learned a lot on that campus—and not everything was in the classroom.

# 18

# LEARNING THE FUNDAMENTALS

MANY YEARS AFTER I'D GRADUATED AND WAS MANAGING marketing and communications for Kodak in Hollywood, a colleague described my job to his nephew. His nephew thought it was a job he'd like to have; he asked what was my major in college?

I hesitated in answering that for several reasons. First, because my job in no way matched my major; second, because I didn't select a major based on the job I was preparing for, but rather for the kind of college experience I wanted to have; and third, because the job I had today would likely change irrevocably by the time he graduated from college. And so, I decided to answer his question in a different way—by encouraging him to look at college not in terms of the specifics college taught, but in terms of the fundamentals he could learn and apply. Requirements for future jobs change—I told him—fundamentals don't. And they would be forever important to his success. Here are some of the fundamentals I suggested:

- Don't worry excessively about selecting a major. Begin with courses that offer a view of the discipline that appeals to you—but then try to find electives that expose you to other subjects you might find interesting. The mix can help you discover your real passions—and may cause you to shift directions.

- Your real purposes of college should be to learn to read more broadly, to write more clearly, to listen more intently, to think more creatively, to act more thoughtfully, and to begin to discover who *you* are and the ways you can make a difference. If you can learn to do all that, you will have the fundamentals you need to compete—and to succeed—in any profession.

- Don't go home for at least the first month of college—maybe more. This is a new adventure and parts of it will be tough, but you have to give it a chance. Learn to swim by yourself without automatically heading to the side of the pool.

- Volunteer—and/or sign up for an extracurricular activity—and show up. You will gain experiences, meet people, learn different ways to solve problems, and develop understanding that you might not in a classroom.

- Whatever college you pick, it won't be perfect. Forget its imperfections; be proud of your school—you chose it and it accepted you. Even the best-rated schools aren't right for everyone; developing a positive attitude about the choices you make—and making them work—will serve you well throughout your life.

- If possible, go away to college. College should be a very different experience than high school and for that, you need to leave your usual support system of family and friends behind.

- If you have a strong interest in a specific profession, go to college in a city where that profession is strong: filmmaking in southern California, automotive design in Detroit, archeology in Utah, government in Washington, and so forth. The schools there are more likely to have working professionals in your field drop in for evening lectures—and you may be able to make contacts that will be valuable later on.

- If you get in trouble of any kind—academic, physical, emotional, mental— tell someone who can at least listen without judging—and who may be able to help. You're not the first one to have this problem; there is a solution.

Don't give up and don't do anything stupid you, your family or friends might later regret.

- Recognize that not everyone learns the same way. Some learn by listening to others; others learn by explaining things to themselves. Some learn in study groups, some don't. Don't be afraid to learn your own way, but above all, don't be afraid to learn.

- Don't go to college looking for others who think and act like you. Go expecting an adventure that will make you uncomfortable at times. Learn to be more tolerant of new ideas, more open to understanding other ways of life, and more accepting of other approaches. The world is a diverse place; you need to accept that.

- When you pack for college, don't leave your values at home. There will be plenty for you to do within the framework of what is right; things that are wrong—are wrong. They're not OK just because you're in college.

- Be proactive in your studies. Don't let work get beyond you. Ask questions often. Don't be afraid to say, "I don't understand." The best professors don't just want to teach—they want to help you learn.

- Don't avoid courses that everyone tells you are hard; don't be afraid to sign up for professors who are said to be tough. If you push yourself to tackle difficult things now, it will give you an edge in life forever.

- Meet your professors personally, as soon as possible. Stop by their office, introduce yourself. At least that will help them associate a face with a name—but it may also enable you to call on them for opportunities, recommendations, internships, or other courses that you may not be able to get on your own.

- Broaden yourself in as many different areas as you can. Attend guest lectures. Learn to speak another language. Take a hands-on course that requires you to use some part of your body besides your brain. You'll never again have the opportunity to sample so much variety—and it will give you a better view of what appeals to you.

- Push yourself to higher goals even when you're tired; learn not settle for OK when you're capable of better. But don't let yourself be judged *only* by your grades; the grade you receive is only one measure of the value of the work you've done. If you want to compete with someone in the classroom, compete with yourself. When you've *honestly* done your best, you've won.

- Expect to be overwhelmed by course work and deadlines. Don't panic; you can do this. Don't let challenges fan out; line them up one behind each other and learn to prioritize your time. That's something you must teach yourself in college; it will be invaluable later on.

- Working on a study or project team? Try to always do more than your share—and not to worry who gets the credit. Eventually, people who can't handle the job will be found out—but so will people who only do what they are rewarded for. You'll learn how to avoid both of those types of people in life; in college, try not to *become* them.

- Put yourself on a budget—and stick to it. Spend more time learning, less time celebrating. When you get your first job, your pay will be less than you expect; one of the great secrets of life is being satisfied with what you have—and learning to live on it.

- Find several people who could serve as your mentors—professors, students, even local businesspeople—who can help you understand the way the world works and can provide some connections for you into it. Get together with them, share your dreams, ask questions, listen to them. Don't be afraid to appear stupid. There is something very refreshing about students who are willing to admit they don't know everything.

- When things get tough—and they will—if you think about dropping out, consider this: It will *not* be easier for you to go back to college, sometime in the future. A college degree is one important 'ante' in the game of life; if you want to win, you need to be in the game. Without a degree, you'll never sit at the table—and, at some point—you may be on the menu.

- Search for internships early—and aggressively. Don't just look for money, look to make connections, to meet people who may be able to help—with advice, with referrals, with later job offers—in your field. Show them what you can do; then keep in touch with them.

- When you have professional people speaking on campus, introduce yourself and ask them: *If I were to work for you, what would I do?* Write down what they tell you, talk to your professors, and make sure you know how to do it; those are the skills you need for the working world.

• When you prepare your resume, your cover letter, or anything else (including yourself prior to an interview), remember this: a company hires you to solve *their* problems—not yours. Position and promote yourself as *their* best solution. And make sure everything you write is error-free; sometimes the smallest mistakes make the biggest difference.

• Be careful what you share. Think carefully before you post anything on social media; someday, those pictures and comments—so funny or crazy right now—could show up to hold you back from opportunities that would otherwise be open to you. There are things the world does not need to see or know; and yes, future employers will see them.

• But through it all, don't lose your sense of humor. Sometimes you'll win, sometimes you'll lose, and sometimes you'll study all night, and it won't make any difference. Smile. Someday, you'll see these times for what they really are: four years of opportunity that helped you prepare for life ahead— and in a way that nothing else could have done.

If you decide to share any of that advice with young people heading off to college, I hope it makes a difference in their educational experience—and in their life. I hope it better prepares them to find a job that fits them well and enables them to build a career that makes them happy. I was fortunate to have my college experiences at Notre Dame; they prepared me for a career I loved, working for a company that provided great rewards for me and my family. But before I went to work for them, I had a series of summer jobs, beginning with one in a company built on marshy land where I used to hunt for pollywogs and snakes back when I lived on Oriole Street.

# 19

# WHERE THE SNAKES USED TO LIVE

**M**Y BROTHER AND I USED TO SCOOP UP tadpoles on the woodsy, swampy land at the western end of Driving Park Avenue. There was always a sign posted indicating that the land was for sale and that it was zoned commercial, but for the longest time, it stood vacant. Finally, by the time I'd entered high school, a building complex had replaced the cattails and the complex had a tenant, the Bernz-O-Matic Corporation. After my freshman year in college, they gave me a summer job.

Bernz-O-Matic made propane cylinders and the tools— such as soldering torches, small portable grills, and other devices—that used them. The company had a small footprint—their headquarters, manufacturing plant and distribution depot were all in a one-floor complex—but they dominated the cylinder market, both under their own brand and under brands they made for others. They paid me seventy dollars for forty hours of work each week—somewhere around $840.00 for a summer's work—good money, back then. Plus, it was just a fifteen-minute walk from home. I worked from seven am until 3:30 pm with a half-hour lunch.

The company was run by a man named Don Clark who, he told me later, always wanted to work for a small company. So, out of college, he joined the Haloid company, a small manufacturer of photographic paper. When they were acquired by the much larger Xerox, Don became a vice president of a large company. To prevent that from happening again, he left and purchased Bernz-O-Matic, a small company of his own.

I was part of a crew of college kids assigned to work for an even-tempered, friendly, but somewhat nervous guy named Tony Vito who managed the Supply department. Our job was to fill orders for the production lines—to bring the parts or cardboard cartons they needed to make and package the cylinders and other components they assembled. In a large cage-like area, we had lots of small component parts; out back, in the warehouse, we had stacks of cardboard cartons—those used for individual products and those used for shipping.

It was a busy place, a good place to work, and every day was different; and our supervisor didn't micromanage us—if the orders were getting fulfilled, he didn't need to watch us work. Which was good because when we went to the warehouse to get shipping cartons, we played a very dangerous game called "tow motor races" on those heavy vehicles with metal forks used to move weighty pallets of materials. They were powerful and dangerous machines—especially when operated by those who hadn't been trained to drive them—and were wearing no safety equipment. That was us.

The game worked like this: one of us would power up a tow motor and put an empty wooden pallet on its forks. Then another one of us would get on the empty pallet and the driver would raise it up as high as it would go—maybe ten or twelve feet in the air. And with his high-riding passenger hanging on, he'd drive at full speed—sometimes cornering on two wheels—up and down aisles as he was being timed. Then passenger and driver would change places—and go again. Tow motors are very poorly balanced; it's amazing one never tipped over; it's surprising no one was killed.

I enjoyed that job and the people I worked with and wanted to return to Bernz-O-Matic after sophomore year, but Kodak paid fifty cents more an hour and I could ride to work with my dad. At that time Dad also worked at Kodak

Park, the huge (twenty-five thousand employees worked there; it had its own railroad) manufacturing complex where I'd be a member of one of the many crews cleaning film machines. I hated every day on the job; I disliked having to meticulously clean anything—and we did because film is incredibly intolerant of impurities including, as just one example, zinc. When Kodak found that some of their emulsion was bad, they traced the cause to an employee whose wife was using shampoo with zinc as one ingredient—and who had touched her pillow sometime during the night. You can imagine how thorough our cleaning had to be—and that wasn't me.

Most days, we were assigned to clean the coating machines that spread light-sensitive emulsion on acetate base in incredibly thin layers, within incredibly tight tolerances, at incredibly high speeds. All completely in the dark. At the end of the line, the so-called "wide-rolls" would be placed in light-tight metal "coffins" and be taken to another building to be slit into narrow rolls, perforated, cut into lengths, packaged, and labeled.

The operation ran twenty-four hours a day and there was enormous profitability in film. One example: In 1963, Kodak introduced the Kodak Instamatic camera, which made picture-taking simple—and hugely popular—because the film came preloaded in a plastic cartridge that just snapped into the camera. Kodak made and packaged every part of that cartridge—from its plastic housing to the film inside—and including the labeling, printing, boxing and shipping. Typically, each cartridge sold for about $3.50; Kodak's all-in cost: eight cents.

Those filmmaking machines were huge, extending from a sub-basement up several floors and to clean them, we used a chemical called 'sevin' which came out of spigots in the wall. We had special cans with closed lids that we'd fill from those spigots, take the chemicals and rags into the machine, and clean all day long. Until…one member of our crew found that 'sevin' killed cockroaches instantly—and huge cockroaches lived in great numbers in the sub-basement of the emulsion-coating building. It was obvious what we had to do: the whole crew had to fill our buckets and chase cockroaches through that sub-basement, dumping massive amounts of chemical on them—and watching them go rigid and dead. It paid the same as doing actual work.

Some of the newer film manufacturing buildings had vacuum systems built into the walls. To vacuum the floors, we'd simply arrive with a wand and long hose which we'd plug into the wall—suction was immediate—and begin working. Until... somebody figured that the vacuum systems had internal filters to collect the dust and other particles—and that if he stuck his end of the vacuum hose into a bucket of soapy water, the suds would be vacuumed into the filters—and he could take a paid break until those filters could be replaced, which took through the end of the day. "Yeah," he'd say when our crew supervisor dropped by, "I don't know what happened. I was vacuuming the floors and the suction just stopped...."

And then there was the day Stewart Dinsmore didn't show up for work until lunch—with a story to tell.

Driving to work that morning, he said, he was stopped at a red light just opposite a hospital when his car was very lightly rear-ended by another driver. A cop happened to be close by, and although no one was hurt, the cop suggested—just to be certain—that Stewart be checked out in the hospital ER right across the street. When Stewart realized it would be paid time off, he readily agreed.

"So," Stew told us, "I signed in and they told me to have a seat. The place was really crowded, and it took an hour or so before a nurse came out and called my name. When I went in to see the doctor, he said, 'I notice that you've been waiting a very long time. What brings you in today?' So I looked him directly in the eyes and I said: 'Doc, I've got a bullet in my heart.' And it was great. Suddenly everybody started running around yelling 'stat' and I had to tell them it was all a joke. Then, they asked me to leave, and I came to work."

But on most days, I didn't like my job any more than Stewart did and the next summer I didn't even apply to Kodak; instead, I went back to Bernz-O-Matic where they asked me to run their Receiving department because their regular manager would be out all summer with health problems. Working for me was an older guy, Joe Shroth, who had been with the company for twenty years and kept a paternalistic eye out for the other member of the department—a short, wiry Hungarian named Aurielius Boris Joseph Bogdan, we called "Bogie." Since I was judged more capable than either of them to manage the department, that may give you a clue about how they approached their jobs: they wanted to get them done and go home.

In Receiving, our job was to unload trucks that were delivering components and other materials needed for the manufacturing processes, to count the materials we received, and to sign for the deliveries. We had special scales that translated weight into quantities; they were very easy to use, very reliable, and greatly simplified the counting process. Using them, Bogie regularly miscounted, or miscalculated, or used the wrong measures, or signed for the wrong count—and just shrugged his shoulders. "They hired me for my back," Bogie told me once. "If they want my mind, that's extra."

But he was just such a lovable guy and in his own little world, that it was impossible to be angry with him. Joe, Bogie, and I all got along well with each other; every day, I'd bring my lunch in a small brown bag and sit with them on a pile of boxes and we'd eat together. And every day, I noticed that Bogie brought the same thing for lunch: three slices of liverwurst. After several weeks of that, I said to Bogie: "I notice that you always bring three slices of liverwurst for lunch. You must really like liverwurst." Bogie looked at me. "Not particularly," he said.

One day Bogie didn't show up for work and Bill Allen, one of the senior managers in the front office came in to explain why. He seemed unable to stop laughing. "Bogie called this morning," Bill told Joe and me, "and said he wouldn't be in today. He said that last night, when he went home, he was very hungry and so he cooked and ate five pork chops. But when he finished, he counted only four bones. Bogie figured he must have eaten one of the pork chop bones; it was inside him and he had to get it out. He decided the best way to do that, was to drink a cup of liquid soap. He did. Bogie says he feels better now," Bill said, "but he says that every time he opens his mouth to speak, he blows bubbles."

That was Bogie. Another small wiry guy who drove me crazy for part of the summer was the main driver named Al King. Every morning, Al would leave headed for Buffalo, NY, driving a tractor trailer loaded with empty cylinders. In Buffalo, the cylinders would be filled with propane and Al would return with them at the end of the day.

We quit at 3:30 and Al would invariably arrive about 3:15 and head off to the break room. There was no authorized overtime, so Joe and Bogie would leave me to unload the truck and complete the paperwork, all for free. I kept thinking that I should say something to Al about trying to arrive earlier or to help with the unloading process, but I never did—and ended up being happy with my decision. Because, as I found out later, the company gave five-hundred-dollar scholarships to three summer employees and Al was on the committee to choose the recipients. And he chose me. "I appreciated," he told me later, "that you did your job every day, without complaint. It made my life easier, and I wanted to thank you for that."

When company president Don Clark gave me my scholarship, he asked me my plans for the future. Would I join a large company—or a small one—after graduation? He saw advantages in both, depending on what I was looking for. In a large company, he said, I could learn slowly, find mentors easily, move through the ranks, gain experience with worldwide brands, have a greater variety of jobs, maybe even work globally. Large companies provide a range of experiences you simply can't get in smaller ones, he told me. And, he said, sometimes the pay is better.

But, in smaller ones, he said, everyone is expected to contribute more fully, to work without a net, to handle lots of responsibility from the first day on the job. There are fewer layers of management, and more a feeling of contributing directly to success, having a greater sense of accomplishment that comes from working with a small team.

He wasn't advising me to join a company of one size or the other—but he did have some advice either way: "three years after you start," he said, "sit down and decide if this is where you want to be." The three-year mark was important, he said. "One year is too soon—and five years are too late because you'll be looking at bonuses and maybe stock options and other things to complicate your decision. Do it at three years—and decide to stay or to go."

I would later join a very large company, Kodak, and would stay for a very long and satisfying career—but that was almost a year in the future. Before I returned to school for my senior year, I invested all my summer earnings in a ring. On August 20, 1968, the night before her birthday, I asked Jeanne Stein to marry me.

# 20

# TWO KIDS FROM THE NEIGHBORHOOD

WHO WOULD HAVE THOUGHT WE'D END UP TOGETHER? There were ninety-six kids in our eighth-grade class at Holy Rosary grammar school and when I received the class picture right after graduation, I wrote everyone's name on the back. There were a couple I couldn't remember; one turned out to be Jeanne Stein. "That's OK," she'd tell me later, "when you were elected president of our high school Sodality and didn't come to meetings, I was one who voted to have you kicked out."

And then there was the year she invited me to a high school dance, and we went together and had a good time—but when my friend Tom Whalen asked me how the evening went, I said, "Jeanne is a nice girl. But she's not for me."

But as it turned out, she was. In recent years, after our kids had all left home but Jeanne and I were still working, I seldom went into the office on Fridays and, whenever possible, she tried also to take that day off. And so, on Thursday nights, we'd turn off the TV, sit on the couch and talk, remember what we had done that week, discuss how things were going, kick around plans for the weekend or for some time in the future. And we would ask each other the same question: *how could we be so lucky? How could we have been so fortunate to have chosen each other for the great shared adventure that lay ahead? How were we ever able to do all we've done together?*

We may have just gone to a Hollywood premiere and sat behind Marie Osmond and her family, or to the EMMYs or even to the Academy Awards; maybe we'd used my Silver pass which gave us free admission to Disneyland, or had been to a special private dinner with Steven Spielberg or someone else from the movie industry. We did all that and much more than we ever dreamed possible.

I was looking at our wedding pictures the other day and as I looked at the last one in the album, the one of us dancing, I thought: *If anyone had told us of the experiences we'd have, we would have laughed and insisted: You've confused us with someone else. A life like that would be impossible, inconceivable for two kids who went to grammar school together then much later fell in love back in Rochester's old tenth ward.*

Although we grew up going to the same church, the same school, and living less than a dozen blocks apart, for virtually all our teen-age years, Jeanne went her way, and I went mine. Until about a week before I returned for sophomore year at Notre Dame. I'd been going out with another girl very steadily but decided I wanted to also date others—although I had no one I mind. I always went to mass on Sunday but on that last Sunday before going back to school, I had arrived at mass late and slid into an available pew, not paying much attention to whom I'd end up sharing it with. It turned out to be Jeanne Stein, the one who had voted me out of Sodality, the girl who was not the right girl for me. But when mass ended, we stood outside and talked for a few minutes before we each headed off to our homes.

When I got home, I thought, if I'm going to date others, why not start now? I looked up Jeanne's phone number and called her; I told her I had to return to school at the end of the week but asked if she'd be available for a movie, maybe on Tuesday or Wednesday night? Jeanne would tell me later that she was a bit miffed by my call. *Who did I think I was calling her at the last minute, expecting her to go out in just a day or two? But then,* she decided, *she'd give me a break; I did have to go back to school, and she was available, and. . . .*

So we went to the Monroe Theatre to see *The Russians are Coming, The Russians are Coming*. The movie wasn't great, but when it was over, I gave her my campus address; she said she would write.

Truth be told, she wrote so seldom that I wondered if she were still interested. Several weeks would go by before I'd get a letter; she really was shy, didn't know quite what she should write and most often didn't. But still, we kept corresponding and when I came home for Christmas, I got a job working at Ester's Liquor Store down on Dewey Avenue. Paul Sayre, for whom I had worked at Holy Rosary when he was a janitor there, was now working at Ester's, but he needed someone to move the heavy cartons, calculate bills accurately, handle money reliably, help customers carry their purchases to the car. He hired me.

One evening before Christmas, Jeanne and her dad came into the store. While he carried on a conversation with Paul—they knew each other from Holy Rosary—and bought some liquor he probably didn't need, Jeanne carried out the real purpose for which they'd come: she invited me to join her family for dinner on Christmas day. Since my family always celebrated on Christmas Eve, I was happy to go.

Her family was easy to talk to; Aunt Jo and Uncle Howie were there also and so there was lots of laughing and good-natured fun. Apparently, that day, at that dinner, Aunt Jo (who always decided things like this) decided that I was right for Jeanne—and Jeanne was right for me. I think she liked the fact that I was tall, laughed at her antics, and went to Notre Dame.

After we had been married for a long time, I asked Jeanne when she knew that we'd end up together. She said that she pretty much knew at the end of that meal. That was surprising; it was quite a while before I knew also.

At some point after that, Aunt Jo bet us two dollars that we would be married by her anniversary (early July) in 1969. She'd lose that bet by about two weeks and somewhere, in a crude wooden frame, against a red cardboard background (red was always her favorite color), is the acknowledgement of her loss: a framed two-dollar bill.

But I went back to school and, sometime that spring, Jeanne sent me her picture. She used to model for a photography studio called Vardens, and they made a hand-painted sepia-toned portrait of her that was stunning. I had a small gold frame on my desk and when I put Jeanne's picture in, it felt like a new beginning in my life. She was, as the expression goes, "drop-dead gorgeous."

Notre Dame always had a Spring dance and to this one, I invited Jeanne. She flew out with Rose Ann Taddeo, Mike Lippa's soon-to-be-wife and we rented a room for both of them to share in a house somewhere down Notre Dame Avenue. Roger Kiley, another friend, also had a girlfriend staying at the same house, and Jeanne remarked to Rose Ann the next day, *"Wow, Roger gets here early. He was already here when I got up this morning."* Rose Ann told her that, actually, Roger was *"staying over."* That never occurred to Jeanne. She was from Rochester.

And so it went through my college years. Jeanne had always been a working girl. When we started dating, she was working for Mr. Sevatski, a tailor and dry cleaner; she waited on customers and removed (and replaced) buttons before clothes went through the cleaning process. She started when she was fifteen and apparently had been underpaid because, at one point, Mr. Sevatski was investigated, Jeanne was interviewed, and she received additional back pay.

She was planning for a career in an office and so, after graduating from Nazareth high school, she enrolled in Rochester Business Institute where, about a month later, she came down with mono. When that led to Bell's Palsy, she had to drop out of school—and quit Mr. Sevatski—to recover. But RBI operated year-round and so she returned the next summer, just before we started dating. During that time, at night and on weekends, she got a job in the jewelry department of Edward's, a major department store downtown, where I would sometimes stop by, give her a ride home after work.

For work that could be more relevant to what she wanted to do later on, RBI helped her get in a job in the office of Stein's Bakery (no relation) and then after she graduated from RBI in 1967 with the equivalent of an associate degree in business, she was hired at Kodak Office. She was the receptionist for Business and Technical Personnel, the Kodak employment office that hired professional or experienced people. Glenn Durkin ran the office; Don Briggs was second in command. If I ever wanted to work at Kodak—and I wasn't sure I did—Jeanne could get me an interview. But that would be in the future.

In the summer after my sophomore year, there was a major world exposition in Montreal, *EXPO '67*, and Jeanne and I decided we'd love drive up together, but her parents' wondered—what would be the sleeping arrangements? It all got settled when my Notre Dame classmate, Roger Kiley who lived in Saratoga Springs, also wanted to join us with his girlfriend, so he and I would stay together—and she and Jeanne would stay together. My mother called Jeanne's and explained how it would work—and we went and had a great time.

At one point, during my junior year, when Jeanne was out for a dance, I remember mentioning marriage in kind of a light-hearted way. I suggested that I wouldn't get married until I had graduated and completed my military service. Those were the days of the draft, and I couldn't think of a reason why I wouldn't be drafted. "Gee," I remember her saying, "I don't know if I'd want to wait that long. Would you?" It wasn't really a question; if there was a 'starting moment' for us always to be together, that may have been it.

We were falling in love—although growing up in the family situation I did, I wasn't even sure exactly what love was supposed to be. I just knew that I liked being with her, that we looked at life the same way, that we had the same values. We could talk to each other and were willing to listen to each other; I figured that, when we had problems, we'd try to solve them together. I never thought we would have much more than our parents did, but what we'd achieve, we'd achieve together. We never had long discussions about how many kids we would have, where we would live, or even what kind of job I'd have; I just thought we'd figure all that out together as we went along.

We were different people—I loved to play the drums, to collect records and books, to travel, to read and even, eventually, to write. She was quieter, liked music, was nice to everyone, was loved by all my friends, was much more likely to listen than to speak. We were both introverts, enjoyed quiet times together; and most important, had the same values. I've come to understand that it's fine to have different interests, but it's critical to share the same fundamentals. It seemed like we'd have a nice life together, that we would be good for each other and to each other, that our relationship would be strong and steady over the long term. She told me once, years later, "I thought you would never hurt me." I've tried hard not to.

I seemed to have passed the test with her parents—and my mother was very clear that she believed that Jeanne was the one for me. The summer after my junior year, we decided to look at wedding rings, "just to see what was available." Auntie knew a German jeweler, Bernie Hensler, who was "an honest man" and so we went to his store, upstairs, in a building downtown, where Jeanne found several that she liked. She would leave the final selection up to me, but that was the only store where we looked. Some days later I went back and paid about a thousand dollars for a nearly one-carat ring that, to me looked impressive but simple. It was a plain silver ring with six prongs holding one diamond. I thought it was perfect. But when to give it to her?

I decided on August 20, 1968, the night before her birthday, but I wanted to do this right, so late on afternoon of August 19, I went down to Briter, the paint store her father ran on Stone Road. "I came here to ask your permission to marry Jeanne," I said, nervously. "I'd like to marry your daughter." Dad also seemed a little nervous. He said something about "knowing that she feels the same way about you as you feel about her" and I'm sure he gave his permission, but I don't remember that, or any other part of our conversation.

The next night, when Jeanne and I were alone in her kitchen, I proposed. I don't remember what I said, but I suspect it was something simple and straightforward. I told her I loved her and asked her to marry me. When she said yes, I gave her the ring.

I should have given my words a lot more thought, maybe even rehearsed them in front of a mirror. I would be taking the most important step of my life; I should have been frightened. I hadn't seen what a good marriage looked like. I didn't know what I was getting into, but truth be told, it didn't seem like a big deal. It just seemed like the next logical next step in our relationship. To me, marrying Jeanne just seemed like the most natural thing to do. And I like to think she said yes because she too felt comfortable and confident that we'd be good for each other.

We told her parents then headed over for champagne with Uncle Howie and Aunt Jo. But later that evening, when Jeanne returned home, her mother asked:

"If you knew you were getting engaged, why would you go out and buy a car? Why didn't you wait?" Her father had co-signed for Jeanne to buy a new blue Pontiac Tempest for $2,600.00, and I think her mom was afraid I'd renege on the payments. We completed the payments together. It was the first car I'd own.

We were married almost exactly eleven months later, on July 19, 1969, in Holy Rosary church, where we had re-introduced ourselves in a pew just a few years before. The glitches were minor. The night before the wedding, Peter Nardone, my college roommate who was one of the groomsmen, and I went out for a final celebration. I was home and asleep when Peter came in, much later, driven by cops who had found him drunk, lost, and somewhere on the streets. He was fine by morning.

And, after Jeanne and I left for our honeymoon, her parents held a small after-party for family and some out-of-town guests, including my college friends. We heard later that Peter Nardone got drunk at that party, took off his pants, and dove into their swimming pool—in front of Jeanne's eighty-year-old, and very-startled, grandmother.

We were driving to New England, but the reception ran late and so for our first night, I just booked a place close to the thruway, a couple of hours drive from Rochester. That's how we ended spending our wedding night at the Town and Country Motel in Utica—and having dinner at the only place that was open, McDonalds. But we did make our way into Boston the next day and that night, on the hotel's black and white television in our room, we watched Neil Armstrong's first steps on the moon.

We spent the rest of our honeymoon in an oceanfront room at the Bass Rocks Inn in Gloucester where the waves crashed on the big rocks and there was a lighthouse just to the north. I can see us driving those narrow streets of that small town and I remember telling Jeanne back then: "I'm glad I married you. I just like being with you." I always have—and I still do.

When we returned home, Jeanne's parents said they had been worried because they hadn't heard from us. Without offering it as an excuse, I think we were realizing that we were becoming our own family, trusting and believing in us. And, in some ways, Jeanne's mother encouraged that. Before Jeanne left to get married, her mom told her: "you and Bob are always welcome here. You are not welcome." What she was saying is: "Don't come running back home if you have problems; work them out together." Great advice. But, even in our first years of marriage, if you were to ask our parents whether we had problems, I suspect they wouldn't know—and we like it that way. In general, parents can only make their children's marital problems worse.

It's not that we haven't had our problems and disagreements, but we can both honestly say that, in all the years we've been married, we've never sworn at each other, never called each other a name, or raised our hands—or even our voices—in anger. We don't bicker or pick at each other; we try never to be overly critical. Jeanne has never liked the fact that I bite my nails—and I wish she would turn off television or lights when she leaves a room—but those are small things. The only potential big thing we've dealt with is—I asked her to stop smoking before we got married, and she quit permanently. Otherwise, when we come up with something we disagree about, we usually end up laughing about it—and then put it out of our minds. We've worked things out, mostly calmly, always without outside help. The way it seemed to me we would back when we first thought about marriage, all those years ago.

I suspect that most marital arguments are about money, so in some ways we were lucky to have so little of it in our first years of marriage. I was in the Army, and we were living on take-home pay of $168.00 a month—for everything. We were unable to afford a twenty-five-cent movie or a ten-cent hamburger, so we spent our time together doing things that cost no money: taking long walks around Milford, a lake in the middle of Kansas, playing bocci balls on the lawn, and just being together, becoming each other's best friend.

I don't know if love grows into friendship or friendship grows into love; I suspect they're really two sides of the same coin. Although there's no question that we remain two different people—she worries about what's wrong while I tend to focus on what's right; she can tell you details of a house we've seen years ago that I can't remember visiting; I can remember numbers and she *definitely* cannot—but we really do enjoy being together. We try to set aside a day each week to go somewhere by ourselves and walk and talk.

I worry sometimes that I've gotten recognition for what I've done—and have been able to stand in the spotlight so many times, that she will get cold in the shadows. That's why it's been so great to involve her in the glitz and glamour of Hollywood and in all that we've been able to do in California.

She's shy sometimes, reluctant to go to some events, worried that she won't fit in, but she always does. I am always intensely proud of her—because all that I've been able to achieve, I've achieved because she has been part of me and my life. When I think back from a perspective of having spent more than fifty-five years together—from the year we re-met—it seems that most of what we have in life is the result of Jeanne saying yes. She said "yes" when I asked her to marry me—and "yes" when Fr. Wheeland asked if she'd take me as her husband—but there were so many other important "yeses" along the way.

She said "yes" when I asked her to leave her Kodak job and follow me as a young soldier to Kansas—and "yes" when I asked her to live on my Army pay, although it would mean eating endless meals of a bologna sandwiches, a few potato chips and water. She said "yes" to having children and "yes" to staying home taking care of them when I traveled most weeks and many weekends for Kodak. She said "yes" when I told her we had the opportunity to move to California, so I could take a job I thought I'd love, even though it would take her far from her own family and friends. And when we both retired and we found we could live more affordably if we moved closer to San Diego, Jeanne again said "yes."

We've been fortunate that the decisions she said "yes" to, have worked out well. She knows I'd never try to talk her into something that didn't make sense— I have too much respect for her and for her judgment to ever do that. Despite her lack of a college degree—which I think sometimes makes her feel inferior— she is one very smart woman. I think our kids get a lot of their common sense, their "groundedness" from her. It's not usual for the phone to ring and it to be one of our very young grandchildren who just needed "to talk to grandma."

I've never felt there was something I shouldn't talk over with her, something she just wouldn't understand. We just try to look out for each other, to take care of each other, to honor the decisions or the commitments the other one has made. When we made the very difficult decision to put our dog, Sophie, to sleep, we made it together.

My mother told me once that the best thing moms and dads can do for their kids is to love each other and I hope our kids would say that we've always shown that we do. I try every day to ask Jeanne: "Have I ever told you that I love you?" She always says I have; but I always tell her again, just to be sure. I never want her to forget.

And I've told her often: She is not only the best, most devoted mother I've ever seen, she is the best, most devoted mother *I could ever imagine*. There's simply nothing she wouldn't do for our kids (and their kids). They come first. Period. It takes real talent, patience, and time to raise great kids, but if you want to see the breadth and depth of Jeanne's commitment, just look at Jennifer, Tim, and Emily.

They couldn't possibly have had a better, more dedicated mom. And now she spends endless hours watching videos of our very young Grant and Liam and Maia. She loves those little kids. And when Brennan or Alex has something special, she's the first one to insist we must be there. Our sadness now is that we don't live close enough so that when any of our grandkids have something going on, we can't be there to show them how much we care.

One night, after we'd left my Hollywood job, Jeanne and I were watching the Oscar telecast where Bette Midler sang *Wind Beneath My Wings*. "You know," I told Jeanne, "sometimes I think that song was written about us. I've been able to do what I did because you were always the wind beneath my wings." "I thought it was just the opposite," she said. "You were always there supporting me."

It's good that we each feel that way, that each brought more to us than we could have ever hoped to have. And so, our marriage continues; it just doesn't seem like a big deal. It just feels like one more step forward. Together. When I look at her, I don't just see the Jeanne of today, I see all the Jeannes she has been through all the years we've been together. And I wonder how I could have been so lucky.

We've come far from those days when I first picked her up at her home on Birr Street where she grew up the eldest of three children of Elmer and Ruth Stein.

# 21

# IN-LAWS AND THE POLISH AUNT

T'S HARD TO BELIEVE THAT JEANNE'S PARENTS—two people named Elmer and Ruth Stein—weren't Jewish. They weren't, they were German Catholics, but when neighbors assumed they were and invited them to attend their child's Bar Mitzvah or Bat Mitzvah, they often went. They loved a celebration, especially if it gave them an opportunity to dance. They liked to do that—they had met back when she had been a dance instructor and he had come to her for lessons—and to laugh and to be together.

The had been married nearly fifty-two years when he passed away; she would live another twenty years. For us they were good parents, in-laws—and grandparents for the kids—because they were always around when we needed them, but willing to stand back and stay out when that's what we wanted. They were as supportive as we needed them to be.

We sometimes asked their advice for some of our bigger decisions—and even some small ones. After the Army was behind me and I had been back at Kodak, I was getting some inquires to go into partnership with friends. Once, long before, Dad had left Kodak and gone into business with a partner; he advised me not to do that. "When you work with another person," he told me, "you never really always have things your way." We also asked him to take a close and careful look before we put in an offer on our first home on Wyndale Road; when he approved, we bought it. And then he mixed endless variations of green paint before we finally decided on a color to paint our dining room there. He was patient that way.

Dad was great at putting up drapes and wallpaper and installing venetian blinds. When our very young Jennifer pulled the upstairs curtains off the wall—molly plugs and all—to protest going to the doctor's, Dad replaced them. Most times, he just did the work, but sometimes he involved me, so I'd learn. One night, he brought his father, and some tools, to help me put a screen on our fireplace. Dad drilled the first hole into the brick, then gave me the drill to make the second. When I broke the drill bit, his father shook his head in disgust; Dad just laughed.

Dad never seemed to be especially close to his parents or to his two siblings—brother Harold and sister Alameda—although we do have one picture of his mother, and two of his father, holding our Jennifer when she was a tiny infant. His father looks more comfortable than his mother.

We lived close to Mom and Dad, and we were at their house on Barry Road often, for birthdays and picnics, usually on Christmas and always for pizza on New Year's Day. For local parades, we joined them in lawn chairs on the Titus Ave. sidewalk; we often shared a pew with them at the five o'clock mass at St. Margaret Mary's Church. They were the first to babysit six-month-old Jennifer overnight when we went to Peter Nardone's wedding in Rhode Island; and when Jeanne went into the hospital to have Emily, Jennifer stayed with them—and decided to cut her own hair—for her first days in kindergarten. And wherever, and in whatever, our kids were involved, including even the smallest events and celebrations, they were always there

They were involved in a very different way in their son Allen's family—they helped to support and raise his three sons, Chris, Marc, and Scott, when Allen and Marie's marriage fell apart. When Al remarried, the situation for his boys was no better, and Chris, despite being only a few years older than his brothers, stepped up to take a lead role—but Mom and Dad were always there to help financially, emotionally, physically, and in every way they could. The boys are all successful today, thanks to Chris's leadership and Mom and Dad's support.

After Dad retired from Briter Paint and Wallpaper, the store he owned with his partner, he and Mom stayed active, going to mass every morning, then bowling, golfing, and square dancing. But as the 1980s turned into the 1990s, he began having serious lung problems. Perhaps a lifetime of smoking had something to do with it; perhaps it was the business he had long been in—using strong chemicals to clean furniture and venetian blinds. Whatever it was, he once passed out in church during Mass and eventually ended up breathing from an oxygen tank. But he never seemed to let it get him down. He was always ready to laugh—or go out for dinner. On Fridays, we'd often pick him up and drive down Nick's or Bill Gray's at Sea Breeze for an evening meal.

But in 1994, it began to look like his end was near. That February, Jeanne and I had the opportunity to go to Norway for the Winter Olympics; Kodak was a sponsor, and we could spend four days there, all expenses paid. But Dad was so sick, we debated whether to go. When Kodak reassured me that would fly us home immediately if something happened, we went—and we found out later, our decision helped to rally Dad. He watched every event on TV, hoping to see us.

Still, his condition was deteriorating, and when Jeanne picked me up at the airport from a business trip one Sunday evening in March, she said, "I'm going back to the hospital tonight. Dad is pretty bad." I went with her. And the last thing he said to me before he died was typical of him; he always liked to give credit to others. "I learned how to be a better grandfather," he told me, "by watching you be a dad." The next morning—March 21, 1994, the first day of spring—he died. He was seventy-nine years old.

He had lived a good life. Elmer Joseph Stein was born in Rochester on February 12, 1915, and grew up in the city, graduating from high school; instead of serving in the military, he joined the Civilian Conservation Corps and was sent to Yakima, Washington where he worked as a canteen steward and newspaper editor. When he married Ruth George on May 2, 1942, he was a lens polisher at Bausch & Lomb Optical; she was a group leader at Kodak. They would have three children—Jeanne Marie in 1947, Kathleen Ann in 1949, and Allen Edward in 1951—and live most of their lives at 426 Birr Street and 549 Barry Road in Rochester. His official cause of death was pulmonary fibrosis.

Jeanne's mom, Ruth Estelle George, was two years younger than Jeanne's dad; she'd been born to John Allen George and Rose Ann Helene Murphy George on March 16, 1917, in Rochester and had also grown up in the city. She had one younger brother, Howard and had graduated from John Marshall high school in the old tenth ward. She had worked at Kodak for several years as a clerk in the research labs and her wedding pictures were taken by a fellow-worker, Jeanette Klute, a professional photographer, using an experimental Kodak color film that had not yet been introduced to the public.

She was a wife, a mother, a grandmother, a great-grandmother, and a great friend, and she was, in her own "Ruthie way," very good at all of them; she had each of her children, grandchildren, and great-grandchildren convinced they were her favorite. And mostly she did that by letting them win at UNO; she liked to play cards. But she had her own life and was happy with it. When Jennifer was very young and Jeanne suggested she might return to work if her mom was interested in babysitting, her mom made it clear she wasn't. But we were always close to her; when we moved to California, she came several times for an extended visit and Jeanne always called her every Sunday night to talk.

To all of us—especially those living outside of Rochester—she often sent newspaper clippings; she seemed especially concerned with the fate of the Buffalo Bills and Kodak. And her clippings usually came with a note written in the perfect penmanship I once thought that only nuns had—but most notes were written on scraps of paper that she had apparently misplaced for a time. When she found them, she'd simply add to the note she had started; it wasn't unusual to get one from her that began on the back of the page, continued to the front, and then went to the back again and maybe up on top—before she sent it off.

She knew a lot of things for sure, some of which may have been true—and she could carry on an intelligent conversation on almost any subject, even when she couldn't hear what the other person was talking about. She *did not* need a hearing aid; people just weren't speaking loud enough. On her kitchen window, she had posted this prayer: *Lord, put your arm on my shoulder. . .and your hand across my mouth.* When she believed something, she wasn't shy about sharing it.

After Dad passed away, Mom stayed for a long time in their home on Barry Road, taking care of that house; in her late eighties, she fell off a ladder washing windows; well into her nineties, she was still driving the big Lincoln Dad had bought, long after many of us weren't sure she could see the road. I once showed her how to pump gas, and forever after she would only return to that station; she worried that pumps at other stations worked differently.

She drove herself—and her friends—to get their hair done, to bowl, or to play golf—and she was actually pretty good at all of them. She got a hole-in-one when she was in her eighties and had a plaque to prove it. We finally took away her car keys when she was ninety-four.

Perhaps because she was a child of the great depression, she always had a lot of essentials tucked away for an emergency. When she finally had to move to an assisted living facility—first to St. Ann's Home and then to Cherry Ridge—she left behind in her attic enough Kleenex, toilet paper, and books of matches to last another fifty or sixty years. Most was so old that the plastic wrapping had disintegrated.

But she did have a competitive spirit, she had a lot of common sense, and she had a lot of very close friends—some of whom had been more outspoken than others; they were mostly all gone—and she missed them. The last time we saw her was just one month before she passed away; we had been in Rochester and on a Sunday had taken her for a ride to Sodus where she had once spent happy summers—and to Bill Gray's, her favorite burger place where ate a half a cheeseburger, most of an order of onion rings (with black coffee, of course), and a full ice cream cone for dessert.

She seemed healthy that day; her final days were mercifully brief. Mom died in hospice care on November 14, 2014, of an intestinal blockage after several bouts of colon cancer and living with a colostomy in her later years.

When we all got together to remember her—at Bill Gray's of course—the evening before her funeral, her grandson Chris told us of his last conversation with her just days before she passed. Among her final words to him: *Enjoy life.*

In her ninety-seven years, Ruth Stein did.

Jeanne had other aunts and uncles—beginning with her father's brother and sister, both of whom had married and were separated and maybe (or maybe not) divorced. We saw them only sporadically. Uncle Harold, her father's older brother, had been married without children and Jeanne never met his former wife. For as long as I knew him, he brought a woman named Anne Bracken to all family gatherings. When they got close to celebrating fifty years of "going together," they got married.

Dad's younger sister, Aunt Alameda had been married to Chuck Steehler, whose job moved him to California long ago—and she chose not to go. They had five married children (some married several times)—Chuck, Patty, Mary Lou, Larry, and Ricky—whom Chuck came back only occasionally to visit. At some point, Alameda began "keeping company" with John Iacona, who came to most of our family gatherings.

But just as with my family, we were closer with those on my mother's side—and in Jeanne's case, that meant Uncle Howie and Aunt Jo. Whenever we were celebrating anything, they were there. Howie was Mom's younger brother; Jo was—loudly and proudly—the Polish aunt. They were proof that opposites not only attract, sometimes they complement each other.

Uncle Howie mostly stayed in the background; he was just quietly there, well beyond the spotlight but always with his dry wit and feigned sense of confusion: "So what does all of that mean?" he'd ask; or "Geez, what's the big deal?" It was all to just add to the fun, to usually play off some outrageous remark by Aunt Jo, who was always front and center and bringing more energy to every party. Uncle Howie was, as we used to say, 'a good man, Charlie Brown.' He even looked a bit like Charlie. He passed away from colon cancer on August 3, 2000. He was eighty-one and had had symptoms for some time but had been afraid to be checked out by a doctor.

We saw Aunt Jo much less frequently after that—she didn't drive—and we missed her "act" that she was simply the "dumb Polack." She was actually very proud of her Polish heritage, and I had a great time playing with that; with my mom's help, I once made her a set of Polish coffee cups with the handle on the inside; on the outside, I painted the red and white Polish flag with the "national bird of Poland"—a pigeon wearing tennis shoes. She displayed the cups proudly in her kitchen for several years. And she loved to hear Polish jokes. We were at dinner one night with Mom and her when a Kodak colleague dropped by our table, and I made the introductions. I pointed to Mom and said, "in-law," and then pointed to Aunt Jo. "Outlaw," I said.

When Uncle Howie was sick, Aunt Jo discouraged visitors—including Mom—and we chalked that up to them being private people, but there may have been something else going on: Aunt Jo was developing dementia, and it finally took over her life. She moved into a memory-care unit under the attentive eyes of her devoted niece Cheryl Wrublewski and spent several years there before passing away on February 3, 2019. She was ninety-six years old.

Of that unforgettable quartet—Mom, Dad, Uncle Howie, and her—she was the last to go; she passed away exactly fifty years after I'd joined that family. That year, 1969, had been, for me, unique.

# 22

# THE TRANSITION YEAR

I N 1969, WHEN ASTRONAUT NEIL ARMSTRONG TOOK "one small step for man, one giant leap for mankind," it felt like I had done a version of that. That was the year I took the many small steps that, together, would become my giant leap into the future.

In June of that year, I graduated from Notre Dame; my degree gave me the key to the professional ranks of corporate America, but the degree from *that* University gave me a key to the "Irish network" at Kodak and beyond—connections that would be influential to my career—and to friends with whom I'd write two books after I retired.

Six weeks after graduation, Jeanne and I got married—and through the years, I've become increasingly convinced that if there is one right someone for everyone, Jeanne is that right someone for me.

It was also the year I joined Kodak, which would not only give me a succession of interesting jobs and an enjoyable career but would also provide a wonderfully rewarding life for my family. And during that year, three things happened at Kodak that would forever change my life: First, I wrote professionally for the first time—and that became the foundation for my success; second, I met Richard Young, who became more than my best friend, he became a source of constant inspiration; and third, I learned to take pictures, which has remained a source of joy throughout my life.

That year also brought some dark days. In September, Pappy, my grandfather, died; he was my last relative from that generation. And, as the year wound to a close, the Selective Service held their first-ever lottery and picked my birthdate as number seventy-three; I knew I'd be drafted by the following March.

But so much of the year was dominated by the fact that, after sixteen years of schooling, I had my first full-time job. I never expected to have a career at Kodak; I took the job just to make things easy until I got the Army behind me. I knew I'd be drafted and most likely sent to Vietnam. If I had taken a job in another city or state, Jeanne would have to give up her job at Kodak, move with me, find a new job, then—when I was sent to southeast Asia—most likely give that up and move back home.

We could avoid all that hassle if I just took a job at Kodak where she already worked—and could stay working until I returned from Vietnam. Then we could decide where I wanted to work when I grew up. I never expected it would be there.

Kodak was wildly successful in those days; they dominated the markets for amateur photography, radiography, professional photography, motion pictures, microfilm, and every other market and application for film. Before digital, everyone took pictures on film, and most people believed that the most important moments in their lives—and the lives of their children—should be captured on *Kodak* film. The company had well over one hundred thousand employees at the time—and they were hiring. Since Jeanne was the receptionist for the office hiring college graduates, it was easy to get an interview.

After talking to Don Briggs, a small, thin man with a slight speech impediment who was mostly smoking during our interview—and being sent around to be interviewed by other managers in other departments—Don offered me a position in the Business and Technical Training Group. I'd be a trainee and would be paid an annual salary of $7,748.00, or $149.00 a week. I took the job and was given Kodak pass number 572317 with my picture on it. We had to keep that pass with us always because, before there were magnetic pass readers, we had to show it to the door guard to enter or leave the office building—although there were times when so many employees were coming and going at once that some got in or out just by flashing their library card.

There were seven of us in the Business and Technical Training Group, all recent college graduates, most with non-specific degrees. Every six to eight weeks, we'd meet with Don Briggs who'd show us a binder of job requests. Some would be full-time positions; others would be short-term projects where temporary help was needed. We'd each pick what looked attractive—and that's where we'd work for the next few months. The hope was that we'd find a job we liked in a department that liked us—and that they'd "make us an offer" and we'd transfer to that department and be off Don Brigg's payroll. The expectation was that would happen within a year, so he could bring on a new group of trainees the next summer.

Of the seven members of our group, at least four—Art Roberts, Mike Morley, Ruth Unzicker, and me—had long careers with the company; I have no idea what happened to Cheryl Arnold, Brian Arnold (no relation to Cheryl), and Gary Paquin—the other three.

At the time, Kodak's Rochester headquarters was home to its core management groups as well as the company's seven markets divisions; my first assignment was with the marketing group that served professional commercial and industrial photographers; the team I joined handled communications with them—including publishing a well-respected magazine called *Applied Photography* edited by an eccentric named Bill Reedy. His office was right across from mine.

Bill refused to attend department staff meetings and "wrote" while talking. "Let's write today," he'd say to his secretary, Carol, who would take out her steno pad and take down everything he said as he paced back and forth in front of her, thinking, smoking, talking, correcting, putting his articles together for the next issue. He was the first really good writer I met at Kodak.

His office was a gold mine of great photographs, the work of highly acclaimed photographers whose work he featured. But then, one day, he apparently tired of looking at the photos because he gathered up all the mounted prints—including signed work from internationally celebrated photographers—and threw them out on the floor in front of his office. "If there's anything here you want," he announced, "come and take it." I took several prints which unfortunately got lost along the way.

Next to Bill's office sat Bob Grunziger, a likeable guy who never lost his sense of humor. One Friday, Bob spoke to a large group of customers, right after lunch when everyone had plenty to drink. The next Monday, I asked him how everything went. "It went well," he said, "until I finished page five. I turned over page five... and there was another page five... and another... and when I kept turning, I found that the rest of my binder was filled with more copies of page five. I threw all the pages in the audience, said a few words, and stopped talking. Good old Ruth," he said, talking about his assistant who had put the binder together, "at least she's fun to look at." You could say things like that, back then.

But here I was, a real employee with a real office—a secretary brought me coffee in the morning—and I wanted to earn the $3.72 an hour I was being paid. Instead, in those first few days, I was given several magazines to read, to learn more about photography. I read them and went asking: *is there no real work for me to do?*

*Well, it turned out, there was one thing. Could I write?* Maybe. I had never taken a course in writing, but I'd be willing to try. What needed to be written? *Well, there was this newsletter for School Finishers—those who took pictures of kids in schools and sold the "packages" to their parents. The newsletter was overdue because nobody else had time to write it; did I want to give it a try?*

If my choice was: write a newsletter—or read more magazines—I said to bring on the writing assignment. My boss explained what they expected; I put a blank piece of paper in my little brown manual typewriter and began; and I discovered I was looking forward to coming to work.

The Legal Department had to review what I wrote—and I was sometimes disappointed when they made modifications that I wasn't sure were really improvements. Eventually I'd ignore their changes I disagreed with; but for now, I learned how to use and protect company trademarks, how not to boast about Kodak products, how never to denigrate the competition or acknowledge other technology. Those were good lessons to learn early and be able to apply later on. The newsletter was printed, and I was flattered to see my work being used, even though I was given no writing credit. I decided I'd try always to "have time" to do writing when others did not; if I could get good at it, maybe I could carve out a niche for myself.

As my six weeks in that unit wound down and I went back to Don Brigg's office to pick my next assignment, I now had a sense of focus I didn't have before. I looked for Kodak jobs where something needed to be written—and found one in a group that served the slide projector market; they were looking for someone to write a twenty-four-page publication to be called "Slides with a Purpose;" it would teach people how to make slide shows. When I finished writing that, it was time for my T-1 photographic training to begin.

T-1 was Kodak's hands-on, three-week training course in photography—its history, chemistry, applications, processes, and products. The company believed: the better their future managers understood all aspects of their business, the better they'd be able to serve customers. The course was our full-time job for the next several weeks; each day, the seven members of our B&T training group came to a classroom and were given cameras and films and chemicals and instruction; we were taught to process black and white and color film; we were expected to make a movie and slide shows; we were given the gift of photography that, for me, would last a lifetime.

When the course finished, I moved to an assignment with a group that provided marketing education—eventually classroom instruction at a modern college-like campus—for Kodak's customers. While that campus was being built on the banks of the Genesee River in Rochester, we developed training materials it would use. I worked in support of two managers—Bob Smith and Gene DuPree—developing creative solutions we would propose to our Kodak clients in regular meetings. After coming up with some ideas my bosses found worthy, I was invited to a meeting with the client—a Kodak senior manager—to describe the ideas to him.

As I went through the approach, it was clear he just didn't get it. He began to suggest different ideas that took us way off course. I thought we needed to get things back on track. "Your ideas are terrible . . ." I began—and Bob Smith asked me to step outside. He explained that I wouldn't need to attend future meetings, that my role would be to work "behind the scenes."

And I did, eventually teaming up with Nick Iuppa, an experienced writer and fellow Notre Dame graduate. He would work for Disney, Paramount, Apple, and other major companies in California after leaving Rochester. Nick and I started a series of graphic instructional booklets called *The How and Why of Photography*. We included some weird humor— "the incredible purple f-stops," for example to explain photographic concepts—and when my assignment ended before we could complete the series, I came over to Nick's apartment at night and we'd write together. He's since gone on to publish several novels, most in the horror genre. He claims they are unconnected to his work at Kodak.

But I was on an eight-week schedule in my regular job and so I again moved on—this time into a group called Audio Visual Services. I worked for Sherm Nelson, an affable, heavy-set bald guy who wore a bad wig; I was a "coordinator" which meant that I wrote the scripts for slide slows, and then coordinated everything else—the photos, music, programming, and even the presentation involved in putting on a show. We billed our time to our clients at the rate of twenty-five dollars an hour.

Fortunately, they had no office available for me in the actual department, so they gave me an office across the corridor in a group called Motion Picture Services. There, I met and eventually worked with one of the MPS directors, Richard Young, who would influence my life. But even as I started on my first audio visual show, I knew I'd never complete the eight-week assignment. The military draft was in full force, and I was classified 1A.

On Friday, March 6, 1970, I turned everything I had done over to another coordinator in AV Services. Two days later, Jeanne and I drove to Buffalo where the Army Recruiting Center was located. On Monday morning, I kissed Jeanne a teary good-bye. She drove back to her life in Rochester, and I walked across the street and into my new job for almost the next two years.

I was trading a business suit and tie for boots and fatigues. I was being drafted into the Army.

# 23

## LIFE IN FATIGUES

FOR 1970, I WAS NUMBER SEVENTY-THREE for the military draft. On December 1, 1969, the Selective Service System conducted the first of its several annual lotteries to determine the order of drafting into military service, men born between 1944 and 1950. The days of the year were written on slips of paper and each slip was placed in a separate plastic capsule. The capsules were mixed in a shoebox and dumped into a glass jar—and one by one, the numbers were pulled out. September 14 was the first number drawn, so all registrants born on that day were assigned lottery number one. My birthday, April 3, was the seventy-third number pulled. Next year, there'd be another drawing.

The Selective Service said they expected to call about thirty numbers a month; I would be called in March. Those were frightening days because the war was raging in Vietnam, and I'd already had two friends killed; I could think of no reason why I wouldn't be sent there. There were other alternatives to the draft: try to join the national guard (nearly impossible and it carried a six-year obligation); move to Canada (kids were doing it, but it seemed cowardly); or—

rumor had it—convince a doctor to remove your spleen. The Army couldn't send you to Vietnam because, in jungle conditions, you need a spleen (maybe; I didn't want to undergo an operation to find out). In the end, I decided that my service would be fair payback for all the freedoms America provided. And that's what I did.

On March 9, 1970, I spent the day in Buffalo, having a physical and waiting around as others gathered. That night, we were put on a plane for New Jersey where we were met at the airport and bussed to Fort Dix. We arrived somewhere around midnight. The Army likes to start you out when it's late, you're sleep-deprived, disoriented, and more willing to take orders. Or, in my case, curious about what was to come.

Within a day or so, we had our first haircut—I was appalled we had to pay for it—and were given meaningless tasks to keep us busy; one example—we had to empty a large dumpster, separate the dirt from the trash, have it inspected, and then shovel it all back in, mixed together.

In the barracks, I somehow ended up in charge of my bunkmates. I was told not to let anyone in or out, but when one kid asked if he could leave to see his brother who was shipping out the next day for Vietnam, I let him go. It wouldn't be the last time I did what I thought was right, even if the Army thought otherwise.

Before leaving for the military, I had talked to a friend who had already completed his military duty. "Imagine your worst experience ever," he said. "Basic training is twice as bad." I figured the drill sergeants were the ones who made it that way, but when one came to talk to us, his words made so much sense I remember his message to this day. "For the next eight weeks," he said, "you're going to do things you never thought you'd do. It's going to be a time like nothing you've had before. You can hate it and resist it—or you can see it as a great new adventure. Whatever you decide, we're going to treat you the same way." *Attitude,* he was saying, *will make the difference.*

After we had been assigned to our company, we were given uniforms and then subjected to a series of tests—math, English, reading, logic, and others; each would be corrected immediately; those who passed, took the next test—those who didn't were sent back to training. I made it all the way to the last test—in a made-up language called ALAT. We were given the convoluted rules of the language—and tested in it. Simultaneously. I got about halfway through; I knew I'd finally flunked an Army test.

But that night, I was called down to the barracks office and asked why I hadn't taken the ALAT test. I said that I did; perhaps the Army just lost it. I was told that the Army didn't lose things; tomorrow, I'd have to take the test.

The next morning, when I got to the testing center, I told my story—I had taken the test—and so I was given a level-2 version. Since I was a little more familiar with the language, I got further on that one before time ran out. But when I took it to be scored, the soldier doing the scoring said: "Before I look at this, let's see how you did with level-1." When he found I had no level-1 score, he said: "I can't even look at this." He tore it up. "You need to take level-1." So I did. By now, I was very familiar with the language—and completed the test. I must have done well because after it was scored, an officer came out to make me "a great offer;" the Army wanted to send me to language school. "OK," I said, "I'll take German."

Ah, that was the problem. The only language available was Vietnamese. The school would be ten months long, so—he said—half of my two-year service obligation would be over; I would have just over a year left. But—I said—since I would already speak the language, I was pretty much guaranteed to spend that year in Vietnam. "No thank you," I said. When I turned down the offer—I had to do it in writing—he told me, "you've made the smartest decision. It's just that I've had this job for several months and you're the first person who's passed that test."

When all the testing was over, things settled into a routine; we went to bed every night at eight, we got up at four in the morning; it seemed like we were always preparing for an inspection. We had three meals in the mess hall and the food was reasonably good although the cook used the same pot to make mashed potatoes as he used to wash his clothes—and when one kid complained about the meat, the drill sergeant wasn't interested. "So, the meat is all gristle," the sergeant said. "What's wrong with that?"

"I don't like gristle," the kid said.

"We can't just serve what you'd like," the sergeant told him.

We had physical training every day—sit-ups and push-ups and overhead bars and even a forced march; we learned to fire a rifle and I would have learned to throw a hand grenade, except that I volunteered for sign-painting duty that day and I was warm and dry in a butler hut while everyone else was out throwing grenades in the rain and bringing me their scores to record on the sign I was making for the barracks. I scored myself 'expert.'

The Army drafted a great mix of young guys in those days; while we were huddled in the back of a truck going out to the rifle range, I was listening to some of the other recruits talk. "What's your middle name?" one asked another.

"It's Philippe," the other kid said.

"Philippe?" his questioner persisted. "How do you spell that?"

"You know," the kid said, "of all my names, that's the only one I don't know how to spell."

We spent a lot of our time in classes where some of the material was boring, the answers were obvious, and I did well on the tests. But then, consider that some of my competition was kids who couldn't spell their middle name.

The rest of basic training went by in a blur. There were cold mornings standing outside shivering in formation, in our summer dress uniform. There were days on KP and nights on guard duty in the barracks, which deprived me of what little sleep the military allowed. I learned to take very quick showers— "There's nothing you got on you that should take more than about a minute to get off you," one drill sergeant advised us—and I learned to be able to fall asleep anywhere, even when I had just a few moments lying on a hard dirt road with a helmet for a pillow.

We had a weekend pass and Jeanne flew into New York City to join me although she almost didn't recognize me—I had no hair and had lost thirty-five pounds. And despite the cold and wet New Jersey spring, I stayed healthy throughout training except for one day when I was on bed rest in the barracks with an upper respiratory infection and I watched as our drill sergeant was carried out on a stretcher; he had tried to commit suicide by slashing himself with a knife.

There was a lot of blood.

Our eight weeks of training ended with one final physical test to prove we were in shape; I passed and as I looked back, none of those weeks had been as bad as I had once feared; it really all had been a big adventure. The longest night was waiting for my orders to come through. In a class where we had learned to disassemble our rifle, the instructor had said: "only a small percentage of you will be going to Vietnam. It may be as low as ninety-eight percent." My worry: would I be one of those sent?

It turned out, I would not. My orders sent me to Fort Riley, Kansas as a 71Q, the designation for a Military Information Specialist. I was thrilled to have a journalism job, to be writing for military publications. If I had only known the truth: at the time Fort Riley was over-staffed with journalists—and it was a regular stop-over point for soldiers coming from or mostly going to Vietnam.

But sometimes, ignorance works out OK and, besides, what choice would I have had? And so, after a short leave in Rochester, I said goodbye to Jeanne and headed west to Kansas. That's how, on that morning in May 1970, I ended up standing in a large room in Fort Riley with about thirty other military information specialists. I was sure they all had more experience than I did; I'd been given my classification simply because I said I wrote for Kodak publications—I had no idea what a journalist even did.

And then my predicament got immeasurably worse. An officer lined us up and told us: "You are all Military Information Specialists, but we only need one; the rest of you will be sent to the infantry or the artillery. So anyone without a four-year college degree can leave the room." When they did, there were still about eight of us left and he addressed us on an individual basis, asking two questions: "Where did you go to college?" And: "Can you type?" I was the third soldier in line.

I told him I had a four-year degree from Notre Dame and yes, I could type. "How fast?" he wanted to know. That was a tricky one. Back in high school, I'd taken a typing course with my friend, Joe, who was an accordion player, so he had very coordinated fingers. Joe could type seventy-five words a minute, so the question I was wrestling with that day in Fort Riley was: *Are there any other ac-*

*cordion players in this room?*

I decided to hedge my bets. "I can type eighty-five words a minute," I said. My questioning officer went immediately to the telephone and called Major Goodrich, the Command Information Officer. "Sir," he said, "I have your candidate. I'll send him right up." The other seven guys were sent to artillery or infantry units.

As I headed off to my new assignment, I now had two worries: back in high school, in that typing class with Joe, I never got faster than fifteen words a minute. So, not only was I was a slow typist; I knew nothing about Army journalism. I hoped I wouldn't be given a typing test—I never was—and that I could find someone who would teach to write in the military style.

At that time, there were levies—requests for large numbers of soldiers—for Vietnam every month, so nearly every unit on the fort was overstaffed with guys who could be shipped off any time. In the Information Office, we had four times the numbers we needed; the first five guys to arrive each day claimed the desks, the next fifteen got chairs, but each day some number of us had to sit on the floor. I have no idea why Major Goodrich wanted one more, but I went looking for the one who'd help me learn the skills I needed to try to secure my future.

As I looked around the office, I saw that SP4 Patrick O'Dell had a "CON-ARC Copy Desk Award" presented for "excellence in journalism." I poked around and found that only one in every thirty-five hundred Army information specialists had one of those, so he must be someone the Army considered to be a good journalist. I decided SP4 O'Dell would be my teacher. I introduced myself, asked what story he was working on, asked if I could tag along. That's why, the next morning, we got on a bus together and went to the buffalo pen at Fort Riley. We started writing together. . .and didn't stop for almost twenty-five years.

In the beginning, when I'd show him what I'd written, his feedback was some version of "this is really awful;" but I got better. My work was soon appearing regularly in the *Fort Riley Post* where I became the Features Page editor; I was writing editorials for the commanding general; and by the time I left the Army after almost twenty-two months in a green uniform, I had won three CONARC Copy Desk Awards of my own.

Patrick and I lived in the barracks on Main Post, but since we considered ourselves professionals, we didn't believe we should be hassled—which is why we were so upset when a Lt. Leo J. Humphries moved in and insisted that we all get up early and clean the latrines before we left for the office. We did, but when I got to the office, I called PFC Adrian Belange. At the time, the Army was drafting some very smart kids and making them lowly clerks—who then spent all their time trying to get even with the Army. Adrian was one. I explained our situation with Lt. Humphreys—and Adrian said he'd take care of it.

An hour after lunch, Adrian called me back to tell me what he'd done. Every soldier had a booklet called a 'shot record'—a list of all required inoculations the soldier had received since entering the military. The record was kept at head-quarters and Adrian called Lt. Humphreys to tell him that his had been lost—so he'd have to receive all his shots over again *that afternoon*. He told Humphreys that the loss was "probably due to his requiring latrine cleaning by soldiers who have access to records like that." When Humphreys received the shots, he was hardly coherent, Adrian told me, "but he said he was cancelling all cleaning operations for the future."

We had some interesting guys living in the barracks with us. Earl Tonklinson was an older guy who kept volunteering to go to Vietnam "to get me some Cong;" Fred Shuttenberg was a tall thin kid who had come back from Vietnam and began giving away his Army clothes, one by one; Jack Koch was an alcoholic who worked in our office and would regularly turn down assignments: "the Army can't fire me," he said; and Gary Warner, to calm himself down at night, would get in his little blue Opel and drive back and forth between Topeka and Salina, a distance each way of more than one hundred miles.

As we approached the July 4 holiday, I asked Gary to drive me to the Topeka airport; I flew home, and we loaded up Jeanne's little blue Pontiac Tempest and drove west. The car had no air conditioning, so I was driving with the windows open and as we were crossing the state of Missouri, I saw a bird out of the corner of my eye. The next thing I felt, the bird flew in—just missing my head—hit the inside of the rear window, and flopped dead on the back seat of the car. Jeanne screamed. I pulled over and threw the bird out. If the bird's flight path had been an inch or two different, Jeanne or I could have been killed.

When we got back to Kansas, we were lucky to find a place to live. The fort was so overstaffed that some soldiers—and their wives—were living in their cars, but we rented a succession of places, first in Herington, a thirty-mile drive from Fort Riley—where we celebrated our first wedding anniversary—and then a basement apartment in Junction City—where, when Jeanne took a bath, the two very young boys who lived upstairs would sometimes wander in. We were in each place for a month before, in September of 1970, we had the opportunity to rent the whole first floor of a big Victorian house in Junction City, right outside the base—but the rent was too expensive for us. There were two bedrooms, so Jack Koch, the alcoholic in our office, offered to move in and split the rent. Since he was being discharged in two months, we let him.

It turned out to be a wonderful home, a place where we felt safe, comfortable, and sheltered from the uncertainties of Army life. Jeanne also had a friend Ruth who lived with her husband Ken and their son Christopher in a small apartment upstairs. Ruthie was a free spirit who took whatever life offered. When she got pregnant with their son, she said, they were practicing rhythm, Ken was using a condom, she was using a diaphragm and was taking birth control pills. Ruth once broke both of her kneecaps when she jumped off a small bridge in a play, *Teahouse of the August Moon*, where she was performing. But if Jeanne ever needed her, she just had to tap three times on the pipes that ran from our dining room into Ruth's apartment. I often think that Tony Orlando and Dawn had Jeanne and Ruth in mind when they sang the song, *Knock Three Times*.

We moved into the house in September and money was tight as it had been from the beginning of our Army days. We had to live on one hundred and sixty-eight dollars a month, which included my salary and Jeanne's government allowance. Our share of the rent was seventy-five dollars, so we had little money for anything extra. Jeanne shopped frugally; we drank water instead of milk; I took a bologna sandwich with one piece of cheese and some chips in a small bag every day for lunch; we could barely even afford the thirty-five cents we paid to the local laundry to highly starch each set of fatigues I wore to work each day. I wore each set for two weeks.

When we were invited to someone's home for dinner—or when they came to ours—it was understood we'd each bring our own food. It wasn't unusual to have a mix of different meat cooking on a grill—and everyone eating something different. We just enjoyed getting together; we couldn't afford to feed one another.

But, perhaps because of those constraints, Jeanne and I found that we were on the same page when it came to money—we were willing to live on what we had because we had each other and with Vietnam raging, I could be gone any day. In the process of taking long walks and playing games on the lawn, we became each other's best friend. It was the best way to spend the first years of our marriage. As Jack Koch told me once, "if someone ever asks me what makes a good marriage, I'll tell them about you and Jeanne."

Meanwhile, Patrick O'Dell was becoming a good friend—and Jeanne also liked him—so when Jack left us in November, Patrick moved in with the same arrangements—we'd split the rent and the groceries, Jeanne would do the shopping and the cooking—we called her our "spoon" —and he'd have full use of our car. In the six months we lived together, we never had a disagreement. One day, lying in our bathroom was a letter I think Patrick wanted us to see; it was from his mom who wrote: "I knew you'd end up meeting someone like Bob and Jeanne. . . ."

We had a lot of fun together. We had a little black and white television set and every afternoon, Patrick and I would rush home to watch *Sesame Street*; often in the evening, guys from the barracks would stop over to watch TV with us; when Jeanne and I got tired, we'd just tell whoever was still there, "turn off the TV and close the door when you leave."

Patrick was very much into the arts and took us—at his expense because we could never have afforded it—to our first professional plays, *Hair* in Manhattan and *1776* in Topeka—during the time we were together. Fort Riley also had an active group of amateur actors, and Patrick——he was a trained actor—and I (an amateur stagehand) —worked together on several productions including *Teahouse of the August Moon* and *Fiddler on the Roof*. Henry Polic—who would go on to a very successful television career before passing away—was a fellow actor, friend, and professional chef who cooked dinner that Easter at Fort Riley for all of us. And at some point, Patrick and I began playing together—just piano and drums—but we called ourselves *The Junction City Philharmonic Orchestra and Pawn Shop*—and picked up extra money playing at the Ramada Inn in nearby Manhattan, Kansas, on the weekends.

That December, Jeanne and I drove back to Rochester for Christmas; the weather was good going home and we made it to Erie, Pennsylvania, that first day—listening to non-stop Christmas music on the radio. It's a big reason why I hate Christmas songs to this day. But on the way back to Kansas, we hit an ice storm in Illinois with Jeanne driving. As she was coming down a hill, she realized she had no control of the car—and was scared to death. At the bottom, she pulled over and let me drive. She refused to drive on a trip—under any conditions—for several years afterwards.

As the new year began, I was responsible for the layout of the features page which required me, every Wednesday, to go down to the *Junction City Daily Union*, where our *Fort Riley Post* was assembled and printed. Those were the days of hot lead type and grizzled old newspaper men—and so when we arrived, our stories would all have been cast in metal type which they'd stack in columns under a headline in wooden cases called galleys. If everything fit, the story ran as written; but if a story ran long, I watched as the "make-up man" pitched the extra type into a trash bin. He'd throw away the last paragraph first, then other paragraphs, if he needed to; he never read anything—and he wasn't up to negotiation. That's how I learned to put all essential information up near the beginning of the story.

Meanwhile, I was writing a diversity of articles—from record reviews (I gave five stars to the Carpenters, *We've Only Just Begun*) to editorials under the general's signature about the dangers of drinking and driving, and the value of traveler's checks (the Military Police became apoplectic when they found my examples sometimes were based on fictitious robberies). I especially liked to write in-depth stories based on interviews—even though I almost always ran into Army censorship.

I figured the Army was a microcosm of youthful society, so if youth had a problem with drugs, so did the Army; I knew a bunch of guys doing dope—and

I decided to interview Major John Roff, chief of the Ft. Riley Medical Hygiene Clinic about their program to rehabilitate addicts and discourage potential users. "So far," he said, "we know that our counselors have kept one man from killing his commanding officer and another from committing suicide." The major described the program and approved my final copy for publication.

My boss, Major Goodrich, disagreed. "This is touchy," he said. "Let's see what the Chief of Staff thinks." The Chief of Staff thought the General should see it. "If we print this," General Linville told me, "we'll be admitting we have a drug problem. We can't admit we have a drug problem." The story never ran.

At the time, Ft. Riley didn't want to admit it had *any* problems. I faced the same obstacle when I got an assignment from *Army Digest* to write a local story about the concerns of Army wives. Every wife I interviewed painted a bleak picture; in my article, I tried to gently air their gripes. When I passed it up through my chain of command, everyone at each level rewrote the women's quotes. Army life began looking better and better for the young Army wife. I decided not to submit the story, so readers never got to see how happy young Army wives were with their rewritten life at Ft. Riley.

In the early months of 1971, there was a change of command at Fort Riley. Major General Linville was moved to a staff job in San Francisco; he was replaced by Major General Edward Flanagan from Fort Bragg who was bringing with him a writer named, SP4 Jim Toms. Jim and his wife Karen soon became friends to Patrick, me, and another writer we hung around with often, Roger Bergson.

The four of us worked together in the Command Information Office for a former major named Bill Obley whom we respected—but when a leavy came through and cleaned out the larger Public Information Office—sending several of its members to Vietnam—Patrick, Roger and I were moved there, working for two civilians who were incompetent. They refused to let us write stories of substance—and as we became increasingly frustrated, we discussed our complaints with Jim Toms. Jim told us to put our situation in writing—and he would take it to the general. We did—and he did.

A couple of weeks went by, and General Flanagan called Roger, Patrick, and me into his office. "I've read your grievances and I've found what I can't do; I can't get rid of civilians," he told us. "Now I'm looking into what I can do." For Roger and Patrick, who were scheduled to be discharged from the Army later in the summer, he found he could make those discharges much sooner. Mine was a different situation; I had another year to go in the Army.

One day I got a call from my friend, PFC Adrian Belange. "What do you think about Fort Bragg, North Carolina?" he asked.

"I don't know anything about it except that General Flanagan came from there," I told him.

"Well," Adrian said, "the general has arranged for you to transfer there—but only if you want to go." I asked him if that was the way the army usually made reassignments—by asking soldiers where they wanted to go.

He said, "It is when the general makes them." But he told me to think about it, "talk it over with your wife."

I asked him what I might tell her about the assignment. "You can tell her," Adrian said, "that if you accept it, you'll never be sent to Vietnam. You won't have enough time left in the military."

"In that case," I told him, "I have her answer. We want to go to Fort Bragg."

So in May of 1971, almost exactly one year after I flew into the Manhattan Kansas airport and reported to Fort Riley, Jeanne and I left Kansas behind. We had rented a small U-haul trailer that we'd packed with my drums and everything else we owned—and headed east. Jeanne cried all the way to Topeka; she was sad we had to say good-bye to Patrick.

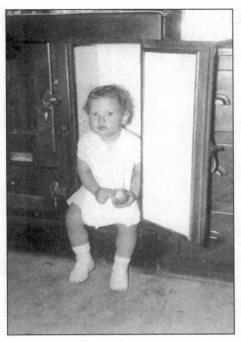

*At sixteen months old, I sit in my grandfather's ice box, looking out on my world.*

*With rice in their hair and dreams in their eyes, my mom and dad leave Holy Apostles Church. They were headed for a small reception on March 3, 1946, their wedding day.*

*This is 234 Oriole Street, the home in the "bird section" of the old tenth ward that provided a happy and secure nest where I'd learn how to fly.*

*Dad's brother Paul and Dad in the only picture I have of their mom, my grandmother, Mary Lane Gibbons. Her death in 1936 so saddened Dad that he never spoke of her.*

*On February 21, 1900, twenty-one-year-old Francis Joseph Koch married nineteen-year-old Theresa Uhl. My mom would be the youngest of their seven children.*

*Pappy, my dad's father, at our wedding. He had his problems, but he always had time for me. Two months after this picture, he passed away.*

*A few days after Christmas 1956, my Uncle Al photographed Dad, Mike, Mom, me, Pat, and Judy in our living room. A year later, I'd trade the plastic trombone for a real drum.*

*Aunt Loretta and Uncle George in 1948. He was quiet and always supportive, a good man; she was our "Auntie," the one who was always there when we were growing up.*

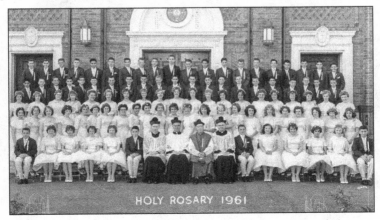

HOLY ROSARY 1961

*My Holy Rosary class of 1961 had forty-five boys and fifty-one girls, one of whom was Jeanne Stein. My dad graduated from the same school, exactly thirty years before.*

For Christmas 1958, Dad gave me his old
Slingerland snare drum. Eventually, he'd give me his
whole mismatched set so I could join a band.

Duvid Smering could play anything the first
time he heard it. We first played together
in our grammar school band.

According to our business cards, The Quintones—with Dave Smering on sax, Gary Cook on accordion, me on
drums, and Allen Fitzpatrick on Fender guitar—played "amplified music for all occasions."

This is the picture of Paula Klos I had on my desk during freshman year at Notre Dame. She was always a beautiful girl with strong values who helped me become who I am.

One of the smartest decisions of my life was to attend Notre Dame. The school would give me a foundation and friendships that made a difference in my career and life.

This is Mom's side of the family. Back row: Uncle Al, Mom, Auntie, Aunt Mag, Dad, Aunt Rose's father Tim. Middle row: Aunt Lorraine, Nancy, Aunt Rose (hidden), me. Front row: Uncle Anthony, Uncle George, Judy, Mary Anne, Pat, Ricky, Mike. Taking our picture was like herding cats.

*John Rank, Dave Pender, Roger Kiley, and Marc Imundo—with Peter Nardone folded up in a footlocker. It was just one of our hijinks during freshman year at Notre Dame*

*Friends from Cavanaugh Hall back for our fiftieth Notre Dame reunion: Bob Wilhelm, John Rank, Marc Imundo, Jim Blakely, Dan Cox, and me. We talk, via Zoom, every month.*

*Jeanne and me on New Year's Day in 1969, the year we were married. Although we never made plans, we built a life we loved, based on trusting each other along the way.*

*On May 2, 1942, Jeanne's parents, Ruth Estelle George married Elmer Joseph Stein in Sacred Heart Cathedral. They loved to laugh, bowl, golf, square dance—and enjoy life*

*Jeanne's grandparents in 1942. From left: Rose Ann Murphy George and John Allen George were Jeanne's mom's parents; Louisa Schönig Stein and Edward Joseph Stein were her dad's parents. By the mid 1970s, they had all passed away.*

*Uncle Howie and Aunt Jo (with Jeanne's Mom) were like a great comedy team.
He was the straight man and she said outrageous things. They were always supportive and fun.*

*Jeanne and I toasting each other on the day we decided to share the future.
More than fifty years later, we still ask ourselves: How could we be so lucky?*

*On our honeymoon, Jeanne left her name in the sand of Gloucester, Massachusetts.
We've gone back there several times—and she's been "my Jeanne" ever since*

*In Army days, Patrick O'Dell—with Jeanne and me in 1970—*
*enriched our Kansas experience in so many ways. We remained close friends for the rest of his life.*

*239 West Fourth Street became our sanctuary from Army strife. Patrick, Jeanne, and I*
*had the whole bottom floor. I was devastated when, years later, the house went missing*

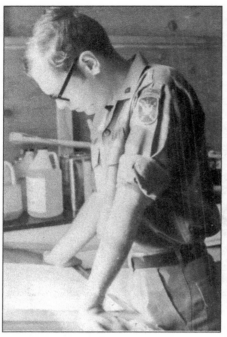

*At Fort Bragg, I put together a new issue of Veritas, the worldwide magazine for Special Forces, every month. My work earned three CONARC Copy Desk Awards from Washington.*

*When Jennifer was just three months old, we took her to her first picnic. After almost five years of marriage, we had our first little one. She had been born on my birthday.*

*Jeanne with Tim riding on his rocking horse in our Wyndale backyard. We called him "the new guy in the neighborhood." For some time, Jennifer thought his name was Guy.*

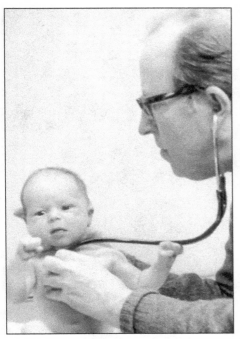

*Emily's first check-up by her pediatrician, Dr. Disney. He told us, "You have addiction in your family genes. Make sure your kids know that —and are always careful."*

*I put ten-month-old Jennifer next to my Notre Dame stool to take a picture when she pulled herself up and tentatively began to walk—and I got this picture of her first steps.*

*After being cut from basketball in seventh grade, Tim put in so much time and effort getting better that he was chosen captain of the Aquinas freshman team.*

*When we rented a cottage for summer vacation, Emily always spent a lot of time in the water. It may be natural that she ended up with a career in the Coast Guard.*

*In 1985, I spent an evening with Bob Newhart at a Kodak event in Houston. He was smart, gracious, easy to talk to, and very different from the befuddled characters he played.*

*This is the crew that made Washington: The Man, the movie that put me in Kodak management. Back row: Dick Quataert, Mel Wright, Bobby Weaver, Bill Douglass, me, Dave Darby, Richard Young, Lorne Greene. Middle row: Sam Scribner, Keith Smith, Craig Nanos, Dick Smith. Front: Don Maggio.*

*Kodak's Journey into Imagination opened in December 1982, where Dreamfinder
(Disney cast member, Ron Schneider) and Figment (a hand puppet) quickly became picture magnets.*

*After so many adventures making movies together, this was my last day with Richard Young, celebrating
his seventy-first birthday with a few close friends: Bob Billheimer, president of Worldwide Documentaries;
Anthony DeLuca, Richard's long-time editor; me, and Richard.*

*Before Emily was born, Eddie and Clara Jordan often invited Tim and Jennifer over for Jiffy Pop,
Tang, and sometimes a backyard conversation. Later, Emily would join them.*

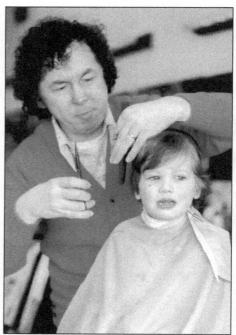

*Jennifer's first day of kindergarten. She had
been staying with Grandma while Jeanne
gave birth to Emily. To prepare for school,
Jennifer had cut her own hair.*

*Tim's first haircut by Ken Mertz, my long-time
barber. Many years later, when he went back to
Rochester, Tim would stop by to see Ken, get
his hair cut, and share stock tips.*

*We were fortunate to live so near to Jeanne's Mom and Dad. We saw them frequently;
the kids loved them—and they loved the kids. Emily especially enjoyed time with Grandpa.*

*With all our relatives so close by, there were always picnics and parties and reasons to get together.
This is Toby, Todd and Tim with some sort of early control device.*

*The cousins on the new playground we built at St. Margaret Mary's grammar school. Clockwise
from the top of the 'climbing tires': Marc Stein, Chris Stein, Jennifer, Katie Fagan, Emily, Peggy Fagan,
Scott Stein, Alyssa Fagan, and Tim. Beth Fagan was too young to be with them.*

*Auntie with Emily, Brad, Jennifer, Tim, and Shauna at St. Ann's Home where we often
took the kids on Mother's Day because Auntie had been like a second mother to us.*

*Jennifer would end up being Kymberly's sponsor for Confirmation. Here they are at a younger age, sometime after we returned from a vacation in Florida where Kym would eventually live.*

*In July 1994, just weeks before we moved to California, Jeanne and I celebrated our twenty-fifth anniversary. It was the last picture we took with my parents; within four years, they'd both be gone.*

*Tony Baxter, Richard Sherman, and me at Tony's home. Tony created* Journey into Imagination; *Richard and his late brother Robert wrote its musical score, along with the scores for* Mary Poppins, Small World, *and other Disney movies and attractions.*

*Jeanne and I attended the Academy Awards twice, the last time at the Kodak Theater in Hollywood. It was one of the many perks of working for Kodak.*

*The Kodak Digital Cinema team that tried to do so much with so little. Left row: Sean Lohan, Drena Rogers, Denis Kelly. Middle row: Les Moore, Lindsay Dack. Right row: Dave Sanderson, Glenn Kennel. The team and monitor are gone now.*

*I had the good fortune to work with giants at Kodak—including Dave Metz, who managed Communications and Public Affairs, and Colby Chandler, the company's CEO.*

*I reconnected with Phil Samper in 2020. He was a decisive leader who understood the Kodak brand.*
*The fate of the company might have been very different in his hands.*

*"Take me along," Sophie said. "I promise to be good." When Emily packed to go back*
*to her duty station, Sophie jumped in her suitcase; she wanted to go, too.*

*When Emily was promoted to Commander, her rank was pinned on her by Captain Pat Culver.*
*He is the Gold Ancient Mariner of the Coast Guard, one of the most highly respected members of that service.*

*This is our "starting five" at my seventieth birthday—when Jeanne and the kids surprised me with a trip to Portland, Oregon. That's the home of Powell's, my favorite bookstore.*

*When Jennifer married Matt Hauser, we got two terrific, instant grandkids—Brennen and Alex. He's headed for a career in archiving; she's attracted to moviemaking.*

The Bake Shop Ghost *played at film festivals where Kathryn Joosten (who played the ghost), Lorette Bayle (who produced and directed the film), and I (who wrote the screenplay) answered audience questions.*

*Back in 2008, the original four Gibbons kids—me, Pat, Judy, and Mike —got together in Judy's Rochester driveway.*

*Jeanne and me in Denali State Park on a 2018 Alaskan cruise. When the boat rocked in heavy seas, I blamed it on the captain buying the drink package.*

*Tim (with Liam and Maia) and Patty (with Grant) on Pier 39 in San Francisco. They're a very active family and the kids are growing up with curiosity, creativity—and confidence.*

*Emily was Sophie's first protector and they always spent time together when Emily was home. Now Emily's family includes Beau, her cat from Key West who hates the cold.*

*In 1982, Jeanne and I and our kids were a young family just starting out.*
*Who knew what great adventures the future would bring?*

# 24

# HEY, IT'S PATRICK

ON MARCH 16, 1995, WHEN I RETURNED HOME to California from a business trip, Jeanne picked me up at the airport. "Catherine called today," she said. "Patrick died."

I had met Bennett Patrick O'Dell, Jr., almost twenty-five years before, when he taught me to be an army journalist in our Fort Riley days; he remained a loyal friend as we both moved across the country and our lives changed through the years since then. Days before he passed, he'd been complaining of heartburn— he was scheduled for tests to determine the cause. On the day he died, he called Catherine, his wife, to tell her he didn't feel well, was coming home from his office in San Francisco. On his way out of the building, he had a massive heart attack. By the time paramedics arrived, he was dead.

His death hit me hard—and lingered long. For weeks and months afterwards, I'd be doing something when Patrick would flash into my mind, and I'd start to cry. It took years for that to go away.

For Patrick, his death was a sudden end to a high-stress life, a life fueled by an active imagination and a never-satisfied sense of curiosity, years spent reaching for everything life had to offer, living just beyond the edge of what he could sometimes afford, wanting the best for Catherine and their young family—Caitlin, Ben, and Meghan—girl, boy, girl, just as Jeanne and I had.

Jeanne, Emily, and I drove up to Marin for his funeral on a cloudy cool spring day; I had written something to say at his service but was too distraught to say it in the church. When others spoke at the gathering afterwards, I decided they hadn't really captured the Patrick I knew and so I stood partway up a stone staircase, held firmly on the railing, and read what I'd written.

> *Almost halfway into his forty-seven years, Patrick came into my life— and I suspect it was for the same reason he came into the lives of so many others: because I needed him. We were soldiers back then, and much younger, from two separate coasts, caught up in an Army we couldn't understand, living in a state far from home. We were so very different and, as it turned out, so very much alike. More than anything else, we each needed a friend, and we found one in each other.*

In October 1970, just months after we'd first met, Patrick and I went with the 1st Infantry Division to Germany on field exercises called *Reforger II*. We spent three weeks living in tents, driving around the countryside, and for the first time, co-writing an article on our impressions of living in the German woods. "We peel back the dew-laden sleeping bags, and our breath crystalizes in the fresh air. It's morning. Somewhere in Germany," we began, before going on to write of fairytale castles and small roads carved carefully into the wooded countryside. We sent our story back to the *Fort Riley Post*, where it was never printed; the editor judged it was not typical Army journalism.

On our first Sunday in Germany, we found that Germans loved to walk in the woods—and Pete Cava, a gregarious member of our office who spoke no German, wanted to talk to them. He asked me, "what would be some good things to say—and could you write them down?" I took a piece of paper and on one side I wrote the English; on the other side, the German. I rehearsed Pete only briefly before he headed to the woods where he proved both fearless and clueless.

He'd walk up to a German, take out his paper and read something, butchering every word he was trying to say; the German was often patient but uncomprehending, so Pete would try again, but generally with no more clarity than before. It wasn't long before Pete and the German were swapping the paper back and forth. Pete would try to read the German—the German would try to read the English—and they'd both laugh. They both seemed to be having fun.

We spent three weeks on those field exercises, eventually ending up camping near the small town of Bamberg where Patrick, Roger Bergson—our mutual friend—and I got an overnight pass. We put on civilian suit coats and ties and went into town; "stay together," our commanding office suggested. And we did. We booked a room in a Bamberg hotel but then got on the train for nearby Nuremberg where we thought there'd be more to see and do. We spent the day seeing the sights and were on the way to catch our train back to Bamberg for the night when we decided to have one more beer before we left Nuremberg.

That's how we ended up in a basement pub called "Die Schwarze Katze" sitting by ourselves when a member of a large and rowdy student group drinking on the other side of the room must have noticed us Americans; he asked the sleepy-eyed organ player to play *John Brown's Body*. When we joined in singing, the student invited Patrick, Roger, and me to join them at their table where we all sang along to more songs from the organist—and joined enthusiastically in playing games that involved drinking copious amounts of German beer. We were way out of our league.

It was only after Patrick had left for the men's room—and not returned—that Roger realized we were going to miss the last train to Bamberg. "And where," Roger asked, "is Patrick?" I was too drunk to notice he was gone.

We left the pub and went looking for him, but soon decided he was on his own; we needed to be on the train. We found seats in a small compartment—six people together with three sitting on each side, facing each other; I must have fallen asleep because I woke up to some old German shouting at me. Apparently, the back-and-forth motion of the train—combined with the amount of alcohol I'd drunk—caused me to throw up all over him. The train conductor was summoned, and I was fined—one mark, seventy-five pfennigs—for "cleaning services." Somewhere I have the receipt—the 'Reinigungskarte'—for cleaning up my mess.

Roger got me back to our hotel in Bamberg where we were woken up the next morning by a call from the Military Police. They had Patrick. He had been found in an apartment complex in Nuremberg, rapping on doors during the night; he thought he was in our hotel and was trying to find his room. Roger "signed for" him and he was released to our custody. Our commanding officer was surprisingly sympathetic when we told him what happened; "that's why I told you to stay together," he said. And then he laughed.

When we returned to Kansas, Patrick moved in to the big Victorian house we'd rented and we spent virtually every waking moment together, playing bocci ball on our lawn—where every few days we held the *World Championship*—writing together in the office, and playing in the snow on the swings and slides at the local school playground on that day in February when the fort closed down because of a snowfall in Junction City. On weekends, we played music together—just he and I—at a hotel across from Kansas State University about thirty miles away.

Patrick was very well read and a better writer than others in our office, including a kid named Dave who one day brought in a piece he said he'd written—and that we all judged to be exceptional. A few days later, Patrick mentioned he'd been in the library and found something he liked. He'd made a copy and wanted to read it to us; it was word-for-word what Dave had written. Patrick never accused Dave of plagiarism; he read the article—and put it away.

Jeanne and I had never been west of Kansas although Patrick talked so enthusiastically about his home state of California—"the difference between California wines and New York State wines," he told me once, "is that California wines aren't bitter"—that we wanted to see it and Patrick gave us an open invitation. By November of 1971, he had been discharged and was living in Los Angeles with a girl named Cathy whom he'd met at Fort Riley. Jeanne and I were still in Fort Bragg, but we had put together a bit of money and flew "military standby" to join them for three weeks.

They lived in a converted garage near the Hollywood Bowl, but his dad, who owned a Ford dealership in Visalia, loaned Patrick a Mustang in which we drove from Los Angeles to Visalia to meet his parents and beloved basset hound, Max ("he has enough skin for two dogs," Patrick said)—to Chula Vista to meet his older sister Janet and her family—and to Berkeley to meet Judith, his younger sister and her then-husband Brian. We drove across the Golden Gate Bridge to see San Francisco for the first time, and to watch the sun set out near Seal Rocks. "Those who want to learn how to make sunsets," I told Patrick, "should do their apprenticeship in San Francisco."

In Los Angeles, Patrick took us to Disneyland where admission was two dollars, but we also had to buy tickets for the rides. Patrick, through a friend, had gotten us tickets for free. Jeanne bought a ceramic wind-chime that hung on the back of our homes through the years; I took lots of pictures. It was a great and whirlwind trip. Late into the evening of November 30, Patrick's friend and landlord, Jim Newton, who was then art director for the *Smothers Brothers* show, hosted a party for our departure; it was the first time Jeanne and I saw how outlandishly openly gay people could dress. We were from Rochester; what did we know?

By Christmas of 1973, I was back in Rochester working for Kodak and in demand as a slide show writer because my work was winning awards; Jeanne was pregnant with our first little girl; and Patrick was in New York City looking for work as a starving actor. We sent him a train ticket to join us for the holidays. While he was with us, I introduced him at Kodak as a "writer who shares my style" and he got so much freelance work that he moved in with us for several months. He wrote—and composed music for—Kodak shows, including a company sponsored show at the Spokane World's Fair. Kodak people loved his writing, they loved his sense of humor, and one even came up with a name for what would become his business, when he said, "Here comes my friend from The Office of the Irishman." When our first daughter was born, Patrick bought a big house in Rochester that reminded me of the home we shared in Junction City.

When Patrick left California, he broke up with Cathy Schultz, but in Rochester, he found another Kathy. Kathy Gramlich was cute, Patrick was lonely, and they were married for several years although they never had children.

Around that time, Patrick suggested I leave Kodak and go into business with him. He planned to move back to California and handle the west coast; I'd stay in Rochester and take care of east coast business. Jeanne and I talked it over—and I stayed at Kodak. He did sell his Rochester home about three years later and move back to the San Francisco area he loved. Within a few years, his marriage to Kathy broke up—and he found another Catherine. In a much-later letter Catherine Hand would tell me:

> On our first date he paused after listening to me yammer on and said, "well, you're just a louder version of me!" When I asked him what he wanted out of life, he said, "to do everything there is to do," and when I asked, "and after that?" "To do everything there is to do all over again!" he said. That was Patrick—Mr. Hopeful!

Patrick and Catherine would marry and have three children. I'd meet them all during my business trips—and spend more time with them after our move—to California. But to continue what I said on the day of his funeral:

> He let me watch—and sometimes help—as he worked his way through his enormous range of talents and tried out his unending string of dreams. In such a very, very short time, he was an actor and a producer, a musician and a director, and always, a writer. But above everything, he was a husband and a dad. He loved looking at life through the eyes of a child—with a great sense of wonder and imagination.
>
> He was a child's child, a writer's writer, and a friend's friend. He could simplify complexity, cut through confusion, and find the humor and the common sense in life. He encouraged us all to look beyond the immediate, to see beyond the obvious, to go beyond the ordinary. He taught us to try new things, to be good to each other. Above all, he taught us to smile.

Through the years, the *Office of the Irishman* in San Francisco produced shows for several companies, including Kodak, Mary Kay Cosmetics and even Apple

Computer. In Rochester, he had access to the creative minds at Kodak—Ed Mitchell for audio and programming, Tom Davis for copystand work, among others—but he lacked that network in San Francisco and it was tough to be on his own. Plus, Patrick's style was to work as close to the deadline as possible. He spent a lot of time thinking but often it wasn't until the night before a project was due that he'd sit at his computer and commit his creativity to a script. That made it difficult to hire him for long-distance work in Rochester and unfortunately, Patrick and I seldom worked together on anything in the later years.

But when we moved to California in 1994, the first person I called was Patrick and we took him and his family to Disneyland as he had treated Jeanne and me so many years before. While we were together, we celebrated Patrick's forty-seventh birthday. We had no idea it would be his last. And so, back to my funeral thoughts:

> *For our three children, they have never known a time when they didn't have a much-loved, Uncle Patrick. He was with us when our first daughter, Jennifer, was born. He and our son Tim shared an interest in computers. And our younger daughter Emily was his special friend. They spent hours on the phone talking about anything and everything— and laughing all the while.*

We still hear from Catherine once or twice a year; their youngest daughter is married; the whole family is doing well although scattered across the country. His son Ben looks exactly like him and is working in the entertainment industry. His youngest sister Judith and I often exchange memories of Patrick on his birthday in August; I learned from her that Patrick had a serious bout of polio as an infant, had lived on ventilators, was expected to be a cripple and was always self-conscious that one leg was shorter than the other; we never knew. His parents and his sister Janet have passed away.

It was so much fun to share our yesterdays with him, if only because he made us feel so protected, so unafraid when Jeanne and I were in the Army so far from home with no one to depend on except each other—and Patrick. He was a loyal friend who shared our lives and our interests—and who had our backs. And so, I concluded my thoughts on that cloudy March funeral day:

> *On those days when clouds cover our lives and fog seems to roll in endlessly off the bay, we need only to listen for his voice, a voice of Peter Pan, the boy who refused to grow up and who invites us still "to fly;" the voice that comes encased in a smile and begins always with ". . . hey, this is Patrick . . ."*

When I finished speaking in that courtyard Catherine's father came up to me. "I had the sense that the words everyone else spoke were for themselves," he said. "But what you said, was for Patrick."

It was. It was my attempt to tell Patrick we always loved him and still do. Our friendship had been sealed long ago in that big old Victorian home in Junction City Kansas.

# 25

# THE HOUSE GONE MISSING

N JUNE OF 2019, OUR DAUGHTER EMILY WANTED to visit Junction City, Kansas. As a lawyer in the coast guard, she had been transferred from San Diego to Key West Florida; the moving van had taken her furniture and home goods, but she wanted to drive separately—she had just bought a new car—and asked me to join her on the trip—if only because she planned a seven-hundred-mile detour through that small Kansas town.

"You've been talking about Junction City ever since I was a little girl," Emily said. Now she wanted to see the place for herself. I told her there wasn't much to see. The only place I'd want to revisit was the home we lived in, the big old Victorian we rented on the corner of Adams and West Fourth Street; that's where so many memories had been made in our first years of marriage, but that house was all gone now. On a previous trip to Kansas in the spring of 2015, I had found only an empty lot where we used to live. Our first real home, an important piece of our yesterdays, was gone

When Jeanne and I had moved into that house nearly fifty years ago, we were far from our family—she for the first time ever. With the Vietnam war escalating—and a good chance that I'd be sent—we didn't know how much time we had together. We had little except each other, but we found shelter and comfort in that house. There was a peacefulness there, a feeling of stability, a sense of balance to the uncertainty of being a soldier. We didn't own it, but it felt like ours.

The house had a large entryway, a kind of parlor which Patrick O'Dell, had turned into a bedroom and shared the rent. It had a living room with curved glass windows, an unfurnished dining room we never used, and our bedroom with a small closet. There was a kitchen with a cracked linoleum floor, a pantry with floor-to-ceiling shelves, and a small bathroom tucked between the kitchen and living room. A third door in the bathroom led to a sun porch; the bare light that hung from the ceiling provided the only bathroom illumination; at times it leaked water from apartments above. The furniture was well worn but there was something magic about that home. And now it was all gone.

Emily and I pulled up in front of that empty lot on a Saturday evening in June of 2019. The grass was full, the ground was even; even the once-mature trees were gone. It looked as if nothing had ever stood there. "See," I said. "Just a minute, Dad," she replied, crossing the street. "I'll be right there."

Across West Fourth Street, an older Black woman was sitting on her porch. "Excuse me," Emily asked, "fifty years ago, when my dad was a young soldier at Fort Riley, he lived in a house that used to be right across the street. Do you know what happened to it?" "I sure do," the woman said. "That old house wasn't torn down, it was moved." She introduced herself as Sarah Sowell; she was eighty-four years old, she said, but her husband was much younger, he knew the details. His name was Wyndale and he was just fifty-eight, a former Marine. "I wanted to marry a younger man, one who could remember things for me," she said.

When Wyndale returned from getting cigarettes, he gave us the names of the new owners and address to where the house had been moved. Emily put the information in her phone and that's where headed the next morning—out of town, off the interstate, past some pastures, over a small plank bridge, down dirt and gravel roads and up a very long driveway . . . to see a partially-reconstructed version of the home I once lived in—and to meet Laurie and Stacey Cooke.

Within moments of knocking on their door and introducing myself as "a soldier who once lived in this house so long ago," we were swapping stories about this place we both loved.

They invited us in and told us the story of the home. It had been built by John Benton Callen who was born in Junction City and spent a lifetime in service there. Among other positions he held, he was a director of the Central National Bank of Junction City, county treasurer, postmaster, a master of the Masons and, for thirty years, a director and secretary of the Board of the Junction City Public Library. In 1887, Callen married Lena Woodson, a schoolteacher and they had two children, both of whom would die young. In 1905, he built the home that we would one day rent, a four-bedroom, single-family house where he lived until he passed away in 1937. His wife and children predeceased him; he had no other heirs.

After his death, the house was sold and carved up into five apartments; it passed through several owners until it was purchased by James and Emilie Archuleta, from whom we rented—and eventually by Gerry and Patty Schoenrock, owners of the largest realty in Junction City. "We acquired it as income property," Patty later told me, "and we continued to rent out the apartments for several years." As Fort Riley downsized, that market dried up; the house sat idle and needed a lot of work. To get it off their hands, they decided to give it away free— to whomever would move it or tear it down.

Stacey Cooke grew up in Junction City; as a young boy, he often rode his bike past the house. Now, he was a science teacher at Fort Riley Middle School, married with a family. For eighteen years they'd been renting a house, saving money to someday build a log cabin on fifteen acres of land they owned in the woods outside of Junction City. "Home-ownership had been a dream," Stacey said, "that I've always wanted to accomplish."

As school was starting in August 2003, a fellow teacher told him of a house that was available—for free. When school finished for the day, Stacey went to Schoenrock Realty and Gerry handed him the keys. "Go look at it," Gerry told him.

"You couldn't walk through it because it had been made into separate apartments," Stacey remembered. "I walked around the outside trying to visualize what it would look like once it was all opened back up as one single house again. When I finished, I went home and told Laurie that I intended to move the house." She had been dreaming of a sprawling log country home, "but he said, 'we've been married for twenty-five years, are you with me on this adventure?'" He took her to the house, and she gave in.

Laurie was a fourth-grade teacher; Lena Woodson, wife of Jake Callen who built the house, had also been a teacher. The Callens had a child who died young; the Cooke's young son would also pass at a very young age. They felt strong connections. "It is my best guess," Stacey agreed, "that the house chose us."

But there were lots and lots and lots of challenges.

"We knew we'd need major funds to move her and begin to restore her," Laurie said. The cost to raise the house off its foundation, move it to the new property and put it in place–along with the tree trimmers and overhead electrical line movers to accompany the house on its journey—was well over fifty thousand dollars. "Our bank didn't have the vision that we did. They weren't willing to do a moving or reconstruction loan. The down payment alone pretty much drained our saving account," she added. They would have to worry about the rest later because first there was a lot of work for Stacey and his volunteers to do. Fortunately, he was very handy.

"We had to remove all of the plaster from the walls, take off all the siding, and take out all the sinks, toilets, tubs, and cast-iron piping," Stacey said. "That would make it lighter. We started opening up the walls in August; that allowed the breeze to flow through and made it a lot nicer. There were six different kitchens and six different bathrooms. The house had sat empty for at least five years and as a result, many of the steam pipes had split. I spent every evening and weekend there from August until March."

There was one very big surprise left. Westar, the company involved in removing wires across the road so the house could pass, had bid $4,500 for their services. Once the house was up on the truck and ready to go, as Laurie remembered it: "Westar decided that, since they'd need to disconnect wires as the house moved down the road, they were going to replace the poles and upgrade their wiring system—and charge us. The new estimate was eighty-three thousand dollars. At that point despair set in."

Until Stacey had another idea. With the house on the truck, he climbed up into the attic and measured from the bottom of the roofline to the ground. It was twenty-four feet, ten inches. Stacey knew that—by code—electrical lines had to be twenty-five feet above the roadway. If he could remove the roof and chimney, the house would slide under the lines by two inches.

Enter Wyndale, Sarah's husband from right across the street. He had been laid off and "one night, I awoke out of a dead sleep," he remembered. "I heard God's voice saying, 'the people moving the house across the street need your help. Get up and go help.'" The next morning, Wyndale began helping Stacey take the roof off the house. Westar wouldn't have to remove lines after all—and finally, the house was ready to go. The *Junction City Daily Union* ran a front-page story that began:

> *A few weeks ago, Stacey Cooke couldn't sleep. Worry kept him awake. Figuring out how to move a free 100-year-old house down a highway will do that to a person. Since August the Fort Riley Middle School Science Teacher Stacey worried about how to move a 5,000 square foot free house from West Fourth Street to Otter Creek Road south of Junction City.*
>
> *He had taken off the siding and the roof. He had removed the portico on the back and the porch on the front. Valley Movers had slid the house from its limestone foundation where it stood for almost 100 years onto steel planks and up onto a truck. The load is 38-feet wide, just over 24-feet tall; it weighs 100-tons. It's all set for its 12-mile journey.*
>
> *House mover Randy Hupe predicts that the move will take about six hours. It will delay traffic or possibly shut down I-70 as it travels to the U.S. Highway 77 exit. At that point, they'll take backroads, cross a few pastures. Hupe added, "A lot of old houses just get bulldozed, but most people don't have the fortitude that Stacey has."*

Two weeks later, after almost seven months of preparation, the house was finally moving. It was 8:30 in the morning on Good Friday, April 9, 2004, and the move became a festive affair. Laurie's aunts and uncles, along with the kids and other family members and friends lined the street. The driver, Clifford, let Laurie get in the cab momentarily and pretend she was driving. Sarah Sowell was quoted in the article: "I've lived across the street since 1983, so I've been looking at that old house for a long time now, and I know a lot of people who have rented in it over the years. It's a beautiful house and I'll miss it."

Watched by what the newspaper called, "lots of gawkers," the load made it over the interstate just a little before noon and was coming across a field and about to enter its final resting place on Otter Creek Road, when, Laurie recalled, "everyone told us they were done for the day. Otherwise, they'd be going on holiday pay and that would increase their fees. The semi with our house pulled to a stop and everyone went home. They even left the keys in the truck. When I questioned that, Randy said: "You think someone will steal this and not be noticed?" They came back to finish the job on Monday.

At four o'clock that Monday afternoon, the bank called; their loan had been approved. "Our theory," Laurie said, "is that they felt the move was too risky to loan money on. Now that it had been moved, their money was safe." The house was left next to the basement hole that had been dug. A few months later, the movers returned to put the house on its new foundation.

The roof was the first thing they replaced; a friend with a crane put the dormers back in place; Stacey had set aside the original woodwork and structural elements and so they put those back; replastered the walls, put the siding back on. They put in central heat; opened up the front and back stairwells—including one originally used by the butler—and removed the one affixed to the exterior. They put a new tile floor in the vestibule with a design by Stacey. They rehung the windows; Stacey had taken special care of them during the move; he didn't want their curved glass to get broken.

In the midst of all that work tragedy struck. The Cooke's only son Clayton who had cerebral palsy had a seizure and went into a coma. After he spent a month in the hospital, they brought him home for his last days. "He passed away on Nov. 1st, All Saints Day," Laurie said, "and we sort of lost our way for a time. We just had no wind in our sails."

The old house was not making things easy. For months, it stood with a four-by-six hole from roof to basement as they looked for someone to put the fireplaces and chimney back together. Several masons turned them down until they met Dave, an old-school mason who said he'd do the job. "He also said," Stacey remembered, "that the reason no one else would do it was because if it wasn't done correctly the house would burn down." Dave worked through the winter, replacing everything "the old way." Just after he finished the job, Dave passed away.

When Emily and I visited in 2019, the house was still a work in progress. "The most difficult challenge," Stacey said, "is time. If there were two of me, I could work them both to death." But they were living there—and maybe sharing the home with other spirits also. "We wouldn't call it haunted because we're not afraid when things strange are happening," Stacey said. "Once while I was working in the basement my cell phone rang and when I walked outside to get better reception, the drill I was using briefly started up. I turned around to look and no one was there." "We believe there are other spirits still inhabiting the Victorian," Laurie added. "On one occasion while watching TV, as I got up to microwave some popcorn, there was odorless smoke floating down the hall towards me. It brushed my face, feeling like a feather. I watched it disappear through the wall at the other end of the hallway."

They're OK with all that. "I think," Laurie said, "that the house is happy that there are new memories being made in her."

When Emily and I pulled out of the Cooke's driveway a couple of hours later, it was the second time I'd left that home behind; the first was almost fifty years before when Jeanne and I were heading to my next Army assignment, in Fort Bragg, North Carolina.

# 26

# EDITING *VERITAS*

I WAS NEVER OFFICIALLY A MEMBER OF ARMY SPECIAL FORCES—I never wore a green beret—but the last military job I had was editing *Veritas*, their worldwide magazine.

Some months before Jeanne and I arrived in North Carolina, General Flanagan, who had commanded the John F. Kennedy Center for Military Assistance at Fort Bragg, had called his information officer, Colonel Charles Siler, and worked out a deal—I'd be joining the colonel's staff in the JFK Center to write for *Veritas*. And then Jim Toms, the writer General Flanagan had brought with him, went further: he called his former landlords, the Piggots, and arranged for Jeanne and me to rent the same small house at 125 John Street where Jim and his wife had lived when they were stationed in North Carolina.

It was a single story, two-bedroom home—one in the front, one in the back—with a living room, dining room, kitchen and bath. Out back was a small building that our landlords—Clarence and Marie Piggott, two wonderful people who lived next door—used as a laundry room. It stood in a small yard where Jeanne once found a snake and refused to go out there again. The rent—for everything, including water and electricity—was sixty-five dollars a month.

We soon learned there is no humidity quite like the humidity in the southeast and the house was not air-conditioned. It would typically rain in late afternoon and all the humidity would stay in the air making it difficult to sleep at night. At first, Jeanne and I would just go down and walk around in K-Mart for a few hours every night because the store was air-conditioned; eventually we invested in our first window air-conditioner for which Clarence Piggot installed a 220-line and never charged us extra for electricity. We put the unit in the front bedroom where we slept and since there were two doors off that room—one leading to the living room, the other to the hall—it kept the rest of the house reasonably cool.

And so, I went to work for Colonel Siler, a small, stocky guy always carrying a mostly unlit cigar. He was calm, confident, a boss who trusted his people. His staff was a mix of soldiers and civilians—competent people, and misfits. In some ways, the colonel's second-in-command was Sgt. Major Jim Davis who'd gotten his stripes the old-fashioned way: he earned them. When I found out he couldn't write, I offered to do that for him—and he paid me back in kind.

When I wanted to take three weeks' leave to go to California, he told me, "When you're discharged, you'll be paid for all the leave you didn't take. Let's not tell the Army you'll be away. When you go, fill out the papers and give them to me. When you return, we'll tear them up—and your leave will never be counted." I ended up with about an extra month's pay; it wasn't a huge amount, but it helped when we moved back to Rochester.

Besides Sgt. Major Davis, the office included several beat reporters and a couple of photographers; they supplied most of what we'd use in *Veritas*, which was put together in a small building next door by two civilians, Tom Walker, an ordained minister who was the editor, and Mildred Hicks, a slight woman who did all the typing. After about a month working for Tom, he realized that if he made me the editor, he'd have more time to do what he really wanted during the day—go bowling. And so that's what he did.

The problem was: I didn't know how to edit a worldwide publication and I wasn't sure that Tom was the best person to teach me; I signed up for the Newspaper Editor's Course at Ft. Benjamin Harrison in Indianapolis. It was a three-week course in August of 1971, and it changed my life.

The course was taught by John Foltz, the former editor at the *Louisville Courier Journal,* a paper that helped establish the look of newspapers in the United States. John knew how to write a story, how to design a page, how to present the news to attract attention, how to get it read. He had the energy of a teenager, the crustiness of a newsman, the confidence that came from success. And his critique of my writing was brutal. "Gibbons," he said, "you're writing in a style that only appeals to people who are so old they're going to be dead in a couple of years. You need to learn to write for a younger audience." He sent me down to the local drugstore with a list of magazines he said I *must read: Earth, National Lampoon, Rolling Stone, Hot Rod,* and others. I did—and I taught myself to write in a very different style.

John didn't just encourage me to write better for my audience, he taught me about the importance of designing better for that audience—making stories look easier to read, giving impact to layout, using illustrations that would catch attention. I came back to Fort Bragg with an idea of how to apply what I'd learned: I wanted to dedicate a whole issue of *Veritas* to a theme I thought would resonate with soldiers—*Freedom of Speech: did it exist in the Army?* When Colonel Siler readily agreed to let me explore that, I went looking for help with photography and graphic design.

SP4 Bob Wornom was a combat photographer back from Vietnam and working in our office but without a sense of purpose; I thought he had talent and when I described what I had in mind, I found it energized him; he began to shoot in a much looser, more imaginative style. After we both got out of the Army, Bob and I stayed friends for several years.

Now, I needed an artist for what I hoped would be a very strong and graphic cover illustration—and I wandered over to our PSYOPS (Psychological Operations) unit where they had designers who illustrated pamphlets. When I looked at their work, one, SP4 Bob Harper, stood out. When we talked, he seemed to be fed up with the military, so I shouldn't have been surprised when he suggested the cover illustration be a graphic image of a soldier standing in front of an American flag—with a steel band over his mouth. He said he'd love to create it, but it would never be approved. I told him I'd worry about that. When I took it to Colonel Siler, he approved it immediately—and didn't suggest anyone above him would need to see it; we were good to go.

On the inside of the magazine, I made stories shorter, cropped pictures differently, drew rules around the pages, and tried to apply everything I'd learned from John Foltz. The October 1971 issue of *Veritas* looked different from any issue we'd printed before. And the soldiers loved it. The publication was available free at several locations and normally there would be a number of issues left on the racks weeks later. All copies of this issue were gone in hours. And as was the practice back then, copies were sent to the Department of Defense in Washington and to John Foltz at Ft. Benjamin Harrison. Foltz loved it; he sent his copy back to me where across the cover page he had written: *Gibbons! J-e-e-e-e-s-u-s!* The Department of Defense was more restrained in their response: they gave me my first CONARC Copy Desk Award; I would get two more for my other work before I left the Army four months later.

Putting together that issue enhanced my credibility and status in the information office; I was asked to handle the highest profile stories and sent out on the most sensitive assignments. I interviewed Sgt. Dan Pitzer, who was a long-held POW in Vietnam; and I talked at length with Captain Chet Jezierski, a kid my age who flew helicopter gunships through the TET Offensive of 1968 and who was painting the Medal of Honor recipients for the Pentagon.

I was the one reporter given a Top-Secret security clearance, so I could attend Secretary of Defense Alexander Haig's speech at Ft. Bragg—and write down what he said, so we could distribute it to the public. I'm still not sure why I needed a high-level clearance for that. And I edited an interview with Brigadier General Henry Emerson, commander of the JFK Center, who rejected my work. "This has to be rewritten," he scrawled across the Q&A; "it reads too much like the way I talk."

But I was enjoying my time at Ft. Bragg, if only because I also wasn't taking the military too seriously. Instead of answering the phone, "Specialist Gibbons, sir," I always said, "Hi, this is Bob. What do you need?" And when a new soldier introduced himself to me as "Sergeant Smith," I asked for his first name. "I'm not too interested in this rank thing," I told him.

Another sergeant came into our small office and laid twenty-five single-spaced, typed pages of copy on my desk. "Here is a story I wrote for your next issue," he said. "This is the first of four parts."

I looked at it briefly and threw it away. "We probably won't use this," I told him.

Jeanne and I never developed close friendships in North Carolina the way we'd done in Kansas, but on weekends we'd head down to then-secluded Wrights-ville beach on the border of the Carolinas and enjoy time together in the ocean; in October her parents came out for a visit and stayed with us for a few days; and we spent most of the month of November on our first trip to California.

Before we left, I had to go before the Army Promotion Board; I was up for consideration to be an E5, the equivalent of sergeant. When I was asked why I should be promoted, I told them it would be to their benefit to do so. "You only have so many slots for E5's," I said, "and I'm definitely leaving the Army in January, so my slot will be almost immediately available for someone else. It's like a two-for-one." The Board must have agreed with my logic; as of 9 November 1971, I was promoted to the rank of E-5.

After more than a year and a half of moving from a trainee (E-1) to a Private (E-2) to a Private First Class (E3) to a Corporal (E4), I had gotten one of the few promotions available. The only reason I wanted it was for the transportation al-lowance; E4s had to move themselves back home after discharge; E5s were pro-vided a moving van.

Although my two years of active duty weren't up until the following March, Vietnam was winding down, the Army was trying to change to an all-volunteer force, and they were moving up some discharges to get short-term draftees off their payroll. My new ETS—Expiration of Term of Service—was moved to 3 January 1972. Christmas 1971 was the first year ever for Jeanne and me to be without family for the holidays. We stayed home on John Street where the tem-perature was eighty degrees and two friends from my office—Ken Wiech and Bill Bush—came over for dinner. Another information specialist—Bruce Ford and his wife Debby—were also with us; they'd moved in with us in December because they would be taking over the house after we left. Debby was young and opinionated, and her presence made Jeanne even more eager to leave.

On January 3, somewhere around 10:30 in the morning, I reported to the out-processing office at Ft. Bragg and after serving for 665 days, I was discharged from active duty. I was reminded that I still had another four years of military obligation and should sign up for a local Reserve unit as soon as I got back to Rochester. Knowing how messed up military records were—and how the conversion to an all-volunteer Army was adding further confusion—I had no intention to do that. I figured, "let them find me." They never did.

The moving van had left with our stuff a few days before; we kept only the essentials we'd need on our drive home. Jeanne kept only a pair of open sandals to wear—forgetting there would be snow as we drove up north. When we stopped to visit her sister in Philadelphia and she bought a pair of boots to wear, the saleswoman looked at Jeanne's frozen feet and said, "Oh, you poor dear." But as we left Fayetteville in our little blue Tempest, it felt like a great obstacle had been removed from our lives.

I was in a grocery store wearing my Army field jacket when somebody asked: "that's a great jacket; what did it cost?" "It cost me," I said, "almost two years of my life." But now, military service was in our rear-view mirror; we were headed for home—and for Kodak.

# 27

## AUDIO VISUAL DAYS

I RETURNED TO KODAK AS A TEMPORARY MEMBER of the Business and Technical Training Group, but I knew where I wanted to work full time. I wanted to join Kodak's Creative Services team, but they weren't hiring.

So, I took a training assignment there and tried to figure out how to create my own job. Creative Services included both Audio Visual Services and Motion Pictures Services and I figured my best opportunity would be in the audio-visual unit where they made slide shows to introduce new company products and services; I thought I could meet the requirements for a writer-producer. There were four writer-producers at the time and since they had no openings, I decided I would need to replace one of them. But which one—and how?

I talked to them, asked them about their jobs. Three out of the four really liked what they were doing; only one—a young guy named Dan—wanted to do something else, but he wasn't sure what. I spent time trying to help him figure that out and whenever he suggested a job he might be interested in, I went to my supervisor in the B&T Training group and told him *that's what I was looking for.* He'd send me on interviews—and I'd bring the information back to Dan.

When he found a match that seemed interesting, he interviewed for the job—and took it; when he went in to tell his boss he was leaving Audio Visual Services, I went with him—and was hired as his replacement. My pay was increased by sixty dollars a week. I had the job I wanted.

Audio Visual Services had a full range of on-staff talent—artists, photographers, audio technicians, programmers, presentation specialists, coordinators, and of course writers—now including me. Many of us were around the same age and we ended up forming the AVUBTC–the Audio-Visual Unofficial Bicycle and Touring Club–-to go riding together on weekends.

And although I'd never been trained to write visual presentations, I figured things out for myself; when my first show—*The New Image*—won awards at a radiography conference, people came to me with interesting projects. I wrote everything from one-projector shows—sometimes with the words of the script right on the slides—to a very elaborate presentation where twelve projectors sat on an island in a sea of mirrors and put on a show that looked like it was taking place below the floor.

A Kodak marketing rep in San Francisco particularly liked my work and he flew me out several times to write for him; as a bonus, he sometimes sent me loose tea from Cost Plus Markets. I was a big tea drinker at the time.

When I saw a new technique called 'multi-image' —which involved the use of multiple slide projectors programmed with a computer to create dazzling on-screen effects—I taught myself how to design shows using that technique and provided writing help to a local producer, Ray Schmitt, who was writing a book on the subject for Kodak. When my work came to the attention of people outside the company, I was elected to the Board of Directors of the Association for Multi-Image International, the group that set the pace for the development of that technique. For several years, I was the MC at their annual banquet. At one, AMI gave me a special award "for giving our association a sense of humor." It was presented by my good friend Ric Sorgel.

Multi-image was complex stuff, but I was working with a small, but very talented Kodak team—Don Maggio did a lot of the original photography; Ed Mitchell did all the audio and programming, Gerry Gregg handled arrangements and production, Tom Davis did the copy-stand work and created the special masking, and I wrote and designed the shows.

Don Maggio was Kodak's fastest photographer; he shot the images for virtually every show I did, but when I showed him the script he'd be illustrating, he never read it. He just wanted me to take him where I expected him to shoot and describe what I had in mind. He'd set up his camera and show me what he saw—and it was always so much better than I could even imagine. He once told me one of his secrets: "most photographers have everything in focus, so people don't know where to look," he said; "in my pictures, only one thing's sharp; I make it easy for them."

On a day off from shooting in San Diego, Don and I went to the zoo where, at one point, he stuck his lens through the wire mesh and began taking endless pictures of one of the great apes—who finally decided he had enough. The ape reached down, took a crap in his giant hand—and flung it at Don. He missed—and Don was nonplussed. "He's probably tired of having his picture taken," Don said.

Don always liked to find an unusual angle. He'd walk into a manager's office, clear his desk, and stand on it to take an overhead shot. He'd climb on piles of boxes in a half-filled tractor trailer, poke his camera inside an idle machine, or use scraps from a trash bin to create an out-of-focus foreground. Dirty, crowded production spaces, or wide expanses of bland factory buildings—Don made great pictures everywhere. And nothing phased him.

We went one day to take pictures of the superintendent of a production building who happened to be in the men's room when we stopped there first. Eager to make the introductions, I said, "Don, this is Dutch Schlosser." Don was standing at the urinal. "I'd shake your hand," Don told him, "but right now, mine is soaking wet."

We called Gerry Gregg our producer because it was usually his Kodak unit that provided the budget for our shows. I met him the day he came into my office and said, "I want to do big shows that let me travel all over the country to places I like to go. Can you do shows like that?" When I told him I could, he said, "good because you're my last resort; nobody else wants to work with me."

One of the first places we went was to San Diego where I fell in love with the city. When I got home, I told Jeanne, "when we retire, I'd like to live at least part of the year there." Jeanne agreed, although she'd never been there. We moved to Oceanside, just north of there when I retired.

Gerry was a private pilot with whom I once flew—contrary to all Kodak rules—to a show we were doing in Washington DC where we were staying at the posh Sheraton Washington. Gerry and I agreed to meet in front of the concierge desk to go to dinner and as I stood waiting for him, I saw him hopping along the sidewalk on one leg, up the stairs and through the door into the lobby. As others watched, Gerry wiped his shoe on the carpet. "Dog shit," he said. It wasn't; it wasn't anything; he had nothing on his shoe—but that was Gerry.

After we'd worked together for a couple of years, Gerry must have gotten bored with his Kodak job because he started coming in very early in the morning, talking briefly to his boss who also arrived very early, and then putting his suit coat on his chair saying "well, I've got to go to work." Where he was actually going was to a small nearby airport where he got in his plane—and flew to his *other* full-time job—at AVL in New Jersey. When he didn't show up there one day—and they called Kodak looking for him—he was fired and ended up teaching school in Texas.

Tom Davis had a job duplicating slides at Kodak when I discovered multi-image and knew I'd need a wizard at the copy-stand to help. I invited him to see a multi-image show in New York City to show him what others were doing and to whet his appetite—and it certainly did! Even on the plane back home, he was designing masks and describing screen effects.

Multi-image had some great talent—Doug Mesney, Chris Korody, Ric Sorgel, among others—and Tom proved he could compete. He could create anything on his copy-stand, often using Kodak products in ways the company didn't condone; some of the on-screen results from his work—the turning pages in the show we created for EPCOT or the pencil-point seamless wipes in our PIT show—have never been duplicated by others. Tom ended up teaching at Kodak and lecturing on the company's behalf around the country.

Ed Mitchell came from Rochester radio where he created the audio for an old-time crime drama; at Kodak, he had a reputation for being tough, demanding, and impatient. After we'd worked together for a while and had gotten to be friends, I told him, "Mitch, you're a mean and ornery old SOB, but you're a lot better than you used to be." In fact, he was my go-to person when I wanted to try something new.

He was wonderful at directing narrators. Once, when I needed an "older voice" for a particular recording, he said to the man in the booth, "Do it again, Jim. But this time, take your teeth out." He was amazing at selecting and editing music. He would sit there with his acetates, dropping the needle and picking it up, remembering what he heard, and later splicing neo-classical with neo-disco in a way that felt right, made sense and was seamless.

And he was terrific at programming—making slides from twelve or fifteen projectors appear to move across and around the screen. We were together that night when he finished programming the first big show we did together—*A Salute to the Broadcast Industry*—and he hit the play button. "Go, you son of a bitch," he said—and it did, splashing the show we created on the screen of his small work room. It was amazing work, and he knew it because, that night, Mitch got up from behind his console and he danced.

Mitch and I created a couple of other much smaller shows that stick in my memory for different reasons. I had, at one point, been asked to create show that had two very firm requirements: it had to describe Kodak's markets divisions— and it had to be under three minutes long. It was going to be used as a "breather" in longer programs. Mitch and I went to work and when we got something we both liked, it was seven minutes long. What to do? "Leave it," Mitch counseled. "Let's show it to your clients."

We did—and they loved it. "How long is it?" They asked. I told them it was exactly three minutes. They said that was "perfect" —and it must have been because somehow, whenever they used it, it always fit into their three-minute slot, despite being more than twice that length.

My other Mitch experience was quite different. He and I taught a course in audio techniques to working AV producers from across the country. To demonstrate how to direct a narrator, we used a script I'd written called *The Wizard's*

*Greatest Challenge*; it was a humorous fable about the invention of the Kodak Audioviewer and involved several voices. We gave copies of the script to students so they could follow along—as Mitch recorded and I directed the narrator.

A few weeks later, after the students had returned home, Mitch gave me a full-page ad in a local newspaper from somewhere in the mid-west. Someone had sent it to him, and he wanted me to see it. *"If you'd like scripts like this, call us"* the headline read—and gave the phone number of a production company run by a student who had been in our class. The rest of the ad reproduced the first half of my script for *The Wizard's Greatest Challenge* —and promised the second half would be printed next week.

I called the number, talked to the student, told him how flattered I was that he thought so highly of my work that he was willing to pretend it was his own. "But," I told him, "unfortunately our Kodak lawyers aren't nearly as pleased. They thought we owned this material. They mentioned a lawsuit." He told me that he didn't say his customers would get *THIS* script; the ad said they would get a script *LIKE* this one. I told him that next week's ad should print a script LIKE others HE wrote. And, as far as I know, he did.

I worked with another Kodak audio engineer, Peter Konnick, on another fable I'd written, this one was about the television industry where, at the time, Kodak film was used to record the news and most other programming. My fable included characters called 'ratings' and I wanted them voiced by rats. "Call Dave Loringer," Peter told me. "He sounds like rats."

Dave came into the studio and we recorded him; "speak as fast as you can," Peter told him—and he did. "Thanks," Peter said, "we got it." "He does not sound like rats," I told Peter, who calmly removed the recording tape, wadded it up in a ball, stepped on it, and put it back on the machine. As it skipped and bounced across the playback head, Dave's voice squeaked and chirped. "I told you," Peter said, "Dave sounds like rats."

Although my job was to write slide shows, when I had extra time, I'd often work on movie scripts; the motion picture unit was also part of Creative Services and I just happened to be working on a screenplay on the day Audio Visual Services was disbanded and combined with another company unit under the direction of Dick Reisem. Our big boss, Bill Pedersen read the name of every member of AV Services who'd report to Dick; my name was not on the list. I had clearly been forgotten so when someone asked Bill, "What about Bob?" Bill improvised.

"What's Bob working on?" he asked. I was working on a movie. "Bob is transferred to Motion Picture Services," he said.

I went in to see Sam Scribner, who managed that unit. "What's my new title?" I asked him.

He took a binder off his bookshelf. "These are all the job titles that report to me," he said. "Pick the one you want."

"How about Senior Audio Engineer," I suggested.

"OK," he agreed.

"Sam," I said, "I don't know anything about audio engineering."

"Then pick something else," Sam said. And that's how, at the end of 1974, I became a Writer-Director of movies.

In 1975, as the country prepared for its bicentennial, Kodak—like many large companies—considered what gift it might give the nation for its birthday. Richard Young and I were in Washington working on another project when we were hit with an idea: Lincoln's words were carved into his memorial—and so were Jefferson's. Where were the words of George Washington? We wondered if they could be "carved" into motion picture film and shown in a theatre on the grounds of the Washington Monument? Kodak had asked their major agencies for gift suggestions, and we added ours for consideration. It became the winning proposal.

I wrote—and Richard Young directed—the movie, *Washington: The Man*, to great accolades from Walt Fallon, Kodak's CEO who then needed a speech written for him to introduce the movie to dignitaries in the capitol when it premiered. When the writing task was given to members of Kodak's scriptwriting team, they passed it along to me. I agreed to do it although I'd never written a speech before; I was later told that it was a combination of that—plus my script for the movie—that convinced our CEO that I should be working for Dave Metz, head of communications for Kodak. The best writers reported to him. Still, Kodak was a big company; everything took time.

One day late in 1979, Neil Stalter, a senior manager who worked for Dave Metz, came to me with a question: *Would I like to join him for a drink after work to talk about new opportunities for me?* I told him I wasn't against alcohol, but I didn't think it helped people make the best decisions; I suggested an in-office meeting instead—and when we met, Neil offered me the job of Coordinator for Presentation Services. I'd manage the company's team of speechwriters, the job currently held by Dick Reisem, who was being moved to a special project.

I told Neil why I was wrong for the job: I'd be the youngest, the least experienced person in that department; I would lack the support, respect, and cooperation from a much more experienced team. He suggested he could be helpful in that area. He told me to think about this opportunity, let him know.

I talked it over with Jeanne who said she would be happy with whatever I decided. So, I talked it over with Ann Finegan, a plain-speaking colleague at work who told me, "it's obvious you're going to be put into Presentation Services, where you're going to work for somebody. Who do you want to work for—you or someone else?" I decided to work for me.

When I told Neil my decision, he took me to meet his boss, Dave Metz, arguably one of the most powerful people at Kodak. "I'm not going to ask you what this job pays," I told Dave, "for two reasons: first, because I suspect you don't know; and second, because I don't care. I wouldn't take this job for the money. If I do this job well—and I'll try to do that—I expect to be fairly paid. And I'll take it with just one promise—I will never let you down."

In return, Dave gave me wise counsel. "This is your first step into management," he told me, "and someday, there may be bigger steps. Every time an opportunity opens, the people above you will vote, but the people below you will vote also." He was saying: *Never step on anyone to get ahead.* Great advice.

As it turned out, the job paid almost thirty-thousand dollars a year and the money was very helpful because we had three very young children at the time. But Kodak also gave me another gift that was important to their growing up years; the company enabled me to work with great photographers who taught me to take pictures.

# 28

# TAKING PICTURES

PHOTOGRAPHY HAS BEEN THE PERFECT HOBBY FOR ME. Over the years, it's given me an excuse to go off wandering by myself with my camera when I just wanted to be alone—or to be the one taking pictures in the celebrations of family and friends when I wanted to be in a crowd; it's let me have an irreplaceable chronicle of the kids growing up—and be able to show them relatives who passed away before they were born. And it was the right focus for somebody like me working at Kodak because free film and processing were always available. It started when I bought my first camera—a Kodak Instamatic 414—in 1969 in the Kodak Office company store, just before our honeymoon— and together, my cameras and I have gone from there.

Growing up, I'm sure my parents had a camera because there are, in old photo albums my mother saved, some pictures of me and my brothers and sisters that she or my dad must have taken, but I never remember their camera coming out at family gatherings. My Uncle Al was the self-appointed family photographer; he had expensive 35mm Leica cameras with lenses, and he mostly shot Koda-chrome slides. Sometimes, when we were at his home, he'd drag his little slide projector out of the living room closet, set up a screen, and show us pictures of us—or of his recent vacation. I remember lots of pictures of trees and some of us kids with our heads cropped off.

When he passed away, Aunt Mag gave me a trunk full of slides; although most were scenics or images of people I couldn't identify, included were some of the only pictures I have of our family and cousins growing up. The picture on the cover of this book came from that trunk.

When Polaroid cameras came out, Uncle Al got one of those also—and he loaned it to me when I went to Florida for Easter vacation during my freshman year of college—but I found it especially tricky to load. My little Instamatic camera solved the loading problem—the film came in a plastic cartridge that was snapped into the camera—and during that one week of our honeymoon, Jeanne and I took about the same number of pictures as my parents had taken, ever, in their lives. Instamatic cameras made picture-taking so easy that we let Jennifer use ours when she was about four years old—to take pictures of her and Tim visiting Santa Claus. Some of her pictures were published in a Kodak book. She may be one of the youngest published photographers.

That might have been the last camera I'd ever buy had Kodak's T-1 course not convinced me that I needed a better one to take better pictures. Kodak no longer made professional cameras, but the Japanese did and when my new Kodak friend, Richard Young, went to Japan on a business trip, I gave him ninety dollars to bring me back a Nikomat, a tier-2 professional camera made by Nikon. The camera was there when I returned from Army basic training, and I began taking it with me everywhere.

Now I had control over the exposure, the shutter speed, the focus, the depth of field. I could decide not only what I wanted in the picture—but also, how I wanted that picture to look. It's the camera I used to photograph our years in Kansas and in North Carolina. It's the one I took on all my adventures with Richard as we traveled the United States together making movies for Kodak. And it's the camera I used to photograph the birth and growing up years of our three children and their cousins and friends. Although I'd have other cameras through the years, I never used any as much as that one.

When we began having children, I had the good fortune to be working with Kodak photographer Don Maggio who gave me some guidelines on how to take pictures of babies and kids. "Get down to their level," he said; "and get close. A longer lens will make them look more natural—and shoot so they're the only thing in focus." We have more than eight thousand pictures of our kids growing up and they're better because of Don's advice.

When Jeanne and I were with the kids, I always had my camera along. "What do Jennifer, Tim, and Emily do after their dad takes their picture?" my sister Judy once asked. Her answer: "They stay where they are—because they know he'll take at least five more." The pictures I shot of Jennifer and Tim's birth—lying on the floor under the delivery table as Dr. Cegelski delivered them—ended up in a slide show in the doctor's office. I couldn't photograph Emily's birth because the hospital was short-staffed—it was Labor Day weekend—and I had to assist with the delivery. But when Emily asked why we had no pictures of her delivery, Jennifer told her because she was adopted.

With a professional camera, there was so much to remember—and I sometimes didn't. At one point, Don Maggio and I were working on a movie I had written starring the television actor, Lorne Greene. "Did you use your light meter for the pictures you took of Lorne and me?" Don asked. "Because you missed the right exposure by about three or four stops." "Remember the problem I used to have with focusing?" I asked. "Well, now I have that figured out, but I'm still working on the exposure thing." But I was trying to learn from everyone.

In 1981, I went with two Kodak photographers—George Butt and Gary Whelpley—to Germany on a research trip; I would write the script for—and they'd photograph—a Kodak slide show on the Bavarian Alps. I had my Nikomat and took lots of slides of our travels. When we got back, I put some of what I thought my better slides on an illuminator where Gary and George could see them—and when they did, Gary asked me, "would you mind if we used some of your slides for one of our instructional shows?" I was flattered—until he explained: "we like to show people the most common mistakes amateurs make when taking pictures—and you've got so many great examples right here."

I'd never be a professional photographer—I didn't have the "eye"—but I was having fun. When I took pictures at my nephew Todd's outdoor wedding, I climbed up on a big rock during the ceremony to get an unusual angle. At that point, most people stopped watching Todd and Stacey and started watching me; they were wondering if I'd fall off the rock. For my friend Charlie Myers wedding, I shot alongside the professional photographer they hired—and I got the only useable pictures from that ceremony. Their photographer thought their wedding was so beautiful, she was crying, and her pictures were all blurry.

I became what Uncle Al had been—the family photographer. I still love to go into homes of family and friends and see—hanging framed and fading on their walls or sitting on their mantel—pictures of their wedding, their children at a very young age, or even pictures of *their children's weddings* and realize *I took those.* I'd often go to a major family event, take several rolls of pictures, and drop the film off for overnight processing. The next day, I would put the best pictures into an album and drop it by as a gift for those who hosted the party; sometimes the bride and groom had their wedding pictures before they even left for their honeymoon.

During my Kodak days, the company had a Camera Club; dues were one dollar a year and for that, they offered darkrooms where we could process our own film and make our own prints; they provided black and white chemicals for fifteen cents and printing paper for free. I spent many evenings in those facilities, enlarging and printing and playing with my pictures. I found photography helped—maybe challenged me—to look at life differently. In 1971, when my friend Roger Kiley was drafted, he was sent to Korea where he was lonesome and lost. Roger was a sensitive guy who was easily discouraged and depressed and he wrote telling me how he felt, and asking how he could cope. I suggested he buy a camera and in his free time, go out exploring. I told him it would give him a new perspective on the very-different country and culture he was in. He did that—and his mood changed entirely.

In the beginning, Jeanne thought our kids should only be photographed when they were clean-scrubbed and shining, but I quickly convinced her otherwise. The pictures we have on them on ordinary days—with cuts and scrapes and runny noses—are among the real treasures in the thirty-nine photo albums those pictures would eventually occupy. We've also had them all scanned—I threw the negatives away; I was sure I'd never need them—to make them more useful. When the kids were married, I put together digital slide shows with music of them growing up.

We've got so many pictures, but I wish we had more. I wish I had pictures of Frank Melville who taught me to play drums and Wally Batog who gave me the first opportunity to play in public. I wish I had pictures of our first band, our now-demolished first home, my first summer job, my first days at Notre Dame. But cameras were often big and cumbersome in those days; you had to plan to shoot pictures, remember to buy film, and bring your camera along.

Technology has come so far from the 1980's when Kodak introduced a line of Disc cameras—and one model had a clock inside. "If we don't market it as a camera with a clock," Kodak CEO Walt Fallon suggested, "maybe we can sell it as a clock that takes pictures."

Now every phone has a camera (and a clock) inside—and the pictures the camera takes are just so remarkably good. And you can see immediately what you have. But in having that immediate gratification, I wonder if we haven't lost some of the magic that came with the anticipation—the waiting for the film to be developed, for the pictures to come back, for the chance to relive the memories sometimes long after those memories may be beginning to fade. Jeanne had a friend who was already divorced by the time she received her wedding pictures—but maybe that's an extreme case.

I swore that I was never going to abandon film, that I liked the way film pictures looked and that I would never shoot digitally. I'm equally sure now I'll never use film again; digital is faster, cheaper, easier, and I'm no longer the family photographer—everyone is. Everyone has a phone and when we go to a family function, everyone is shooting pictures. But I still print my favorites—I like to crop and adjust them myself and hold the results in my hands, put them in albums, and in frames. I sometimes make those pictures into birthday cards and other cards for friends. Some of my older pictures bring back memories for them; I tell them I have so many old ones, they'll never be safe.

And maybe through the years, I've even gotten slightly better at taking pictures—if only because I took so many. And although the pictures I took of our kids and family always comprised the vast majority of those we had, running a close second were those I shot on my travels with Richard Young.

# 29

## ADVENTURES WITH RICHARD

H E CHANGED MY LIFE AND MY KODAK CAREER; he was an incomparable friend. And I still miss him. Richard Young and I met on a fall day back in 1969. He was almost eight years older than me, trained as an artist, but moved himself into a position as a Kodak cinematographer and director, one of several making movies to promote the company. The other directors made straightforward films to sell Kodak products and services; Richard's were more subtle and visually stunning—work that often ended up shown on public television as a donation from Kodak. He brought a sense of imagination to everything he did.

I was a young trainee at the time, had discovered that I liked to write, and had a temporary assignment working on slide shows; Richard convinced me to try writing a movie, he took me in mostly rusted Oldsmobile out to a studio Kodak had rented on McKee Road, so I could see where Kodak movies were shot.

He was different from anyone else I met in the company; he had an impeccable sense of style—he bought his hand-made white shirts in Toronto; he wore bow ties and blue jeans to work; he seemed to dream different dreams, have different ideas, look at the company and his job in a different way. He wanted to make movies no one expected.

We kept in touch through my Army days and reconnected when I returned to Kodak in 1972. We first worked together in January of that year when he asked me to help script a movie that he was editing on the Florida everglades. It went well; we liked working together. Three months later we traveled together to Mobile, Alabama to make a movie on the Junior Miss pageant where we had to wear tuxedos to film near the stage during the final televised performance; Richard listed the tuxes on his expense account as a "helicopter rental" —he thought it would be more fun that way.

Before we began working together, I didn't know what I wanted to do, had no idea what I had talent to become. If at one time I thought Kodak would be a temporary job, Richard convinced me otherwise; in a very short time, I couldn't imagine working apart from him. In a world where so many enabled me to get what I've got; Richard was one of the few who helped me become who and what I am.

From the beginning, we had separate but overlapping roles; I looked after the words and he looked after the pictures—although I'd often suggest what to shoot and he knew what he wanted the words to say, sometimes only after he heard them. I was fine with that. For the *American Cowboy* movie, I wrote—and we recorded—three separate narration tracks, each of which we played against the movie. Richard liked bits and pieces of each and so that's what we sent to Tex Ritter who recorded the final narration.

Although Kodak commissioned some movies to introduce a specific product (Kodak Disc cameras), honor a sponsorship commitment (America's Junior Miss), or celebrate a certain event (Kodak's centennial), the purpose of most movies we made was to promote picture-taking. Kodak dominated the market for film, so anything that increased picture-taking raised Kodak film sales. And film was so profitable, Kodak could afford to have us make several movie series; one was called *Legacy Americana;* another, *Know the Land and the People.* In each series were four or five movies that encouraged viewers to enjoy the natural beauty and history of the mountains, the seas, Old Sturbridge Village, St. Augustine—and other places that offered plenty of opportunities to take pictures. Kodak also had a close working relationship with *National Geographic*—they shot a lot of our film—and we sometimes made movies with the same title as their best-selling books: *The Mississippi River*, or *American Cowboy*—although there was no overlap in content.

Our working process depended on several factors—including how much we knew about the subject we were tackling, or even what form the final movie would take. For example, if the movie included an on-screen narrator, we had to have a finished script before Richard began filming.

But in most cases, I'd do a bunch of research, mostly in books and periodicals, then Richard and I would talk things over and swap ideas. He usually knew at least the "kind" of sequences he wanted to include, so before I wrote a final treatment, he and I would head off on a several-day research trip to see what was available, make contacts, and select people to be included in the film when he came back with a crew.

Unfortunately, most movies we made are no longer available anywhere; the company made very few copies and those were on film that has deteriorated; the negatives were thrown out somewhere along the way. Only the two movies we produced for America's Junior Miss—*Be Yourself* in 1972 and *Sharing* in 1977—can still be viewed. They're both on YouTube.

When we travelled, Richard and I always shared a room, simply because we enjoyed being together. When I suggested that hotel clerks might think we were gay, he said, "we're not, so that's their problem."

Richard was a romantic, always in love, sometimes working things out with women over the phone from a hotel room in the middle of nowhere, while I drifted off to sleep. In 2001, he married his thirty-year life partner Pamela Nesbitt; they had nine more years together. But when I first met him, he'd been married to his first wife, Rose, and they had a daughter, Jackie, he adored. One night, I drove him home and left him in a drunken sleep on his living room floor where he awoke to find himself surrounded by lit candles Jackie had placed there. "Daddy," she said, "I thought you were dead." He always laughed about that.

"I'd love to have the highs in your life," I told him at one point, "but I'm not sure I could survive your lows." On *Sports and Competition*, he was too depressed to even go into the editing room. "Just keep it in sync," he told me as I cut it together. He revived for the final edit.

Making a movie on *The Mountains*, he and I shared a small tent above tree line in Colorado's Sangre de Christo range when a fierce lightning storm came up in the night. Our metal tent pole was the highest point for miles around. I was wet and cold in a soggy sleeping bag when I heard Richard's voice in the darkness: "the next time we see lightning," he said, "let's hold hands and see if we can get our hair to stand on end."

On a flight to shoot the *American Cowboy* movie in Jackson Hole, Wyoming, winter weather caused us to get stacked up over connecting cities while the airline served us free drinks. When we got off at our last connection—Bozeman, Montana—we were so drunk, we thought we were in Jackson Hole. We checked into a motel and were shocked to find out where we really were in the morning.

On that same trip we filmed a cattle branding where I discovered that calves do exactly what you would do if somebody tried to brand you with a hot iron; I ended up with cow plop *inside* my shoes. And when one old cowboy showed up to be photographed, he was so drunk that Richard worried Kodak might be liable if he fell off his horse.

In Colorado, Richard and I went flying in a hot air balloon with a pilot named Joe Woods. On the day Richard flew, Joe miscalculated the landing and instead of touching down gently, they hit the ground going about twenty miles an hour. Joe, who weighed about three hundred pounds, fell on Richard, who cut his elbow and dented his right kneecap. But Richard laughed it all off. "Joe," he told me, "is just a terrible pilot."

Driving with Richard along the Blue Ridge Parkway in Tennessee, I tried to exit the road too quickly, lost control into a tree and did so much damage to the rental car that we couldn't open the passenger doors. When we returned it to the airport, Richard parked the car with the smashed-in side facing away from the rental office and went inside to check in. "We had a little trouble in a grocery store parking lot," he said. "People run into cars with shopping carts all the time," the check-in kid told him, "don't worry about it." He never looked at the car.

In Florida, we filmed a professional fisherman who asked us what we wanted him to catch? He went into his freezer, thawed out an already-caught fish, threaded it back on his line and threw it in the water. With the phony—but vigorous—struggle that fisherman went through, no one could tell that fish was already dead. On another day, for a different movie, we took a small boat into the Okefenokee swamp where our guide, Johnny Wilcox, told us to "pay no attention to bumps, we're just hitting alligators in the water," but to "sit in the center of the boat, so you don't get bit by the snakes that hang down out of the trees."

One time, at the Minnesota State Fair, my job was to hold Richard into the lead car on a roller coaster. He was riding backwards, filming the people screaming in the cars behind. I did a better job than he did—because once when he was guiding Geraldo, a cameraman who was walking backwards as he was filming, Richard walked him through a sizable pile of dog poop—and into a lamppost.

Richard loved to eat and to suggest new foods. At his suggestion, I tried shoo-fly pie and funnel cakes on a trip to Pennsylvania. And if you ate too much and didn't feel well, Richard had a remedy for that, too. "If your stomach is bothering you," he advised me once, "you've got to punish it. Put some hot stuff in it. Show it who's boss."

We flew into New Mexico on a flight with Jesse Owens. We were there to film a contest where Indians climbed a greased pole to carry down a pig stuck on top. But that year, there were budget cuts; the Indians had replaced the pig with a pork chop. And Richard decided not to film.

He had such a respect for people, especially for those he considered "authentic." For the *Mississippi River* film, Richard went down to New Orleans to shoot the Preservation Hall Jazz Band. *"Music is more authentic,"* he said, *"when it's played by old guys who don't have any teeth."*

When Richard cast Lorne Greene as the central character in *Washington: The Man*, we flew to Greene's summer home to introduce him to the script. Every word he would speak would come directly from Washington's writings, and Greene was impressive with his quick understanding. "I may sound like this," he said, reading with a touch of sibilance, "because, you know, Washington has those damned false teeth, and they're hurting him, and he's talking very slowly."

He was flipping through the pages when he came to what I've always believed were the lines that made Washington the most human—and best described all he had done for his country. Greene stopped; his Hawaiian shirt rustled in the breeze. He seemed lost in thought.

And then, with a sense of exhaustion, he seemed to drag himself to his feet. He slowly hooked his reading glasses over his ears. Every movement was difficult, painful: his voice was a hoarse whisper. "Gentlemen," he said, looking from me to Richard, as if he could barely see us. "Gentlemen," he said again, "with your permission, I should like to read my thoughts to you on this occasion. For I have not only grown gray, but almost blind in the service of my country."

He took off his glasses and sat down. "So," he said matter-of-factly, "I may play it something like that." Richard and I looked at each other. We decided he'd be worth the $25,000.00 we'd be paying him for his three days of work in our movie.

Richard was at ease around well-known people because he quickly earned their respect. Through the years, he filmed the Dalai Lama and the head of the United Nations, Kofi Annan; he shot actress Glenn Close and actor Will Smith, the singer and humanitarian Bono from U2—and so many others. In Hollywood, as he prepared to film an interview with celebrated cinematographer, Owen Roizman—who shot *The Exorcist, French Connection, Tootsie* and other movies—Owen asked Richard what shooting technique he'd be using. When Richard described it, Owen said: "I've only seen that used once before and it's very effective."

Through the years, Richard and I ended up going to more than forty states together. Counting our time at Kodak and later, doing some small projects with each other, we worked with one another for about forty-five hundred days— talking, laughing, making movies, dreaming dreams, telling each other stories. Even when we each lived on a different coast, we never lost contact with one another; we always looked forward to being together—and found reasons to be; there was something magical, always, about working with your best friend.

After twenty-five years at Kodak, Richard left to point his camera into the darkness of global problems needing to be solved, to bring attention to those needing to be heard. He photographed *I'm Still Here: the truth about schizophrenia* and, with Worldwide Documentaries, two powerful movies: *A Closer Walk*, a film confronting the AIDS epidemic; and *Not My Life*, a feature-length documentary on modern day human trafficking. Before Richard passed away, he and Bob Billheimer were planning their next movie together, an environmental film that for Richard would have a prophetic title: It was to be called: *Take Me Home.*

His end was much too sudden and came way too soon. In October 2010, Pamela wrote me that Richard was very sick; I knew he'd had a nagging cough for some time but now he'd been diagnosed with cancer; x-rays and a CT scan showed a tumor in his bronchial tube and a mass on his liver and on the lymph node closest to his right lung. I was on a business trip in Florida and flew immediately to Rochester where he and I had dinner together and shared our favorite memories from our adventures long ago. When I dropped him off afterwards, I could tell he was tired, but as he unfastened his seat belt, he turned to me and said something that we had both known for more than forty years; "I love you," he said. "And I love you," I told him. We hugged and cried, and I told him that he had long been my hero. "And you," he said, "are mine." And then, for the last time, we said good night.

I was home in California two months later, on December 16, 2010, when Pamela's note came in an email:

> *He was very peaceful, Bob, when he crossed over last evening at 10:16 pm. Please know that he loved you and admired you and while we will mourn his passing all the rest of our days, we will always celebrate how lucky we were to love him—and to be loved by him.*

Six weeks later, I gave his eulogy in a packed church on a snowy Rochester day; and on the first anniversary of his passing, I sent Pamela and Jackie a binder of my favorite adventures he and shared so long ago. I titled it *You Should Have Been Here Yesterday*, and concluded it with these words:

> *In his time with us, what a gift he gave us all. For long into the future, those of us who had the great privilege to know him and to love*

*him, will be able to tell others: "If you wanted to meet someone who truly will never be forgotten . . .well, you should have been here yesterday."*

Kodak officially sent Richard and me in two different directions in the early 1980's. He eventually left the company while I moved into management where I would become Kodak's chief speechwriter, a role the company would judge to be more important than the writer of screenplays I'd been. But none of my good fortune would have happened—and I would never have shown the talent the company needed me to show—if, once upon a long time ago, I hadn't had all those adventures with Richard.

# 30

# CHIEF SPEECHWRITER FOR KODAK

AS 1981 BEGAN, I WAS THIRTY-THREE YEARS OLD and in charge of Presentations Services, Kodak's team of speechwriters and others who produced presentations for the company.

And I was still a bit in shock over it all. "Can you just imagine," I told people, "how desperate Kodak must be? They put me in management." Why do you think the company did that?" they'd ask. "I made three lucky guesses in a row," I'd say. "Kodak considers me an expert."

But an expert in what? No one ever fully explained what I was expected to do. I was in my first day on the job when I got a call from Paul, the manager of one of Kodak's markets divisions who asked: "Can Presentations Services develop themes for sales meetings?" I had no idea. "Sure!" I said, but since I'd never done that, I said, "It would be helpful if you could give me some themes you've used for previous meetings."

"Three years ago," Paul said, "we had several new products, so our theme was: *Products Make the Difference*. Two years ago, we developed programs to support them, so our theme was: *Programs Make the Difference*. And then last year, we decided to focus on our people, so we used: *People Make the Difference.*" "Based on what you're telling me," I told him, "I already have an idea for this year. How about: *Nothing Makes Any Difference?*" There was silence on the line. "No," Paul said finally, "no, that wouldn't interest us." I told him I would keep thinking.

I may not have been a typical manager, but I also didn't have a typical group. I had writers who couldn't write and hired others to do their jobs for them; I had producers who drank their lunches and seemed sleep-deprived in the afternoon; I had assistants who were sometimes off wasting everyone's time elsewhere. When Cletus, a member of our team retired, he gave a very short but insightful speech. "Working with all of you," he said, looking around the room, "has been unbelievable."

I had freelancers who set up their own permanent offices in our unused rooms, expecting secretarial support and full access to office supplies; and I had people who were moved into my department in lieu of being fired for incompetence. Only at Kodak would things like that be tolerated; only someone like me—who didn't know what he was supposed to do and hadn't been trained to do it—would try to change the situation.

George was a most interesting case. He was a kind of delivery man; he carried things between our group and others that were part of our production process. Within a short period of time, people from other departments were asking me if I could stop George from coming to visit them because he was wasting their time. When he told me he was "feeling overstressed by having too much to do," I invited him to join me in a conference room with a whiteboard on the wall. I went to the board and told him I wanted to write down everything he did during the day—and how much time it took to do it. He suggested some things and I suggested others; when he told me how time each task took, I increased the time "to allow for delays."

When he agreed we had a complete list of his daily responsibilities, it was clear to both of us that he had no more than three hours work on his busiest days. "Looking at things this way," George suggested, "I could be doing a lot more." And we gave it to him, and he did it—and somehow his stress went away.

In our group, we had some talented people also. Tom Ward and Tim Hughes were "go-to" writers who would never turn me down when I needed help; Bob Sandle and Dave Barone and Don DeBrine could make any show run reliably;

Connie Thayer and Billie Grunzinger got stuff done. And there were others. I convinced myself that I wasn't going to worry about the incompetents; they were at least fun to watch.

Neil was my immediate supervisor, and he could be very supportive, but also very demanding. When I had my first performance review, Neil rated me highly, writing I had "high potential." I told him, "If you have extra money for raises, give it to someone else. I'm well paid for doing this job."

"When you go to the grocery store," Neil said, "do they expect to be paid in money or in potential?" I always wanted to be rated higher than I was paid—to be seen by the company as offering "good value."

But since I was "in management" I was able to have my own secretary and I found a great one in Mary Moore. Mary was young and came out of the division's "secretarial pool;" she was smart, shy, seldom said much, and just sat there doing her work, and never making a mistake. She could read my scribbled writing and flawlessly retype it on her big and cumbersome manual speech typewriter before sending it to management for approval.

She and I got along great, but one time she did something that left me exas-perated. "Mary," I said, "it's a good thing you're pretty because you sure are a lot of trouble." Right after I said it, I knew I shouldn't have; she could have easily reported me for sexual harassment, but instead, she said: "You know what I think, Bob? I think you should go fuck yourself." Mary said what was on her mind and went back to work. We never discussed it again.

When Mary worked for me, a woman named Jackie worked for my boss, Neil; both women were good friends and Jackie, especially, liked to have fun with what she saw as my naivete. One year, several of us worked the company's annual meeting in Tennessee and were flying back the next day. Before we boarded, I told everyone not to be offended; I was tired and would sit by myself in the back of the plane to sleep on the trip home. When Jackie found an empty seat next to where she and Mary were sitting, she wanted me to join them. I shook my head, I wanted to sleep. But Jackie was insistent and, standing up in a crowded plane, she asked in a loud voice, "Bob, why you won't sleep with Mary and me?" And then she realized what she said . . .

Through the years, I had other secretaries, some shared with other managers, and most were good, but the quiet and very efficient Penny Sarsfield was the best until Linda Russell came along. In the beginning Linda was not happy to be working for me because she knew we were opposites. She was neat, decisive, very organized. My office was a mess; there were lots of things I just didn't worry about, I mostly wanted to be left alone to write. I had a happy marriage; she was in an unhappy one. We each needed help in different ways—and we took care of each other.

Linda helped to organize my life inside—and outside—of Kodak. Whatever I needed, she was there, and I came to trust her completely. In return, I tried to provide the support she needed to get her life together—and she did. But make no mistake: she did all the heavy lifting to turn her life around, to find things to look forward to—and people who deserved her. She just needed someone to believe in her—and I was proud to be that someone. We remain friends to this day.

Little by little I figured out that I had two jobs: on the one hand, I was managing the team—writers, producers, and others who put together company presentations; on the other, I was the chief speechwriter for the company president, Colby Chandler. Later, when he was promoted to CEO, I wrote also for his replacement, Kay Whitmore as well as for our Executive Vice President, Phil Samper. Colby, Kay and Phil comprised what Kodak called "The Office of the CEO" and they each had a very different speaking style.

Colby spoke formally, seemed quiet and easy-going, patient, and thoughtful. He didn't use contractions, would sometimes repeat phrases for emphasis, and had a strong internal rhythm to his speeches. But he was deceptively smart. "When people make presentations to Kay and me," he told me once, "after they get about ten minutes in, I ask them: 'If, at the end of your presentation, Kay and I could agree to whatever you want, what do you want?' In most cases," Colby said, "they do not know. They just want to make a presentation."

Kay was casual, sometimes seemingly indifferent, but very comfortable with himself. He liked to get to his points obliquely, to wander around a bit, and sometimes to poke fun at himself with a dry wit: "My mother was amazed to find there were also *women* named Kay," he'd say with a straight face. He had a reputation for dozing off in meetings—but waking up suddenly to ask the question that cut to the heart of the matter. I asked him about that once. "When people are giving me the information I need to make a decision, I listen," Kay said. "But most of the time, they're just talking; I have no interest in that."

Phil was incisive; he had a very sharp mind and was always the best-prepared one in the room. He liked to focus in quickly and drill down relentlessly on the issue at hand. He scared some people because he could be blunt, but I loved working with him. I was never afraid to disagree with him, but he knew what he wanted and refused to settle for less. He would never accept less than the sixth draft of any script—although I do admit that in some cases, I left out numbers three and four and went from the second version immediately to the fifth. "Very close," he would say, "but we need excellence. Let's do one more draft."

For one Board meeting, Phil needed to speak to the directors about changes at Kodak Park, the company's twenty-five-thousand employee film manufacturing complex in Rochester. He asked me to call the head of Kodak Park and get the specific information, but when I made the call, the general manager there told me that he "preferred not to give me that information—he didn't care who was really asking." When I relayed that to Phil, he said. "Oh, is that what he's decided? Perhaps I should speak with him directly." Apparently, Phil did because the next day, the general manager called me back, "singing like a bird."

In those days, Kodak had two Gulfstream corporate jets based in Rochester and I flew often on them with the senior managers on the way to make presentations. It was a great way to travel. The plane was ready to go when everyone was onboard, and it always went non-stop. We could wander freely about the plane, go up into the cockpit to talk to the pilots, get something to eat in the galley—we never had a steward or stewardess, but there was always good food or snacks—or just sit and talk.

On a flight with Kay Whitmore, I asked him about his assignment as general manager in Mexico—and how his wife, Yvonne, liked her time there. "She didn't like it at all," Kay said. "She just never got used to being robbed." Apparently, it happened often. "Yeah," I agreed, "that's tough for anyone to get used to."

When Kay became CEO, he decided to refurbish the Kodak Office lobby and he asked for suggestions. I proposed installing a merry-go-round with a sign: *If you like this ride, you will love a job at Kodak.* I'm not sure Kay understood my sense of humor

One night I flew to Toronto with Phil Samper—just to get time to talk about an upcoming presentation. He took another airline to Europe; I flew home. On another morning I flew with two Kodak senior managers to a top-secret meeting with a key customer in Texas. One of the managers, Doug, was a very large man with a voracious appetite. There were a dozen donuts in a box on board; the other manager had a donut, I had one—and Doug had the rest. But I always felt safe on that aircraft after I was talking to the pilots one day when there was a storm predicted around the Rochester airport. "Will that be a problem for us?" I asked. "Are you kidding?" he said. "This aircraft is so over-powered we could stay at forty thousand feet on one engine."

The pilots were terrific and attentive. On a night flight back from Washington, one came back to tell us, "the northern lights are very bright tonight and the sky is unusually clear. When we get up over Pittsburg, we'll shut off all the lights on the aircraft and turn the plane so you can enjoy them."

And sometimes on the plane, you could hear a lot just by listening. At the time 35mm cameras were complicated and fully aimed at the limited professional market. On the plane one day, I listened to one senior manager tell another that he had just come back from Japan: Nikon was interested in making amateur 35mm cameras under the Kodak brand. Kodak turned them down to introduce Disc photography, which was quickly a failure. Meanwhile the amateur market for 35mm photography exploded. But that may not have been Kodak's biggest error.

I was in Phil's office one day discussing a speech to introduce new Kodak film at an industry convention. With me was John Simonds who managed the Physics division of Kodak's research labs and John brought along some family pictures he wanted Phil to see. They were snapshots and John asked Phil, *if those were his pictures, would he be satisfied with the quality?* Phil said he would, but he wondered why John was asking. "Because," John told him "those were taken with a little experimental camera we developed in the labs. It's digital." "Be still my heart," Phil said. That was 1982.

Many years later, Phil told me, "I recall telling Colby and Kay that we had to develop a separate company for digital—but sadly not in Rochester due to talent pool needed. Kay accused me of being focused on destroying Rochester. Life is never fair."

With more than sixty thousand employees in the city, Kodak was critical to Rochester, but senior management never flaunted their positions. Kay told me once that when he was signing up for something in the Rochester suburb, Mendon, where he lived, he was asked his job title. "I'm the President," he said.

"Of what?" he was asked.

For six years, I wrote the company's annual meeting presentation, and it was always a challenge because I had to write it before I had access to the final sales and earnings numbers, and it was tough to find the right tone without that information. When I sent my drafts to management with the results left blank, nobody filled them in; so I tried a different tactic: I simply made up the numbers. That resulted in an immediate call from Paul Smith, our head of finance. "Where did you get that sales number?" he asked. "I made it up," told him. "Bob," he exploded, "you *cannot* make up numbers for the company. The sales were actually . . ." And he told me. "Thank you," I said.

In addition to writing for senior management, I also wrote other big shows for Kodak. In 1980, the company sent me to the Alps to research and later write a multi-image travelogue Kodak presented to camera clubs around the country. With two photographers, I flew into Munich and then traveled by small bus to five countries—Germany, Austria, Yugoslavia, Italy and Switzerland—eating so much rich food in every place, for every meal, I thought my heartburn would never end. We visited Castle Neuschwanstein, spent a cold morning in Vienna's Spanish Riding School watching the training of the famous Lipizzaner stallions and an afternoon with the Director of the Vienna Boys Choir where the choirmaster told me, "Today, the quality of young boys' voices is worse—because mothers don't have time to sing to their children."

In then-Yugoslavia, we visited a farm so far from anywhere that the old farmer said that during the 1940's, he didn't even know that World War II was going on. That's where I drank their version of moonshine called 'slivovitz' that I thought would blow my head off. To cushion his stomach, the farmer ate lard on bread. We went across the top of Italy, where I found that spaghetti and meatballs are NOT served together—and into Switzerland, where we ended up getting very drunk on scotch with the British curling team in a forest cave in a snow-storm.

Three weeks after entering Germany, we flew back home into LaGuardia airport where I was asked if I had any food to declare. I said I didn't. "Open your camera bag," the inspector said—and when I did, a loaf of dark German bread fell out. He laughed and waved me through.

Nineteen eighty was the year of the Kodak centennial, and our little group wrote dozens of presentations that were given to major customers, at industry events, and to other groups across the country. Besides those, we were writing all the presentations being delivered by company management, everywhere. For sales meetings, we were competing against outside agencies and winning jobs based on the creativity of our ideas and approaches; but at one point, I decided that too many of the ideas were coming from me; I needed to do a better job of getting input from my people.

One day Darlene, one of our writers, came to me to ask how to approach a particular script. "What I'm really interested in," I said in reply, "are *your* ideas. How would you do it?" "It's too late in the day for me to have ideas," she said. "What should I do?"

I always insisted I brought "portable ignorance" to every assignment I tackled. I asked questions and listened. Some suggested that I was setting policy for the company, but I disagreed. "I write words on paper," I said. "it's only when Colby or Kay or Phil say them that they become company policy."

One of our markets division managers was especially plain speaking. "What I want to say in my talk to our dealers," he told me, "is: we don't give a shit what you think of our new products; if you stock them, your sales will go through the roof. Now," he said, "clean that up and get it back to me. This speech is all written except for the words—and that's your job."

I wrote for a lot of different audiences but here is something I found a bit ironic: many of the speeches I wrote for Colby were intended to be delivered to his middle management team—and since I wasn't at that pay grade, I wasn't al-lowed to listen to those speeches I had written.

Later, when I'd been promoted to middle management, the company was going through some difficult times. "I think Kodak has too many middle managers," I told Jeanne, "maybe I should volunteer to step down." "Do you have your period?" she asked.

My job was to write speeches, not to make them although when a group that comprised the CEOs of the top US companies and the presidents of the major American universities had a meeting in Rochester, Colby—who was a member of that group—asked me to talk to them about communications. I decided to have some fun with my approach, to tell them something perhaps no one else would. The title of my presentation was: *How to be a Failure in Communications*—and I gave some ideas, with examples, of how they might botch communications in their organization. They reprinted my speech in full in their publication.

Those were the days before computers, and I wrote everything in pencil on legal pads. I needed quiet to be able to write so I'd go by myself into a conference room without windows with just a pad or two of paper, some sharpened pencils, research materials—including any tapes—and a wristwatch. I'd divide the speech into sections—an annual meeting always had four parts—and set a time to finish writing each part. Then, I'd draw a line down the middle of each page because I found that one half of a page, in my writing, equaled one minute of speaking. I wrote on the right side only—on the left side, I made visual notes. I liked to change slides six times a minute.

Every few hours, I'd bring out a few pages to be typed. I have no idea how many speeches I wrote in the eight years I had that job—sometimes there was more than one short one per day—but I do know that despite never having had any training in writing speeches, I seemed to have a natural talent for them, and got lots of satisfaction out of writing them. I've kept only one or two I've written.

Every year in January, I wrote the speeches for the dinner Kodak sponsored for the Football Coaches Association—to thank them for all the Kodak film they used shooting their games. One year, the dinner was in Houston and Kodak hired Bob Newhart as the talent. I went in the limo to pick him up from the airport—which was a long way from the hotel—and when he arrived with his manager, his manager jumped in the front seat. "Why don't you and Bob sit in back and get acquainted," he said. Since we got stuck in traffic, Bob and I had a several-hour conversation about a myriad of subjects. He was a bright and inquisitive guy, interested in everything—and very different from the often-befuddled character roles he played.

He adapted his material to his audience, but before going on stage, he asked how long we wanted his routine to be. The dinner organizers suggested twenty minutes. Just for fun, I timed him; he ran twenty-three seconds over.

While I was writing speeches and running the presentations group, I picked up responsibility to manage the company's motion picture and video teams; we were among the first companies to install video monitors in the hallways throughout our buildings. To keep employees informed, our video group produced a weekly broadcast of company news hosted by my first secretary, Mary Moore.

Even as I took on more responsibility, Kodak decided that I wouldn't be in my job forever and they needed someone to replace me. I agreed that no one on staff was qualified, so we looked elsewhere. We were turned down by one candidate whose wife believed "the cost of living is too high in Rochester"—before we found Mike Benard who had the talent, experience, and confidence to deal with senior management.

In his first days on the job, I took Mike to meet Dick, Phil Samper's assistant—and asked him to give Mike "his perspective on Kodak today." Although I usually took notes during any discussion, Mike just sat there with a slightly amused look on his face. Finally, after about twenty minutes, Dick asked Mike if he understood what he was saying. "I don't know," Mike said, "so far, all I've heard from you are buzzwords and bullshit."

I was moving on, but just as a "first" anything, my first job in management would always leave an imprint on me not only because of what I'd been able to do, but because of two senior managers who provided so much enthusiastic support during that time. As President and then CEO, Colby Chandler gave me ready access to him—and his full attention when we were together. And Dave Metz, the company's senior vice president for Communications and Public Affairs was also a writer at heart and he gave me the full benefit of his wisdom and counsel. I need to talk more about each of them.

# 31

# WORKING FOR DAVE METZ

WRITING IS THINKING," THE AUTHOR-HISTORIAN David McCullough once said. "To write well is to think clearly." Dave Metz demonstrated that daily; he thought decisively, he wrote succinctly, he enabled and insisted Kodak speak with one voice to all constituents they served. He led a 625-member communications and public affairs team at a time when Kodak was a multi-billion-dollar company, when a "Kodak Moment" signified one of the most meaningful events in someone's life, when Kodak was an enviable company with a brand known, respected, and trusted worldwide.

During my formative years at Kodak, I was fortunate to work for him, privileged to come under his mentorship, and to have benefitted from his guidance. I was one of many for whom he opened doors and provided opportunities we never could have found or earned on our own. But he was always both demanding and supportive: he made it clear: good wasn't acceptable; he expected our best—but he'd be fully engaged to help us achieve that along the way.

"Gibbons," Dave told me once, "you're unmanageable. When I tell you how

I want something done, the only thing I know for sure is that you won't do it that way. But when I see that gleam in your eyes, I know you have a better way in mind." He motivated his people by trusting their instincts and relying on their talent. I liked that.

He made my writing sharper, my sentences shorter; he was an impatient man who wanted me to get to the point sooner, more succinctly; he crossed out hazy ideas and connected smarter ones. He turned bad suggestions into teaching moments. I brought him, once, an idea I was sure would be effective. He said: "let's think about this together—from the perspective of our shareholders and employees, from the point of view of management and our suppliers, communities and customers." And he pulled up a chair. By the end of that "thinking," my idea had morphed into something very different, something that could work for everyone.

He was a large and imposing man and I told him once that I thought people were afraid of him. "Good," he said, "I want some people to be." Maybe, but he could be very empathetic. When Kodak was downsizing, there was a woman slated to be let go whose situation I thought he should know about. She was a young mother in an abusive marriage and with no other support. Dave found a way to keep her on the payroll.

He loved his company, his profession, and his Notre Dame. We were both proud graduates, but a Fighting Irish football loss could color his mood for a week while he couldn't understand my lack of interest in the team. He'd often come in on a Friday morning dressed in Irish plaid and heading to a game in South Bend. One week, he asked me if I'd be interested in attending the USC game. "I don't know," I told him, "who is USC playing?" In addition to being unmanageable, that day he found me "hopeless."

When Dave retired, I asked Father Monk Malloy, Notre Dame's president if I might do a video interview with him about Dave. I was prepared to explain Dave's connection to the university when Monk cut me off. "I know Dave Metz," he said, and the interview began.

Long after everyone else was writing with a computer, Dave would sit at his manual typewriter at a small roll-up metal table in the corner of his office facing the wall, smoking, thinking, crossing out, typing over, writing words for others to speak and to send, crafting messages and policies to drive the Kodak brand forward. He loved to write and seemed to take every opportunity to do so.

One day I found him modifying quotes from George Eastman—who had been dead for more than fifty years; I shouldn't have been surprised. Eastman's original words were most likely written by Louis B. Jones, Kodak's legendary copywriter. Dave was simply carrying on his legacy, making the older work stronger, sharper, and more relevant. "Someday," he told me, "when you get a little better, I'll let you write for Mr. Eastman, too," he said. At one point, I did.

I learned so much from Dave, just by our regular interaction. "I was never very good at the formal stuff," he told me once. "I suppose that's because I felt my daily-weekly-monthly interaction was frequent enough—maybe fervent enough—to provide clear signals and good guidance." One year, as was required, he said he'd written a formal appraisal of my performance—but could no longer find it and wasn't sure it was necessary. "You know what I think of your work," he said. I did.

When he retired on August 3, 1993, I wrote him a long letter telling him it was an honor and a privilege to have worked with and for him; I thanked him for the great difference he made in his profession, in our company, and in my life. "Someday," he wrote back, "my children will see your letter—and their children also." He said my thoughts touched him deeply. "He was always very proud of you," his wife told me at his funeral.

His guidance continued after he left Kodak; he wanted me, at some point, to return to Rochester and teach writing at Nazareth College where he was a member of the Board—and he set up an interview. He also brought the Board of the George Eastman House to Los Angeles—and asked me to give them an introduction to digital motion pictures. And every time he visited California, we tried to have dinner together. On his last visit, one of his friends suggested a restaurant and Dave and his wife, Jeanne and I went there. "I'll pay for dinner," Dave offered—until he looked at the menu. "Holy God," he said when he saw the prices; we split the bill.

"Do I miss Kodak?" Dave wrote after I also retired, "of course. I miss the people; they were the best. I miss being on the bridge, in the middle of the important action. I delivered newspapers at ten and at twelve worked as a stock boy in a grocery store. I retired fifty years later. It's not the right thing for everybody, but it was the right thing for me."

His being at Kodak was also the "fortunate thing" for me and for so many whose lives and careers he touched and who benefited from his probing questions and perceptive counsel, his challenges and his coaching, his support and nurturing and friendship.

David J. Metz, a boss who became a mentor and then a friend, passed away on August 28, 2019. When I went to his funeral, I spent time talking to Colby Chandler, the former CEO for whom we both worked. Colby told me, "Dave was in the Navy, and I was in the Marines. We didn't have our own boats, so we depended on the Navy for transportation. I came to thank him again for helping us get where we needed to go." He could have been talking about Dave's career in the military—or at Kodak.

But Dave's funeral was the last time I saw Colby Chandler; nineteen months later, Colby too would be gone.

# 32

# WRITING FOR COLBY

HE FIRST QUESTION COLBY CHANDLER ASKED ME WAS: "How would you graph a speech?" He was the President of Kodak, a ten-billion-dollar company; I had just become the new Coordinator of Presentation Services and discovered that I was responsible for writing his speeches. When I went to his office for the first time, he took out a piece of graph paper and asked that question. It was probably logical for him; he was trained as an engineer. I was a liberal arts major and had never been trained to write speeches or anything else. I had no idea of the answer.

"I think of a speech as a kind of relay team," I told him. "The strongest point goes first, to catch everyone's attention. The next best point goes last, to finish strong, to stick in people's minds. The other two points go in the middle—and there are only four because most people can't remember many more." Colby put the graph paper away. "I believe that will work," he said. And that's essentially the process I used to write virtually every major speech he gave during the next six years he served first as Kodak's president and then as the company's CEO. To write for him was a central honor and privilege of my Kodak career.

He had a sense of rhythm to his speaking that was so strong, I knew when I had the words right before I gave him the copy. He would strengthen the cadence by underlining words, drawing arrows and boxes and other graphics on every page. They reminded him—he said—of how he wanted to read different lines, how he wanted to connect adjacent words, where he wanted to put his emphasis. He even sometimes recorded his speech and listened to it as he drove back and forth to the office in his truck from his farm in Mendon. Preparation was important to him. "When you bring me the final copy," he often said, "bring me a list of questions that might be raised, including some I would not want to answer." He wanted to be ready for anything.

When he became Kodak's CEO, he was also on the Board of the Digital Equipment Corporation. DEC was making a series of commercials featuring well-respected leaders in business and in sports having an "on-camera dialog" about leadership. Colby was to be paired with John Thompson, then head basketball coach at Georgetown University. I wrote Colby's part of the dialog and was with him on the shoot in New York City, where they photographed him speaking against a plain background. There had to be at least twenty assistants on the set. "There were a lot of people involved," Colby observed to me later. "Did they all had something to do?"

In those days, Kodak was known for its classic TV commercials—*Turn Around, Green Green Grass of Home,* and others—and I'd inserted one into a speech he was rehearsing prior to a presentation. But I didn't tell him which one, so when he got to that part in the script, he simply looked at the screen. I'd chosen *American Family* about a small Korean girl who thanks her adopted parents in her valedictory speech, as pictures of her life play in the foreground. When the commercial finished, I waited as Colby took off his glasses and wiped his eyes—and I saw he'd been crying. "I always liked that one," he said.

He brought a sharp intellect balanced with common sense to all his observations. "No matter how many times we ask focus groups," he told me once, "they tell us they want their cameras black. Too often people define what they want by what they think is possible." Another time, on another subject, he advised, "You don't have to tell an audience everything *you* know about the subject, you just have to tell them everything *they* need to know." And a third example: "when a company looks to eliminate what makes them unprofitable," he said, "they need to be careful to retain what makes them unique." That's one reason why Kodak kept pictures on company business cards, despite the added expense.

He was a gentleman's gentleman, both decisive and humble. On the company plane, he would announce: "My rule is the senior man serves everyone else. What can I get for you?" When he was President and Walt Fallon was CEO, outside observers would have seen Walt as the bad cop and Colby as the good one. Those who worked closely with both said it was Colby who made—and carried out—some of the more difficult decisions.

Still, Colby maintained a posture of humility. In 1980, the year of the Kodak Centennial, both he and Walt were often out making celebratory presentations around the country. One of our projectionists, Dave Barone, noticed they'd each be giving the same presentation to different groups in the same city, a few nights apart. "Was there any way," Dave asked Colby, "that the two groups could get together—and then Walt could do half the presentation and you could do the other half?" "I don't know," Colby told Dave, "but if they could, Walt could deliver the whole presentation—and I could stand there and nod my head."

He had a dry wit. He told me once about the annual Kodak marketing meetings that he and Walt Fallon used to attend together. "Our marketing managers always wore camel hair blazers," Colby said, "but one year, Walt also showed up wearing one. When it was my turn to speak, I said, 'I am not surprised seeing all of you in your blazers, but I am surprised seeing Walt in one. I did not know Sears carried them.'"

At that time, we had two very small children and one day, when Colby and I were talking about family, I told him that I liked to rock our kids at night and tell them all the good things they'd done that day. "I want them to go to bed feeling good about themselves," I said. "Would you ever," Colby asked, "be available to come over and rock me?"

He was helpful to me personally. When I was working on my master's thesis, my subject was advertising and I wanted to interview the senior ad manager at P&G—then world's largest advertiser with eighty brands—but they had turned me down. When Colby asked me about my progress, I mentioned that to him. "They said they don't participate in student projects," I told him. "Perhaps if I call John Smale (then CEO of P&G), they might," Colby suggested. He called—and they did. "Who did I want to see," they asked me, "and when?" They'd be available.

As Colby neared retirement, in one of the last times I was up in his office, I asked him how he was able to move from the depths of Kodak Park to become the CEO of a hugely successful company. "Whenever I was offered a new job, I never considered what I would be doing," he said, "I always considered whom I would be working with—because when you work with good people, you can do anything." That was "so Colby"—to pass the credit on to others.

We reconnected after we had both been retired, in the fall of 2018, when he invited me to share a long lunch with him in Rochester. The first thing he said to me when we met after about thirty years was: "I owe you a very belated thank you for all you did for me during my Kodak career." I told him, "you have that exactly backwards." But what I remember most from that lunch are the tips he gave me—*if I ever had to judge cows at a state fair*. He had done that in his home state of Maine and remembered the experience in detail and with great enthusiasm. He was ninety years old and still a country boy at heart.

"If you asked others about me," he once said, "they may tell you a lot of different things. But one thing I hope they will not say is: *Colby did not understand how good I wanted to be*." I suspect I wasn't the only one Colby helped *"to become as good as they wanted to be"* along the way. I was a raw kid who didn't even know how to graph a speech; he was the CEO who always gave me his full attention; when I was with him, I never felt that he had more important people to talk to, more important decisions to make. Physicist Sir Isaac Newton once wrote, "If I have seen further, it is by standing on the shoulders of giants." I felt that way writing for Colby.

Colby Hackett Chandler had died in Rochester, New York, on March 4, 2021. He was 95 and had been in hospice care. His wife of 72 years, Jean, passed away nineteen days later. After a very brief time apart, their enduring love story continues. "He is still a mystery to me," she wrote to me back in 1997, in response to a letter I had written to him. She now has eternity to "figure him out."

When the *Wall Street Journal* called the Chandler family for input into their obituary, the Chandlers sent the reporter to me. Although I had a long conversation with him, it was clear—even during our discussion—that he had decided on his approach, and that my efforts to convince him to emphasize Colby's humanity, humility, and sense of humor wouldn't change his mind. I was disappointed with what the *Journal* wrote.

Colby was unique, and I wanted others to see the man and the leader I knew. He had meant so much to me in so many ways; but from the first, being his speechwriter meant I'd be paid at the level where Jeanne and I could afford to buy our first house.

# 33

# A SUNDAY MORNING BIKE RIDE

FROM ROCHESTER TO JUNCTION CITY TO FAYETTEVILLE back to Rochester—in our first five years of marriage, we lived in eight different places; now that we were starting our family, we were looking to buy a place of our own.

We had a realtor, Gene Cassatta, who took us out "looking" every weekend, but we hadn't found anything we both liked—and could afford. Interest rates were high—well into the double digits then—and Jeanne and I tended to be conservative; we didn't want to buy something we couldn't handle. I had made charts where we could determine our monthly payments by aligning house prices, taxes, and loan rates to determine what was in our range; we were afraid to look at anything outside of that. Gene was on the same page. "Don't buy a house you can't afford," he told us, "because every day, when you have to make other compromises in your life, you'll resent that house." Everything considered, we needed to be looking at houses "in the high $20,000s—or low $30,000s" —less than the cost of many new cars today.

But then one Sunday morning in September 1974, I was out for a bicycle ride in West Irondequoit, a northern suburb of Rochester, a neighborhood of small homes on tree shaded streets. Jeanne's parents lived close-by and although her mom had made it clear she had no interest in being a full-time baby-sitter, we thought we'd like living closer to them. And there, on the lawn of a small white colonial at 95 Wyndale Road was a For Sale sign. I called our realtor. It looked about the right size for us—it would turn out to be about 1536 square feet—in good shape, and was priced at $34,900, at the very upper end of our price range, but taxes were reasonable; maybe we could stretch into it. The house had been sold, but the deal fell through, and it just went back on the market. "Could we see it?" I asked.

We could—and that day, carrying our five-month-old Jennifer and inviting Jeanne's dad and mom to join us because we had never bought a house and didn't know what to look for, we went through that little house with white aluminum siding and fell in love with it.

It was owned by Ed and Vera Doyle, who had raised their family there. Their girls had grown and moved away and now Ed had been transferred to a job five miles farther from West Irondequoit and wanted to be closer to work. We offered them $33,000 and because we had no contingency of a house to sell, they accepted. But when I went to Eastman Savings and Loan, the bank that served Kodak people, the loan officer said: "This is a sizeable amount for a person earning your salary." I agreed, but I was a bit cocky and confident. "I'm a pretty smart guy," I told her, "so I expect to be making a lot more in the future."

With help from my brother and friends—and a borrowed truck—we moved in on a cold December day. As Jeanne watched from the kitchen window, someone dropped her washing machine off the back of the truck into our driveway. A few months later, we replaced it with a Maytag that lasted for the next forty years.

Our neighbors, the Jordans, who were the original owners of their house next door, told us the story of ours. Back in the late 1930's, an old German carpenter bought three lots on Wyndale Road—theirs, ours, and one across the street. After he built each house, he sat in a chair on the lawn until the house was sold; when it was, he took the money he made and built another one. When he finished all three, he left the area.

That carpenter built a sturdy house, but he built it to his specifications; nothing was standard and so when Jeanne wanted to have a built-in dishwasher, all the counters had to be replaced; they were too high and not deep enough. Some rooms—the kitchen, dining room, and den off the back, even one of the three bedrooms upstairs—were small, but the living room and two bedrooms, including ours, were good sized. There was only one bathroom—but that was typical of homes back then. On the front of the house, we had a porch with floor to ceiling screens that was a peaceful and quiet place to sit on the long summer evenings. There were no streetlights on Wyndale Road and so after dark, there was lots of privacy out there.

The house needed some work—in one place, the carpet in the dining room had been torn and worn through—but we only had money to do a little at a time. Over the eleven years we lived there, Jeanne's dad helped us with paint and some wallpaper; my friend Charlie Myers installed carpet remnants in the upstairs bedrooms; we hired a carpenter named Matt Sims to put plywood flooring in our small attic so we could use it for storage. We did some remodeling in the kitchen, but our big expense was air conditioning; when we found the duct work was already in place, we had central air installed and we've never been without it since.

Down in our basement, a big tank held the oil that heated the house in winter. There was a small fruit cellar down there also and, for times when I needed a quiet place to write, I set up a desk below the stairs. Eventually we put in a bathroom and shower in the basement, also.

I was often down there writing in the evening. I was taking every writing assignment I could get at Kodak—I was trying to get better at my craft—as well as other freelance work to try to bring in some extra money we needed. But I was writing everything on paper with pencils. Those were the days of electric typewriters and I needed one for home, but we couldn't afford it.

At work, I asked my boss, Sam, if I could borrow one from Kodak. "No," he said, "I'm not authorized to provide you a typewriter for your home." Obviously, I'd asked the wrong question, so that day when I finished work, I unplugged my

typewriter, wrapped the cord around it, and caried it out the door. The guard—
Kodak had guards at the door checking people in and out in those days—just
nodded. "Have a good evening," he said. The next day, I told Sam: "I have a
different problem: I have a typewriter for my home, but I don't have one for my
office." "That," he said, "I can authorize," and one was quickly delivered.

The driveway on Wyndale led to our detached, single-car garage. The garage
was narrow, tough to drive into and out of. One day, I was sitting in the den
when Jeanne drove the car out of the garage and misjudged her clearance on one
side. She ended up ripping off the molding that served as a guide for the garage
door—and it came off so loudly that she knew I could hear it, even with the
doors and windows closed. So, she stopped the car and came in. "I won't need
anyone asking any stupid questions," she said. I didn't.

It was the right house for us—and in a great walking neighborhood. We had
one child, Jennifer, when we moved in; Tim came along seven months later, and
Emily was born four years after. At night, with some combination of bicycles
and strollers, we'd wander up to the library, or to Cooper Del, or even across
Hudson and Titus Avenues to Baskin Robbins for an ice cream cone. On Memorial Day and the Fourth of July, there'd be parades along Titus Avenue; we'd
walk up and set up lawn chairs and always be joined by Jeanne's mom and dad;
there were fireworks on those nights. Jeanne's sister Kathy and her family lived
just a bit north of us where our kids would often be over swimming in their pool
on hot summer days.

It was a small friendly place to live but its best feature was our neighbors.
They were all considerably older than us when we moved in.

The house across the street was owned by Bob Kelly, a man in his 80s who
one day went up on a ladder to trim a limb on a very large tree in his front yard.
Unfortunately, he had propped the ladder against the limb he was cutting—so
down came the limb, down came the ladder, down came Bob Kelly—and along
came the ambulance. Bob never got around very well after that.

On the east side of us lived George and Bernie Thibault; he apparently had
been a heavy smoker because in all the time we knew him, he carried an oxygen
tank. When we decided to fence in our yard, we hesitated to tell the Thibaults

because we knew they loved having our young kids run all over theirs. They passed away a few years after we moved in—George first and a few years later, Bernie. When we went to the funeral home and I stepped up to George's open casket to pay my respects, our other neighbor, Eddie Jordan, joined me. "Look at him," Eddie said; "he looks like hell."

Eddie and Clara Jordan lived in the white house to the west of us; they had a massive pine tree in their front yard and every night when I pulled in the driveway, I paused—and left all my work problems in that tree. I didn't think our young family should have to deal with them. I'd pick them up again in the morning if the wind during the night hadn't blown them away.

Although the Jordans never had children of their own, they were like a third set of grandparents for ours. After Clara finished planting her marigolds that first spring, Jeanne turned her back on our young Jennifer for a few minutes—and Jenny picked the flower off most of the stems. "Oh," Clara said when Jeanne tried to apologize, "she loves my flowers. She can come over and pick them anytime." As the kids got a bit older, Clara and Eddie would invite them in for a glass of Tang and some Jiffy Pop or hoist them up in their back yard lawn chairs to join them in the sun.

Eddie had been in World War II and apparently, he talked about that with our very young Tim, who asked: "Dad, did you know that Mr. Jordan was in the war?" I said that I didn't know that. "He was," Tim said, "and I think his team won." He paused, thinking, considering, wanting to be sure. "No," he corrected himself, "I think it was a tie."

Eddie, who had come from a very different generation, told me one day: "I have never seen a father pay so much attention to his children." I told him that I believed a dad who doesn't pay attention to his children when they're young has no right to expect them to pay attention to him when they're older. And besides, I said, paying attention to our kids was one of my favorite things to do.

Every year, for their birthday, the Jordans gave our kids coins—quarters and fifty-cent pieces; for Christmas, they gave them small ornaments that we still hang on our tree.

Although Clara and Eddie always seemed to be upbeat, she had multiple medical problems and, in April of 1983, when she was seventy-four years old, Clara passed away. At some point afterwards, Eddie brought over the engagement ring he had given her so many years ago; it was a man-made emerald and he wanted Jennifer to have it—in case anything happened to him. And unfortunately, he seemed to go quickly downhill from there. He started drinking heavily and seldom came out of the house. We'd see him through the window that faced our driveway; he'd be just sitting there, with a bottle by his side. But then, when we returned from that summer's vacation, we found he'd sobered up. "When I saw you pull out of the driveway with your family," Eddie said when he caught me outside a day later, "I thought that if I kept drinking the way I was, it would be the last time I would ever see all of you. And I didn't want that." I told him that we didn't want that, either.

Nevertheless, the damage had been done. Eddie died in April 1984, almost exactly—to the week—one year after Clara. He was seventy-seven years old and was buried next to his wife. In their will, Eddie and Clara left a little money for each of the kids—and his family invited me to go into their home and take anything I wanted to remind me of those wonderful people. I took a book of O. Henry stories because the warmth of those stories reminded me of the warmth of Eddie and Clara. And then, when Jennifer reached the age where she would be confirmed—and could add a Confirmation name to Jennifer Marie—she added Jordan to remind her always of the times she spent with them.

The Cummings, the family that replaced the Jordans, were very different; they were much younger with two very young children and a cat named Pickles. One night, for some unknown reason, Pickles somehow crawled up under the hood of our car; it was impossible to see her, but she was apparently there when Jeanne turned on the ignition—because the fan blade hit Pickles, and the bloody cat fell out from under the engine.

Jeanne screamed and we got the cat to the vet, but Pickles had to be put down. That night, we heard the Cummings wake up their two very young children and take them out back to bury Pickles. When their daughter asked what happened, her mother told her, "Jeanne killed your cat." A few weeks later, as we were getting ready for a picnic, Jeanne asked me to go in the basement and check what we had in the fruit cellar. "We have plenty of mustard and ketchup," I told her, "but the pickles are all gone." She did not think that was funny.

We loved our home—and even hired an architect to show us how to enlarge it—but we figured we'd never get our money back from a major addition; plus, with neighbors like the Cummings, our days there were numbered. In August of 1985, not quite eleven years after we first moved in, we sold it for $79,000.00— more than twice what we paid for it. But I would try to honor it forever by making it my email address: wyndaleroad@gmail.com. It was my favorite real address, why not make it my virtual one?

But we were moving on from this magical place we would always associate with so many good memories of our children's childhood. Jennifer, Tim, and Emily were growing up.

# 34

# AND ALONG CAME THE KIDS

O N AUGUST 21, 1973, JEANNE'S TWENTY-SIXTH BIRTHDAY, we found out she was pregnant. We knew we always wanted kids. At my graduation, a month before we were married, we bought a pair of tiny Notre Dame booties for a child we might someday have. Would we have more than one? How many? When? That never came up.

It turned out that we had the perfect number for us; we are incredibly proud of who they are and what they've accomplished, how they lead their lives. We told them years ago: "Always remember, you are not just *any* kids, you're *our* kids. That doesn't make you better than anyone else, but it does mean you'll always have our love and support. We'll always believe in you and always be there for you."

At the rehearsal party before Jennifer's wedding, she talked about that. "Whenever one of us had a game or a show or anything else, we'd look up in the third row and there would be Mom and Dad cheering us on." Of course. If it was important to them, it was important to us. It still is.

After we were married, it took nearly five years for Jennifer to arrive. Although we originally planned to wait until my military service was over, Jeanne stopped birth control pills long before that. One reason—as she told me later—was that she figured if I were sent to Vietnam and killed, she wanted "to have something of me left." But getting pregnant wasn't easy. Her doctor suggested it may have been because she had a tipped uterus, or maybe not. But after we returned from the army, Jeanne had gone back to work as a clerk in Kodak Park Medical, working for a no-nonsense boss. Since we only had one car—and I worked at Kodak Office—she often took the bus to work and one day, in a huge snowstorm, busses were delayed, and she arrived ten minutes late to work. Her boss docked her a full hour. "Late busses are your problem," her boss told her, "not Kodak's."

But right about at holiday time, Jeanne started having false contractions and the baby was too small to be born. Her doctor's recommendation: drink one ounce of alcohol every three hours; it worked. The contractions stopped: "That's good," Jeanne said. "I'm attached to this little guy; I don't want to lose him." We didn't know the baby's sex; we thought she was having a boy.

As we got closer to her due date in mid-March, I wasn't sure I wanted to be in the delivery room. "You were so anxious to be at the conception," she said, "I want you at the delivery." We went to childbirth preparation classes and on the night of April 2, the contractions began; we had decided we would tell no one when Jeanne went in to deliver because we thought it would put added pressure on her. But by five o'clock the next morning when I called her doctor with the exact time of every contraction during the night, he told us to come to the hospital. I grabbed my camera, and we went.

Jeanne's obstetrician, Dr. Cegelski, was an amateur photographer himself and so rather than have me stand at her head as her coach, he let me lay down on the floor under the delivery table as her photographer. As he delivered Jennifer, I got very close-up pictures of her birth. We were thrilled that we were wrong—she was a little girl—and after debating about calling her Jennifer Lynn, we named her Jennifer Marie. She was born on my twenty-seventh birthday; she was the best present ever.

We took it as a good sign that there were other coincidences: I'm six feet two inches, she was born six pounds two ounces; and because she was born when I was twenty-seven, one other fact would always be true: beginning with her first year, the sum of the numbers in our ages will always be equal. As it turned out, the sum of the digits in the years she and I graduated from grammar school, high school and college were also equal. Yeah, I know, esoteric stuff, but kind of neat.

Jennifer was a very small baby, "colicky," who cried a lot and liked to be carried and cuddled before she would settle down. She was known to scream steadily on long car trips; I carried her around our apartment on Clay Avenue endlessly singing "Daddy's Little Girl." We were so proud of her. When my mother took her out the first time in her buggy, a neighborhood woman looked in the carriage and said: "Oh, what a beautiful boy." "A boy?" my mother asked. "What are you—a moron?"

But we did have a boy less than fifteen months later; Dr. Cegelski suggested that if we wanted more children, we try to have them before Jeanne's uterus "tipped back." She may have gotten pregnant with Tim when we left Jennifer with Jeanne's parents and went to Rhode Island for my roommate Peter's wedding. When we had just one child, Jeanne was thinking of going back to work; now that we'd be having our second, we decided she'd be a full-time mom. It would prove to be a great decision; she was awesome at it.

On June 30, after a few months of Jeanne being on partial bed rest, Timothy Robert joined our family. At first, to get attention, Jennifer began "playing with her poop" —smearing it all over everything; to clean and disinfect her crib, we went through countless bottles of Lysol—but things soon settled down and the kids began getting along well. We called Tim, "the new guy on the block" and for a while, Jennifer thought his name was Guy.

At some point, during his first year, Tim developed a lump in his eyelid. It was a dermoid cyst, benign, but it would have to be removed when he was old enough to undergo general anesthesia—and so, in the summer of 1976, Tim went in for surgery and everything turned out well. We were concerned that he was slow to talk in understandable words until his pediatrician explained: "Watch Jennifer when Tim makes any sound. She understands what he wants—and gets it for him. He doesn't need to learn to talk; he's got his sister."

Meanwhile, Jennifer was prone to lots of ear infections, some of which we never knew about because she had a high tolerance for pain; but with two kids, it seemed like whenever we made plans to go out with another couple, we had to cancel at the last minute because one of the kids was sick. At the pediatrician's, we were on a "payment plan." Still, we thought we'd like to have one more child and early in 1979, we found that Jeanne was pregnant again. By this time, we had decided that, with our two-syllable last name, we'd continue our tradition of a three-syllable first name and so, if our next was going to be a girl, we decided early on to name her Emily Michelle.

Emily was born on September 1, 1979, a few days before Jennifer was to start her first day of kindergarten, so we left her with Jeanne's parents where, the day before school was to begin, Jennifer cut her own hair. It wasn't ideal . . . but neither was Emily's delivery. Dr. Cegelski was out of town, and his partner had neither the skill, nor the experience. Plus, since it was Labor Day weekend, the hospital was overcrowded so Jeanne delivered in a labor room, on her side, and I had to help hold her leg. Unlike Jennifer and Tim's birth, I couldn't take pictures. As a third child, she has fewer pictures in our photo albums, but from her very first days, her young life is well documented. She was our little "Scooter."

A year or so after Emily's birth, a colleague at Kodak was working on a Kodak book called "Picturing the Times of Your Life" and when I showed him some pictures I had taken of Jennifer's first few years, he asked me to write a chapter around them. He added another chapter using pictures I took of Tim's first hair-cut—and then I gave our original Instamatic camera to Jennifer to take her own pictures of Santa; those were in the book, also.

With three kids, our family was wonderfully complete—and active. When she was very young, Jennifer went to ballet class on Saturday mornings, sometimes with mixed feelings. It wasn't unusual for me to tell the instructor, "Jennifer does-n't think she wants to dance today." And some days, she didn't. But as she got older, she joined the local cheerleading squad and by the time Emily was ready to join, Jennifer was a coach. On Saturday mornings, the kids bowled at Maiden Lanes. Tim took guitar lessons for a time and played soccer; Emily also played soccer, and every year they all marched in their uniforms in the Irondequoit

Fourth of July parade.

The kids all went to St. Margaret Mary's grammar school in Irondequoit where Tim was on his sixth-grade basketball team, but they were a small school and let everyone play. When we moved to Greece and he went to seventh grade at the much larger Mother of Sorrows, he went out for the team—and was devasted when he was cut. I told him what the coach had told the parents: "I'm not here to teach your son to play basketball; I'm here to win games." I suggested to Tim that he didn't have the skills to play under those conditions. He disagreed. "Next year," he told me, "I'm not only going to make the team, I'm going to be one of the starting five. I'm going to start practicing now."

We had a basketball backboard in our driveway, which was then covered with snow. Tim went out, shoveled off the snow, and began shooting. He practiced—sometimes by himself, sometimes with others—every night and every day, until the tryouts the following year. That year, he was one of the starting guards on the Mother of Sorrows team and, the following year, when he went to Aquinas high school, he was team captain. He later played for the junior varsity and varsity teams. I went to every game, and I sometimes disagreed with the referees. At one game, I apparently disagreed too loudly, because the ref blew his whistle and came over to talk to me. "Before you say anything," I told him, "I think you're calling a good game. But with my help, I think you could call a perfect one." If he wasn't laughing so hard, he might have thrown me out.

Jennifer went from Mother of Sorrows to Cardinal Mooney, a school that closed after her first year; she ended up at Aquinas where, she got involved in something called "winter guard." It was a combination of marching, music, and dance and although their instructor, Mr. Monicelli, was a bit of a psychotic, he put together a terrific program. In Jennifer's senior year, the Aquinas Winter Guard went undefeated in multiple competitions. We traveled around to sometimes distant schools—often on very snowy Saturday nights—and saw some very entertaining shows. Jennifer also joined the Aquinas Color Guard that made a bus trip to Florida to march in a Disney parade. It solidified her love of all things Disney and she worked in Disneyland one summer before we moved to California.

Before the kids were old enough to have summer jobs, we usually spent a two-week vacation at a rented summer cottage on the finger lakes in New York State. We often went with Jeanne's sister Kathy and her family, and with Jeanne's brother Allen and his. All our kids were roughly the same age—Kathy and Dick had four girls, Allen and Marie had three boys—and the kids spent endless hours fishing, using hot dogs for bait and catching dozens of very small fish—or maybe the same fish dozens of times—and always throwing them back.

When our kids got older, we often took a family vacation at Easter time— sometimes to Disney World and other theme parks in Florida; sometimes to historical sites—Mt. Vernon, Gettysburg, Washington—where I'd been filming with Richard Young and wanted to show my family; and sometimes—after Emily discovered a love of roller coasters—to parks that had the highest or scariest ones. Jeanne's mom once said that we were being unfair to our kids, showing them places they could never hope to see again. I think we were giving them a love of adventure that continues to this day.

In 1994, when Kodak offered us the opportunity to move to California, I asked Jeanne's opinion and Emily's before accepting the offer. Jeanne was fine with the move; Emily said, "when I went to high school, I had to make a whole new group of friends; I think I can do that again."

And she did, at LaReina, a terrific all-girl's school in Thousand Oaks, where she quickly decided, "the most popular kids are the nicest kids" and she was determined to fit right in. Being tall, she decided to go out for the basketball team. She knew nothing about the game and was cut after a few practices, but she took it philosophically. "Most of the kids on the team have played before, so they're probably as good as they'll get. Since I've never played, I could get a lot better." Apparently, the coach didn't recognize that potential.

But Emily had some great teachers, including a wonderfully influential English teacher named Betsy Potts, who assigned a three-page paper every week. Emily loved to write, but soon ran out of approaches to take; when she asked me for ideas, I offered her a reading list of authors who wrote in very different styles. What she learned from reading Paul Harvey and Kurt Vonnegut, among others, she uses to this day. And she always spoke her mind. When she showed up late for a meeting of the yearbook staff, the teacher berated her. "Mrs. Coe," Emily said, "I can't change the past. Would you like to talk about the future?"

Meanwhile, Jennifer and Tim were in college; she was at Niagara University, rooming with her best friend Sara Bergin from high school, and majoring in Tourism and Hotel Management, for which Niagara had a well-respected program. When they recognized Jennifer's ability to speak well in front of groups, they sent her out to recruit for the school.

Tim had several schools under consideration when Lou Holtz, a legendary Notre Dame football coach, came to Rochester and Tim had a chance to meet him. "Where are you going to college?" Coach Holtz asked Tim. Tim admitted he wasn't sure. The coach asked him if he did well in school; Tim admitted that he did. "Well," Coach Holtz said, "a lot of schools will give you a very good education. If you go to Notre Dame, you'll get a great education."

When he chose Notre Dame, Tim probably did get a great education, but it was the wrong school for him. Tim is a competitor and will do what it takes to come out on top. But at Notre Dame, he was in classes where many other students were their school's valedictorian; in those situations, the only way to win is to compete against yourself, and Tim hadn't learned to do that at that age.

After also being accepted by Notre Dame—and deciding she didn't want to follow Tim, Emily chose the University of San Diego, a Jesuit school, where she made some inseparable friends in Jacqueline, Vicky, and Elena. She majored in English and taught at her high school, LaReina, for a few years where one of her students was Tom Selleck's daughter—but Emily was getting restless. She had taken a college course in maritime law and loved it; when she found that the professors who wrote the books on maritime law taught at the University of Hawaii, she applied and got in.

While she was in law school, Emily began temping at a local law firm where she asked permission from one of the partners to cite their cases in a paper she was writing. He gave her permission, but when she told him the approach she was taking, he told her emphatically, "I wouldn't even read a paper like that; that's not the way law papers are written." But of course, that's the way Emily wrote it—and when she received a good grade, he asked to read it. He did—and offered her a job. "If you can write like that," he told her, "we want you writing for us."

She turned him down. She didn't know what she wanted to do, but she didn't want to do it in Hawaii. He offered her an idea: the Coast Guard, he told her, had a highly competitive program where they directly commission a few lawyers to practice law as officers in the Coast Guard. Emily was interested; she graduated—we spent a week with her in Hawaii—came home, took and passed the California bar on her first try—highly unusual—applied to the Coast Guard . . . and heard nothing. She was working at a small law firm handling wills and trusts, when the Coast Guard called. They had an opening; if she turned them down, they'd never ask again.

She decided she'd accept their offer. And so, one early morning in May 2008, we drove her to the local Coast Guard station at Point Mugu to take the oath of office. She was soon off to basic training where she was president of her class and the main speaker at her graduation. Her first assignment was Norfolk, Virginia where worked for the defense—and for the prosecution—and gained more courtroom experience than most lawyers in either the Navy or the Coast Guard. "When I can hear the jury sobbing behind me while I'm giving the closing argument," she told me, "I know I've got them."

But the work was not easy. She's seen things that we, as parents, did our best to protect her from. When she moved into her office, somebody put a large empty trashcan next to her desk. "This," he said, "is for you to throw up in, when you find what you're going to have to do."

For a while, she was married; by the time the marriage was over, she'd been assigned to teach law at the Coast Guard Academy, based partially on the recommendation of a senior officer who initially told her the job would not be available to her because she wasn't an Academy graduate. In her second year of teaching, she was named "Teacher of the Year," an honor voted on by the entire student body of the Academy. But even better was yet to come. In October 2010, I sat in chambers in Washington as Emily was introduced by a senior Admiral in the Coast Guard to the nine judges—and sworn in, to practice law before the Supreme Court. It was one more of her accomplishments to make a dad very proud.

And for her, it was one more thing she never would have done in civilian life. She's also been up in a Coast Guard helicopter, and she's gone into the mouth of a hurricane in a small boat with other Coasties. She escorted then vice-president Biden when he gave a graduation speech at the Coast Guard Academy, and she's worked also in New Orleans, Key West, and Milwaukee helping to deal with a variety of maritime situations. It's not unusual to get a text from Emily saying, "I can't tell you what I'm working on; it's better if you don't know." But in her words, it's sometimes also "a shit-load of work."

When Jennifer graduated with a degree in Tourism and Hotel Management, she returned to California to take the job as front desk manager for the Westlake Inn, an upscale boutique hotel—where she found the job came with twenty-four-hour responsibility. One night, when the computer system failed, she designed a fully manual record-keeping system to make sure the hotel lost no money because of the failure.

But she found, she had no life. When the demands of the job became excessive, she went into retail (she always loved to shop!), working for *Structure* until she was recruited by *Pottery Barn*. When *Pottery Barn* opened their new Las Vegas location, they asked her to move there as an assistant manager and she did. She ended up in their Call Center—as a supervisor with responsibility for business sales. Jennifer has a talent for managing people and situations.

When she married Matt Hauser on September 24, 2011—giving us two great grandkids, Brennen and Alex—she moved to Ridgecrest, California where she's a business manager dealing with contractors working on the China Lake Naval Base. Jennifer and Matt both work for the government.

Tim set off on a path of his own. With a degree in biology, he thought he might become a doctor—but only because he couldn't think of anything else he'd rather be. "That," I told him, "is like deciding to be a priest because you can't get a date. It's not a good reason." He was home in California, waiting to take the MCAT test for medical school when Cinesite, a Kodak subsidiary that created special effects for the movie industry, offered a training course. Although Tim had no computer expertise, he also had nothing to do, and so he joined the course. He must have showed promise because Cinesite offered him an internship working nights for eight weeks for free.

Every night, he'd work in a large room filled with geeks at computers; a few, like Tim, were working on the very basic tasks, but some were doing rotoscoping—using 'computer scissors' to put actors and other movie elements in different backgrounds—and Tim wanted to learn that. No one agreed to teach him because rotoscopers had enough problems of their own; the software they were using was shaky and every night, as Tim worked, he listened to them complain about it. So every morning, after he finished his work, he stayed to try to solve their problems.

And he did. He got so good, Cinesite hired him and made him the head of the rotoscoping department—and sent him on assignment to London to work on a television show. His first on-screen credit was for *Air Force One*; for *Double Jeopardy*, he rotoscoped Tommy Lee Jones' hair underwater. Tim would eventually have more than sixty end credits—most as a digital compositor with ILM, George Lucas's company that handled most of the big movies at that time.

He had long wanted to work there, but when they offered him a job, he kept saying, "maybe" until they gave him a signing bonus that would cover his first six month's rent in San Rafael where ILM was located. The job paid well and he ended up writing a book on how to get a job in the special effects industry—but by 2012, he was spending part of his time training people in lower-cost countries—India and China—to do a lot of the hands-on work so it could be shipped in via digital pipeline. Plus, he was working twelve- or eighteen-hour days, six days a week.

Tim married Patty Chang on June 13, 2009, and soon after their first son, Grant, was born in 2013, he left the effects business, "because," he said, "I wanted to know my son." He went into finance—Patty is in finance also—and he became a senior research analyst at Franklin Templeton. Tim and Patty would have another son, Liam, in 2015 and a daughter, Maia, in 2019.

When our kids were very small, I once told Jeanne's mom and dad that I thought of our children as animals. Jennifer, I said, was a cat. She was equally happy with you or by herself. She seemed to accept the world as it came, without complaint. Tim, I said, was a dog. He was interested in whatever you were. And he was incredibly loyal; he's still friends with those he made in the early years of grammar school. Emily, I said, was a bird. She wanted to sit and sing her song and she was OK whether you listened or not. But along the way, she also wanted to help other injured birds and that's caused her to fly in some different directions. Time has proven that my analogies were overly simplistic but at least a starting point. The kids have, over time, become terrific people.

Jennifer is a natural leader with a bullshit filter that's world class. If you're trying to convince her of something that's not right, you're talking to the wrong person. She's also patient, understanding, willing to listen, but thinks things through. When she and I stood in the back of the church waiting to walk down the aisle where she'd marry Matt Hauser, she said: "I've never been more scared, but I've also never been more sure that what I'm doing is right." I told her that I agreed; they seem right for each other—and continue to prove that.

Jennifer is willing to work hard for what she gets and doesn't think the world owes her a living or that life operates on her time schedule. She learns quickly, is willing to bend but not break, and has more common sense than a person has a right to have. The other kids sometimes "check in" with her and I'm sure that Brennen and Alex have benefitted from having her in their lives.

Tim seems to know a little about most things—and can figure out the rest. Technology, biology, business, whatever you want to talk about, Tim's able to contribute to the conversation—but he's always had a special interest in finance. At a very young age, he liked to discuss investments with Jeanne's dad. And when the kids would visit me at Kodak Office, our receptionist, Pamela Young told me, "Tim would sometimes ask if he could take the issue of *Fortune* or *Forbes* with him. He was the only high school kid reading magazines like that." But what he's most interested in is his family. He's a very hands-on dad and he and Patty are raising three very bright kids.

From the beginning, I've called Emily "Scooter" because on her very first night home, we put her in the middle of the cradle next to my side of the bed and she slept through the night, but in the morning, we found her "scooted" all the way to the top. When one of her high school classmates called her Scooter, she told him, "Only my dad is allowed to call me that," She has long called me

"Vati," the German word for "Daddy" as would be used by very young children.

Through the years, Emily has become very well read—she especially loves the writing of Joseph Conrad and Shakespeare and an eclectic mix of other writers on a variety of subjects, including witches and Norse mythology. She loves quotes, writes very well, and finds that words stimulate her, excite her, calm her down, give her ideas.

Emily learned to drive in California, where one night, she said, "Vati, you would be so proud of me today. I did the perfect merge." She's applied that same ability to other parts of her life. She has merged her sense of creativity into a love of painting, knitting, and sewing; we each have unique photo quilts she's made. She's merged her love of reading and writing with a love of the outdoors; she bikes, she runs marathons, she swims and camps and hikes. She's merged her love of being by herself—or with her cat, Beau—with a willingness to stand in front of groups, including juries, to speak for what she believes is right. "America," she says, "is the land of second chances." And she has merged her love of maritime law into a continuing career in the Coast Guard where she helps to protect the sea that Conrad once wrote so articulately about.

In some ways, each of our kids is like Jeanne—and each is like me. From her, they get a sense of steadiness, an attention to fundamentals; from me, they get a restless enthusiasm to try something different. But we both try to instill in them the same values we developed as children—and the realization that they should believe in themselves because we always would. We've tried to listen, to guide, to suggest, to support, but then to step out of the way as they went off on their own adventures. And, in the process, they've achieved more than we could ever have imagined.

From their earliest days, I told myself I'd remember everything they did and said, but of course I didn't. Fortunately, I took pictures—and kept notes. And oh, the things they said.

# 35

## OH, THE THINGS THEY SAID

WHY DOES IT SEEM LIKE THEY WERE SO SMALL just a moment ago? Wasn't it just yesterday when I was holding Jennifer or Tim or Emily in my arms, rocking them to sleep, burping them over my shoulder? How did we get from yesterday to today so quickly? And aren't we fortunate that kids, unlike many adults, seem to always want to be happy?

When Jennifer was very young, exploring her world, she was playing with two keys on a chain and put one key into each socket of a wall plug. The charge of electricity blew her backwards across the room. Tim went from crawling—directly to running. We had a blacktop driveway, and he fell—often. Jeanne had to have his chin stitched so frequently that the doctor suspected child abuse. And it's surprising that Emily didn't put herself in as much peril back then because Tim's most frequent complaint was, "Mom, make her stop copying me."

"Pay attention to them when they're young," my mother advised. "Those years go so quickly."

They do. In addition to the pictures I took, I wanted always to remember the funny things they said, so I began writing notes on scraps of paper and tucking them away in folders for "someday." Someday is here; I'm dragging my notes out now, to again remember what they said.

Jennifer went to morning kindergarten, and it was my job to wake her up for school. One morning after I'd called her several times, she opened one sleepy eye, looked up at me, and asked: "Daddy, how can it be morning here when it's still nighttime in my dreams?"

On another day, when I was waking him up, Tim had his own version of Jennifer's thought: "Oh Daddy," he said, "if you just let me dream one more minute, I could have had us a puppy."

Once, at my sister Pat's house, Tim obviously had something to eat that disagreed with him. "My stomach hurts real bad," he told me, "but I think I can shake it."

When I was traveling frequently, it was clear that our very young Jennifer didn't understand what was going on. One morning, after a long trip, when I came down to breakfast, Jennifer gave me a stern command: "Daddy," she said— and she was mad, "don't run away again."

On a business trip to San Diego, I bought Tim a black sombrero. One night, after a bath, he put it on and ran through the house naked. When I finally caught up with him and asked him what he was doing, he looked up at me with a big smile and said: "La Cucaracha." I have no idea what he thought that meant.

When Jennifer asked me how long an upcoming business trip might be, I told her. She seemed to think about my answer. "I'm not sure," she said, "that I want to be without you for that long."

Even at a young age, Tim must have had a sense of what I did for a living because one day he said: "Daddy, when I grow up, I'm going to be a writer just like you. Except I'm going to be popular."

One night, Tim was offering an excuse that seemed far-fetched, but when I questioned him on it, he said, "If I'm lying, may lightning strike me dead." I told him we didn't want that to happen. "OK, then thunder," he suggested, "may thunder strike me dead." I told him that thunder could not strike him dead.

"How about rain?" he asked.

During a thunder and lightning storm, Jennifer came into our room and woke me up. She was afraid, and we let her stay with us until the storm passed. "OK," I told her, "I can hardly hear anything, so it's time for you to go back to your own bed."

"The thunder may be quiet in here," she said, "but it's considerably louder in my room."

Tim had his own room for a while before Emily came along and he woke up one night crying. I went in to see what the matter was. "Daddy," he said, "I'm having a little trouble with my dreams."

One night, as the crickets were chirping, I asked the kids what they thought they were hearing. Jennifer said, "It's the sound the moon makes when it moves across the sky."

Tim thought it was "the sound of the stars crying— because they get wet in the rain."

On a walk home from getting ice cream, Tim picked up a branch and stuck it in his mouth. I told him to take it out because there were so many germs on that branch. When we got home, Tim and Jennifer went to our upstairs bathroom and Tim came out a few minutes later with his mouth foaming. "He washed his mouth to get rid of the germs," Jennifer said. "He used toothpaste and a little bit of shampoo."

When Tim was in kindergarten, his teacher sent home a note advising that we talk to our pediatrician about Tim's "lack of small motor skills." He had trouble using scissors. It turned out that Tim didn't have a problem, the school did: he was left-handed, and they hadn't realized that—maybe because, at that young age, Tim would sometimes color simultaneously with both hands—using his left to do the detail work and scribbling in the broad strokes with his right.

When Emily was about a year old, Jeanne took her to the pediatrician to ask about her reluctance to walk. As Emily stood off to the side—with Jennifer and Tim—Dr. Disney said, "Watch her. As soon as she makes any motion for something, her brother or sister gets it for her. She likes people to wait on her; she can walk—she just doesn't want to."

On a winter Saturday, Tim and I were ready to leave the house when I suggested he go to the toilet first. "Let's both go," he said, and as we stood together in our upstairs bathroom, Tim still had on his unbuttoned long heavy coat. "Let's go on the count of three," he said, and without unbuttoning his coat, he counted quickly and started to pee—inside his coat. As I watched the urine drip down from the coat's edge, he looked at me with panicked and pleading eyes. "Daddy," he said, "make it stop."

A few years later, I spent an evening with Bob Newhart whom Kodak had hired as the talent for a dinner we were sponsoring for the College Football Coaches Association. After his performance, Bob came up to the Kodak suite and, as we sat talking, I told him that story about Tim. "Kids are funny about bathrooms," he told me. "They think bathrooms have a secret door that lets you leave the house forever."

One day I came downstairs to find Emily playing with a calculator. "Dad," she asked, "what year were you born?" I told her. "And," she asked innocently, "what year will you die?" I told her I had no idea. "Oh, don't worry," she said, punching some numbers into the calculator, "I can figure that out." I sometimes wonder what happened to that calculator.

As we were getting ready to leave for a party at Uncle Dick and Aunt Kathy's, Jeanne said, "Bob, come talk to your son."

I asked Tim what was going on. "I told Mom a joke," he said, "it's about a dirty dick."

"Tim," I asked, "do you know what a dick is?" He told me that a dick is a penis. "Right," I said, "but I don't want you saying 'dick' again."

"OK," he readily agreed, but then he asked: "Dad, can I say, 'Uncle Dick?"

"Yes," I agreed, "you can say 'Uncle Dick'."

Tim seemed thoughtful again. "So," he said, "I really have two dicks."

"Tim," I said, "we're all going to a party. If anyone tells a joke about a dirty dick, you're going to be punished."

Jennifer came into the kitchen one day and said, "I don't know what's going on in his damn house anyway." I told her we did not want her talking like that— and if she said 'damn' again, we'd wash her mouth out with soap. "How much soap?" she asked. I told her I didn't know. "And will you get that soap from the kitchen or the bathroom?" she wanted to know. I told her that I wasn't going to answer a lot of questions about soap; she was just going to have to stop saying 'damn.' And she did.

"Tim," Jeanne said when I walked in the door from work one night, "tell Daddy what happened to you in kindergarten today." It turned out that Tim was standing next to another little kid named George at the school urinal and they got into an argument. George turned around—and hosed Tim down. "It was a bad day, Daddy," Tim said.

As I left for a parent-teacher meeting with Tim's first grade teacher, Sister Dorothy Mary, I asked Tim: "Is there anything you want me to tell your teacher?"

"Tell her that I'm trying hard," he said.

"OK," I said, "I'll say, 'Sister, Tim is trying very hard'."

"Not very hard," Tim corrected me. "Just hard." I asked him when he would begin trying very hard. "Not before next week," he said, "because I still have a few bumps in my brain left over from summer."

But a few weeks later, he was apparently working to his fullest ability—and not liking the effort. "Today," he told me one night after school, "I tried so hard, I think I broke my brain."

"When Tim grows up," Emily announced one day, "he's never going to be married. He's going to be a spatula." I told her the word was "bachelor." "Bachelor, spatula," she said, unconcerned with the sound-alike words, "he's just never going to get married." At their rehearsal party I congratulated Tim's soon-to-be-wife Patty for saving Tim from becoming a long-handled cooking spoon. As a gift for their wedding, Emily gave Tim a spatula.

In our den was a bookshelf where, one night, I came home to find a very young Jennifer rapidly pulling books off the shelf and throwing them across the room. "Young lady," I said, "you put those books back right now."

"You put them back," she said. "I'm busy."

When Emily was tiny, Jennifer and Tim saw all the attention she was getting and, on our way to get them ice cream one night, they told me, "Daddy, we want to be babies like Emily."

"OK," I said—and I turned the car around.

"Where are we going?" Jennifer asked.

"We're going home," I told her. "Babies have to be in bed—and they don't eat ice cream."

"We don't want to be babies,"Tim said.

I had a beard for the first six years of Jennifer's life—and five-year-old Tim was with me the night I went to the barber to have it shaved off. I had told Jennifer beforehand: "I'm thinking of shaving off my beard," I said.

"I can just imagine what you'd look like," she said, "and I wouldn't like it."

Tim was sitting in the barber waiting area when he looked up—shocked—to see my beard gone. "Dad," he said, "where is your beard?"

"Gone," I said, "do you miss it?"

"Yes, he said, "and I think it misses us."

But Jennifer had the best comment when I arrived home clean-shaven for the first ever in her life. "Dad," she said, "I think you look positively ridiculous."

Once Emily was here, we knew our family was complete and Tim was in third grade. When Jeanne went in the hospital for a hysterectomy, she received hand-made get-well cards from all the kids in Tim's class—except Tim. His teacher held his back—and gave it to her much later because she thought Tim's message would upset her. The card said:"Mom, everybody tells me that you will get well but I think you are dead."

When we took the kids shopping, it was clear they remembered TV commercials. "Here, Daddy," Jennifer said, giving me a package of gum, "shake up your mouth." That same night, she gave me a *People* magazine with a cover picture of Cindy Williams and Penny Marshall. "Daddy," she said, "look—Laverne and cereal."

I sometimes called our young kids the "JET squad" after their initials and so I knew "squad" was the word Emily wanted me to guess when we were playing "hangman" one day. She had written five blanks _ _ _ _ _, so it was a five-letter word and had already filled in S _ _ A D. "Q," I said.

"No, she said, "no Q."

I guessed "U"; wrong again. I finally figured it out: SKWAD—exactly like it sounds. As Mark Twain once wrote:"Only a dull person can think of only one way to spell a word."

In the very early '80s, cars had seat belts, but we had grown up without them and seldom used them—they were for little kids. But they must have been talked about in school because when she wasn't more than six or seven years old, and driving somewhere, Jennifer told me, "We have to wear our seat belts." I said we'd be OK without them. "Do you know how many people who were killed because they weren't wearing their seat belts?" I didn't, but she did—and she told me. She had all the facts and figures; she was very convincing.

We learned a lot from our kids at a very young age—and now we're listening to our grandkids. "Only leaves can see the wind," our three-year-old Grant, Tim and Patty's son, observed one day; he also came up with an imaginative excuse when he was caught sucking his thumb after his parents tried to break him of the habit: "It just fell into my mouth; I was trying to get it out." At about the same age, his brother Liam told me, "Grandpa, if you keep sleeping, you're going to miss me."

I don't want to miss him—or any other part of sharing childhood with such smart kids. They're sharing their imagination with us and if every story they tell isn't always true, it could be. Like a story I wrote about Emily a month or so after she was born.

# 36

# THE CHRISTMAS STORY
# WRITING CONTEST

T BEGAN WITH A PHONE CALL FROM MY MOM in September 1979, a few weeks after Emily was born. My mother had seen a notice for a Christmas story writing contest sponsored by *Upstate*, the magazine that came with the Rochester *Democrat and Chronicle* Sunday newspaper.

"First prize is two hundred and fifty dollars," she said. "You like to write; you should enter." When I said I'd think about it, she told me to think fast; the deadline was coming up soon. I've always hated to disappoint Mom and so, when I found myself alone on a business trip from Los Angeles back to Rochester, I decided: when the plane lifted off from LAX, I'd start thinking—and, hopefully writing; when it touched down in Cleveland—an intermediate stop—I'd stop writing. I would edit what I'd written on the connecting flight to Rochester. Once I got home, if I had a story, I'd type it up and send it in.

If I had no story, I'd be able to tell my mother that I had tried. But a story did jump into my head that day, a story of our three children—Jennifer, Timothy, and Emily—and their adventures on one magical night. Several weeks after I dropped it off at the newspaper, one of their editors called to tell me: they had received one hundred and eighty-one stories, including one from a nine-year-old with a note: "typed by her father." In fact, the editor said, *Upstate* had received so many entries, they decided to offer two first prizes—one for the best general interest story, the other for the best story for children. I had won first prize in the children's category, she told me. She invited me to come down to the newspaper to tell them a bit about myself, and to let them take my picture.

When I went, they asked me about my job. They asked me about my family. They asked me if I had any children. I asked them if they had a chance to read my story. "Oh," the woman asked who was interviewing me, "is this story about your children?"

I told her it was. And I said that, despite this being a fiction writing contest, "my story was true." She smiled—and wrote that down.

My story was published in *Upstate* magazine, on December 23, 1979, the Sunday before Christmas that year. On that morning of publication, our phone kept ringing from people calling me to tell me how much they enjoyed reading what I had written. The most suspect call came from a man named Bill McCarthy, who said he remembered being my English teacher at Aquinas and said how proud he was of all that I learned in his class. I can prove I never had Bill McCarthy for English, but I didn't tell him that. I thanked him for his help and told him I was glad he enjoyed my story. Here is what I wrote on that flight long ago.

## A Present for Emily

Someone was moving around downstairs. Timothy bolted upright in bed and listened. That sure sounded like the crackle of paper rustling against Christmas tree branches; someone was dragging heavy presents across the room. And then, much softer than Timothy had ever expected, somebody chuckled the most familiar chuckle in all the world: "Ho, ho, ho."

"Santa!" Timothy almost screamed the name into the darkness, but that would have ruined everything. His mom and dad would wake up and scold him; his new baby sister probably would cry, and his big sister

Jennifer might start fighting with him. But worst of all, Santa would hear him—and would disappear up the chimney with a bound.

Santa didn't like children awake when he was leaving presents; Jennifer, who was five-and-a-half and a whole year older than Timothy had made that clear the night before. "Come on," she had said, "if we're not asleep, Santa might skip our house." Then she got into her nightgown and under the covers faster than Timothy thought possible.

Timothy had struggled into his pajamas. His pajama tops kept getting inside out, he couldn't find the sleeves, and Jennifer turned out the light just as he was putting on the bottoms. In the darkness, they had felt funny; Timothy guessed he had them on backwards.

But now he had more important thoughts on his mind. He lay awake and worried.

He wasn't so much afraid that Santa would see him awake; Timothy could pretend he was sleeping if he had to. He was worried that Santa would forget to leave a present for Emily, his new baby sister.

Emily was just three months old and was too young to visit Santa. Timothy knew she wanted a doll and, because he was her big brother, told Emily he'd ask Santa for her. But then, when he finally got to see Santa, a few days before Christmas, things didn't go as planned.

Timothy had gotten very nervous. He hardly remembered his name and whether he had been good all year. He stammered and whispered that he wanted a truck and a train. He had completely forgotten about Emily's doll.

He had remembered when he was riding home, but by then it was too late. "Don't worry, dear," his mother had said, "you can write Santa a note." Timothy had sent the note to the North Pole the next day, but he was never sure that Santa had received it.

But now, Santa was *here*, downstairs. Timothy could talk to him, ask him if he got the letter, remind him to leave a present for Emily.

That would be easy; Timothy would simply walk downstairs and explain the situation. Santa would dig into his pack, pull out a beautiful doll, but *wait a minute*. That wouldn't work at all. The stairs creaked, his dad would wake up and tell him to get back into bed. Santa would hear the noise—and leave.

Timothy needed some advice and he rummaged in his bed for Benjamin Bunny. Benjamin had been with him from the beginning, and they did everything together. When Timothy was afraid, Benjamin gave him courage; when he was sick, Benjamin made the hurt go away. Tonight, Timothy needed to know what to do—and in his own magical way, Benjamin Bunny told him to ask Jennifer.

Timothy crept over to her bed. "Jenny," he said softly. "Santa's downstairs."

Even in the darkness, he could see her eyes widen with fear. "Go back to sleep," she whispered. "If Santa hears us, he won't leave any presents."

"But Jenny," he said, "I just know that Emily wants a doll and I forgot to tell Santa. What if he didn't get my letter? If I go downstairs to ask him, he might hear me coming—and leave. What can I do?"

As Jennifer thought, Timothy heard sleigh bells, loud . . . and *right outside his window*. He slowly lifted the shade. There, on the porch roof, level with his window, was a red sleigh and eight reindeer. "There's only one thing to do," Jennifer whispered. "We've got to go out and wait in Santa's sleigh until he comes out. Then, we'll tell him about Emily."

Timothy grabbed his bathrobe and Benjamin. "You're the bravest," he told Benjamin. "You can help me talk to Santa." Jennifer put on her robe and took Mandy, the doll with whom she shared all her secrets. "With Benjamin and Mandy," she said, "we'll be OK." They raised the window, slid into the darkness, and climbed into the sleigh.

The front seat was bare except for a few heavy blankets dusted by lightly falling snow. The back seat, the seat that always held the toys in the pictures that Jennifer and Timothy had seen, had some giant packs, but the packs were empty and thrown about. *This was Santa's last stop.*

Jennifer and Timothy crawled under the packs to get out of the snow. It was warm and dry there, with the beautiful smell of newly painted toys. It was so comfortable that they did something they never expected to do: they fell asleep.

Timothy awoke with a start. He knew that voice. "On Dasher, on Dancer, away Rudolph," it called, and the sleigh lifted off the rooftop with a gentle bump.

Jennifer awoke too and they peered out to see that they were already climbing into the night sky. They were over Amy's house, then over Shawn's . . . and then everything became a soft white blur. They were passing through snow clouds on their way with Santa back to the North Pole.

Timothy hugged Benjamin closely, and Jennifer held Mandy. Then, very softly, the children began to cry.

"Ho, ho, ho," said Santa's jolly voice, "do I hear somebody crying back there?" Turning around, he lifted off the packs and found Timothy and Jennifer, Benjamin and Mandy, huddled in the darkness. "Why, it's my friends," he said. "Come on up here and keep warm with Santa."

Quicker than a wink, the children were in the front seat, bundled in blankets, and not afraid anymore. Timothy explained to Santa about Emily's doll.

"Well," said Santa, scratching his beard, "I'm not sure what we can do. You must have sent your letter too late because it didn't get up to the North Pole before I left on my journey. I sent all my elves home, and I took all the toys they made. I don't know where I can find a doll for Emily, but let's go back to the North Pole. Perhaps Mrs. Claus will have an idea."

It was still dark and snowing when the sleigh touched down and Mrs. Claus rushed out to meet Santa. She was surprised to see Jennifer and Timothy and their friends, but when Santa explained the situation, she invited them in for cookies and hot chocolate.

While Santa fed the reindeer, Timothy told Mrs. Claus about his new baby sister. "Oh dear," said Mrs. Claus, "poor Emily. I don't think there are any toys left in the workshop, but when Santa comes in, we'll go out there and check."

It seemed like forever before Santa drank his hot chocolate and finished his pipe. Then Mrs. Claus bundled the children up again and Santa led the way to a long, low building, covered with new-fallen snow. A wooden sign over the door read: *Santa's Toyshop.*

Santa turned the knob and the door swung open. He and the children stepped inside. At first it seemed as if they were alone, but then they heard a soft noise in the darkness. Jennifer thought she saw a faint glow in the workshop and Santa lighted a lantern. "Follow me," he said, "but be careful you don't fall. This place is a mess."

The workshop looked as bad as Jennifer and Timothy's room on a rainy afternoon. Scraps of cloth, pieces of plastic, and chips of wood were everywhere. Paint cans had been left open; hammers and brushes littered the floor. But Jennifer had been right: there *was* a light at the back of the workshop. As they drew closer, they saw a tiny elf bent over his workbench.

"Hobbles," said Santa in surprise. "Hobbles, what are you doing here?"

Hobbles was the oldest of all the elves. He was always quiet and very shy, but he wanted everything just right. While the young elves each made hundreds of boats and planes, kitchen sets and dollhouses, Hobbles worked all year on just one toy. He had been with Santa for a long time: this might be the last toy he would ever make. He had tried so hard to finish it before Santa left, but he just couldn't do it.

The other elves laughed at him and said that nobody would want his toy anyway. But Hobbles stayed in the shop, working. When the fire had died in the fireplace, Hobbles shivered and pulled his sweater tighter. His fingers were numb, but he kept sewing and he finished just as Santa came up to his workbench.

The oldest elf was afraid that Santa would be angry with him for working so slowly. Maybe the other elves were right; maybe nobody *would* like his toy. But Santa had just asked him what he was doing, so he had to show him. Shyly, he held it up.

Timothy almost yelled with happiness because there, in the hands of Hobbles, was the perfect present for Emily: the most beautiful doll in the world.

Santa chuckled. "It's very beautiful, Hobbles," he said. "You've done the best job of all and I'm very proud of you. I know that doll must be very special to you because you've worked so long and so hard to make it the best you could. It wouldn't be right to ask you to give it away. Perhaps Timothy and Jennifer have something special of their own to trade you for it."

Jennifer and Timothy looked at each other. If they had thought of this before, they could have brought their piggy banks filled with pennies and nickels and dimes. But it was too late for that now. This was the last present left and it was just perfect for their sister. They had to have it.

Timothy did the only thing he could. With tears in his eyes, he held out his friend—Benjamin Bunny. "Here, Mr. Hobbles," he said. "I'll trade you Benjamin for your special doll. He will help you be the bravest in all the world. He's been my very best friend and now he will be yours."

"And take Mandy too," said Jennifer. "Mandy helps me to go to sleep at night and she knows all the best secrets. If you're ever scared when it's dark or worried about anything, Mandy will understand."

Jennifer and Timothy cried as they handed over their friends and took the special doll from Hobbles. "Good-bye, Benjamin," said Timothy. "I'll miss you."

Santa put his arms around the children. "Come," he said, "we must get you back home before your mom and dad and Emily know you're gone." With that, he bundled them into the sleigh, hitched up the reindeer, and once again took off into the snowy night sky.

It seemed to be only minutes before the sleigh touched down on the porch rooftop outside their bedroom window. "Hurry into bed," Santa told them. "I'll slide down the chimney and put Emily's doll underneath the tree. . .and Merry Christmas."

Both Timothy and Jennifer fell asleep as soon as they tumbled into their beds. The next thing they knew, light was coming into the room and their mom was standing there in her robe, holding Emily.

"Time to go downstairs to see if Santa got your letter and left a present for Emily," she said. Jennifer smiled and Timothy winked at her. They started for the stairs.

Under the Christmas tree, presents were everywhere and in the center was Emily's very special doll. Emily laughed and waved her arms. "Santa must have received your letter, Tim," Mom said. "But what else do I see next to that doll?"

Mom bent down and picked up two presents. "One is for Jenn and one is for Tim," she said. "I wonder what they could be?"

Quickly the children tore off the paper and found their biggest surprise of all: Mandy and Benjamin Bunny, the two faithful friends they had traded away the night before. Mom and Dad looked puzzled, but then Timothy found a note. It said:

> *Dear Jennifer and Timothy,*
> *It's a wonderful thing to share what's important to you and to be willing to give away your favorite things to get a present for your new baby sister. Hobbles loved Benjamin and Mandy, but he thought they belonged with you. You have made Emily's first Christmas very special by your love. Take care of each other always.*
> *Love,*
> *Santa*

That was the story. In my files I've kept a couple of copies of the original publication and for several years afterwards, I read the story to Emily, who always cried. But even as it was published, I was enjoying an equally exciting adventure of my own: I was working with Disney.

# 37

# A JOURNEY INTO IMAGINATION

On A COOL, OVERCAST NOVEMBER DAY IN 1971, Jeanne and I made our first trip to Disneyland. I had grown up as a fan of Walt Disney movies and television shows. I'd cried watching *Old Yeller* in a Rochester theatre so crowded that many of us kids had to sit on the floor. I'd walked home in a raging snowstorm after seeing *Toby Tyler* when my bus had gotten stuck in the snow. I stood in a long line at the small neighborhood Liberty Theatre to see *Davy Crockett* when I was just eight years old. And on our small Philco television, I watched *The Mickey Mouse Club* and *Disney's Wonderful World of Color* where, in his raspy, fatherly voice, Walt Disney spoke sometimes of Disneyland. It looked like a magical place, but back then I'd never been more than a hundred miles from home. I never thought I'd see it. And I never imagined I'd ever work with the Disney Imagineers who created it.

In the late 1970s, when the Walt Disney Company was planning EPCOT— their Experimental Prototype Community of Tomorrow in Florida—they approached Kodak to be a sponsor of a major pavilion. They asked for ten million dollars, payable over ten years. Initially, Kodak turned them down; but at the time,

Kodak CEO Walt Fallon was on the Board of General Motors and when he went to their meeting—and they bragged about being a sponsor—Walt asked his people at Kodak, "why don't we do something like that?" The Kodak people who initially said no, invited Disney back.

Disney proposed that Kodak sponsor the "Space" pavilion at EPCOT. I was a young writer of slide programs at the time, but people knew I liked to stick my nose into creative projects and so one day, Kodak's manager of sponsorships asked me to look at Disney's proposal. I did and on March 30, 1979, I wrote a four-page memo in reply. Its essence was this, *Kodak is not about space, Kodak enables people to express their imagination through photography. Imagination should be a vital part of the Kodak EPCOT experience.*

I turned in my memo and heard nothing—until I was invited, several weeks later, to a meeting where Disney management flew to Rochester to make two proposals—one about space, the other about imagination. The space proposal was polished; the imagination presentation was sketchy and led by a young Imagineer named Tony Baxter; he was my age and had just been promoted from their model shop. But it was clear to everyone in the room that Tony had world class talent—and Kodak wanted to work with him. At the end of the meeting, when Kodak president Kay Whitmore told Disney management that we would support the imagination approach, Disney invited Kodak to send a few people to California to work with them, so the finished concept would make sense to Kodak as well as to Disney. It was the summer of 1979; Disney planned to open EPCOT on October 1, 1982; they needed to move this project forward.

Kodak's head of communications, Dave Metz, decided the Kodak team would be Greg DiNovis as business manager, me to watch over creative, and Neil Stalter, my direct boss to (I think) watch over me. Dave told me later, "we considered you our resident creative genius"; he didn't want Disney recruiting me. "But," Dave told me, "don't get your hopes up, Bob; this is one trip, one time." Neil would soon leave the team; Greg and I would fly back and forth to California at least once a month for the next several years.

The trip was magical. We stayed at the Sheraton Universal where we saw at least one TV star every morning at breakfast; we ate at the best restaurants—where we took turns pretending it was each other's birthday so we could get free desserts—and Tony explained how the great Disney effects were done—*Haunted Mansion*, for example—and showed us conceptual art for the other EPCOT pavilions.

When our meetings ended early, Disney would give us books of tickets for Disneyland where *Peter Pan's Magic Flight* was my favorite ride. Tony loved that ride also; he had started as an ice-cream-scooper in the park before "graduating" to become an operator on classic Disney rides. As an Imagineer, he'd later lead development on many of the new Disney classics.

One night, Disney took us to our saved seats for the Disneyland electrical parade. "We're actually saving these for the President of the United States," the rep from Guest Services told us. "Since it doesn't look like he's coming, we're giving them to you."

But there were two immediate disconnects. The first: Kodak people showed up in suit coats and ties; Disney people wore casual shirts and slacks; a day later, the Disney team wore coats and ties and the Kodak team had on open-neck shirts; we decided casual attire would be best. But the bigger issue was, Disney wanted to brainstorm, and between the Kodak team and theirs, we had way too many people to do that. When the first overcrowded session achieved nothing, someone—I think because of meeting conflicts—decided there would be just four people involved in the next session: Tad Stones, Barry Braverman and Tony Baxter from Disney—and me.

Tony began the session by tossing out ideas, to see if anything would stick; the goal was to create a ride that played with guests' imaginations. At one point, Tony had everyone inside a hollow log where guests would hear a thumping sound that got progressively louder—as if they were about to be run over by galloping horses. But then, they could look out through a knothole in the log and see they were hearing cattails slapping together in the wind.

It would be fun—except for, I suggested, small children. They might be scared and cry. We had two very young kids at the time: "I can tell them a frightening bedtime story and they're OK with it because I'm with them," I said. "We need a storyteller to protect them."

Tony understood immediately. He left the room and came back carrying a small model of a Victorian gentleman that had been carved for another project; on his shoulder was a small green flying dragon. Disney had ruled that EPCOT would have no characters, but Tony never let a corporate edict stand in the way of a good idea. "This is our storyteller," Tony said. He would eventually be named "Dreamfinder" and symbolize the rational side of imagination; the dragon would become Figment, who brought a child's sense of curiosity.

There was one major problem: Figment was green—the corporate color of Kodak's main competitor for film. Making him red or yellow (Kodak's corporate colors) didn't work for Disney—so purple became his compromise color. "Let's go," Tony said, climbing up on a table and voicing Dreamfinder; I got up on a chair and played along as Figment.

From that session forward, the pavilion began to become—led by Tony's talent— an adventure in three acts: a unique ride reminding guests of the tools of imagination, an interactive exhibit area enabling them to use those tools, and a movie that provided an imaginative bridge back to the real world.

In the beginning, we simply called everything 'the imagination pavilion,' but one night back in Rochester, I was taking our son Tim for a ride in a cart around the block when a plane flew overhead. "Daddy," Tim asked, "where is that plane going?" Having no idea, I said, "it's on a long journey to wherever you can imagine"—and it struck me: "journey . . . imagination;" they sounded good together. I proposed "Journey into Imagination" at a subsequent Disney meeting in Rochester. "We like that," Marty Sklar, Tony's boss said. "Can we use it?" "Sure," Kay Whitmore said. Disney artist Dan Goozee's concept art showed *Journey Into Imagination* as two crystals—reminiscent of two silver halide crystals, the fundamentals of photography. I helped put together a presentation for Walt Fallon to show the Kodak Board what we'd be doing.

When Kodak signed on for EPCOT, we also became the "official photographic supplier to Disney." According to industry figures, visitors on Disney property took 260 million pictures annually back then, about 2.5-percent of *all* pictures taken in the US during the year; Disney estimated they'd take an additional sixty million pictures at EPCOT during its first year of operation. So,

Kodak would be the only company selling film and cameras where people were going to take more than three hundred million pictures. The Disney sponsorship was such an easy decision, I suggested, "even a Kodak vice president could make it."

Disney built a scale model of the pavilion and set it up on a huge table where we could walk around it and, using a special miniature upside-down periscope, we could view everything as if we were its same scale. But Disney worked from the inside out; the final dimensions of the building would be determined by the story they were telling on the inside—and that, in turn, enabled Tony to play with guests' imaginations from the start of the ride: when they first met Dreamfinder and Figment, everything was on a giant turntable where what's stationary appeared to be moving—and what's moving appeared to be stationary. From there, it was a ride through the Dreamport where building blocks of imagination were stored, then on to the creative realms of arts and sciences where new ideas came to life—all told with Tony's sense of childish delight.

Figment was loved even before the ride opened. Tony was in a Disney store, watching a mother interact with her child. "You're just going to have to decide," a mother told her young daughter, "do you want the Mickey Mouse doll or do you want the purple kangaroo?"

The ride would all play to music and, Tony decided to let the Sherman Brothers have a go at composing the score. Once, they were Walt Disney's favorites—he called them "the boys" —and they'd written the soundtrack for *Mary Poppins*, *Small World* and so many other Disney classics. One day after lunch, we went into a room with a beat-up piano—and in walked two guys who looked like they had taken the subway direct from vaudeville. Dick played the piano, Bob clapped his hands, nodded along, and they both sang—and *One Little Spark* became the song we'd use for the ride.

The ride was act one; act two would be a hands-on playground for guests' imaginations led by Dreamfinder and Figment; both acts were under development, but there was still some question about act three. Disney proposed an IMAX movie, but I wasn't sold on the idea. IMAX was big, but not unique; I told Disney that Kodak needed a format more imaginative.

One day, Marty Sklar, Tony's boss, called to ask if I'd be willing to fly to Florida to look at the work of a New York filmmaker named Murray Lerner? He'd made a 3D movie called *Sea Dreams* and Disney was impressed with the quality of his work and thinking the 3D could work for us. At that point—long before digital technology made them commonplace—3D movies hadn't been in theatres since the exploitations movies of the 1950's and I'd never seen one. I thought it sounded intriguing. And so John Simonds, the head of physics for Kodak Research labs who joined our team as technical adviser, and I—along with Tony and Barry Braverman—met Murray in Florida where his movie was playing at Marineland in St. Augustine. With his ever-present cigar and Brooklyn accent, Murray appeared to me to be a New York City cab driver.

When we went into the theatre to see his movie, we were with, as it turned out, an audience of senior citizens, sitting in front of an older couple. At one point in the movie, two kids were playing with a frisbee on a beach . . . and the frisbee appeared to be floating in slow motion directly out into the audience . . . at which point, the woman behind Barry tried to catch it . . . and instead grabbed a handful of Barry's hair and jerked his head sharply backwards. She was apologetic—and I was sold on the imaginative aspects of 3D. John Simonds made a few calculations on a theatre napkin to show Murray he'd need to shoot it on 65 mm film and print it on dual strand 70mm film; it was one of the very few 70mm 3D movies at the time. The camera Murray used to shoot the film was built by Steve Hines, then a member of the Kodak Research Labs. And again, the Sherman Brothers wrote the music. *Magic Journeys* was, in Bob Sherman's words, "one of the most imaginative songs we ever wrote," and, in Dick's words, "one of the most musically complex."

But still, the brothers weren't done. While guests were waiting in a dark room in a queue to enter the theatre, we at Kodak wanted to "show them some pictures" —to entertain them with a multi-image show. Disney agreed that would be a shared responsibility: they would hire the Sherman Brothers to write the music, but Kodak would produce the show. We knew the theme would be picture-taking, but it had to be showcased in a non-commercial way. I sat down with Bob and Dick to share my joy and enthusiasm for photography—and they got it immediately: "it's all about takin' pictures," they said, "and takin' pictures is makin' memories" —and they were off and running with a song that had a bouncy, ragtime feeling.

When Kodak lawyers suggested that too many lyrics— "birthdays disappear," for example—raised issues about the dye stability of film, I got Kodak's chief technical officer, Dr. Herb Rees, involved. "This is a song about the joy of photography," Dr. Rees said. "The lawyers need to stop their nonsense." And they did.

When the Sherman Brothers recorded "Makin' Memories," they signed the lead sheet: 'To Bob Gibbons. Thanks for your inspiration. Your friends, Bob Sherman and Dick Sherman.' They sent us an audio tape of the recording and Ed Mitchell, Tom Davis and me—my Kodak creative team—went to work gathering pictures from several sources; in the library of the University of Rochester, we found old family pictures; we licensed images of historical events from the Bettmann Archive in New York City; and I hired Andy Olenick, a local photographer to create one special image, that I'd once seen and I wanted him to replicate.

Two days later, Andy came back with a slide of a red-headed, freckle-faced boy looking through a camera with a long lens—and there, at the end of the lens, sitting on the lens hood, was a bird looking back at him. "I bought a stuffed bird from a taxidermy company," Andy told me, "then I drilled a hole in my lens hood and wired the dead bird to it. The hardest part was finding the right kid." It was exactly what I had asked for—and had imagined.

Meanwhile in California, *Journey into Imagination* and the rest of EPCOT had a deadline always looming. In a Disney conference room, a note tacked to a corkboard said: "October 1 is not the problem. 1982 is the problem." *Journey into Imagination* formally opened in early December of that year when Kodak CEO Colby Chandler stood at a lectern in front of the entryway to the ride and read a speech I'd written for him on the power of imagination. I still have my ticket from that day; admission was twelve dollars; I had a free three-day pass.

More than three years—and uncounted trips—after I first met Tony in a Kodak conference room, the ride quickly became everyone's favorite attraction. Figment and Dreamfinder were the only original characters ever created for the park—and they were a huge hit. Ron Schneider, a Disney employee, dressed up as Dreamfinder and with Figment as an appendage on his arm, he charmed visitors and appeared in zillions of pictures. For Walt Disney World's 50th Anniversary, Figment was honored with a gold statue—one of only fifty characters from the worlds of Disney, Marvel and Lucasfilm to be so honored.

From the beginning, I admired Tony's creativity—and his humility; we spent a lot of time together. He would go on to create several rides—*Big Thunder, Indiana Jones, Splash* and *Star Tours;* he'd have overall responsibility for Disneyland Paris; and after he retired as a senior vice president of Creative Development for Imagineering in 2013, he was given his own window on Main Street in Disneyland. When he was recognized with an award by the Themed Entertainment Association, Kodak put a full-page ad in the event program with a color picture of the original *Journey into Imagination* pavilion, signed by Kay Whitmore, Neil Stalter, Greg DiNovis, and myself—the original Kodak team.

In an article about us in *Kodakery*, the Kodak newspaper, Tony would say that he and I were "kindred spirits, creative types not wrapped up in a corporate structure and job advancement priorities." "Tony," I said, "is one of my creative heroes." We remain friends.

After EPCOT opened, we took the kids there several times to see what I had been working on during their earliest years—and got them special Figment dolls wearing Kodak shirts. But back home the kids were growing up, and we needed more room; we were moving from Wyndale Road—and I was going back to school.

# 38

# PADDLING DAYS

In SOME WAYS, THOSE YEARS IN THE LATE '80S AND EARLY '90S seemed like a time when many of us were doing our best impression of a duck—looking calm on the surface with lots of furious paddling going on underneath.

Jeanne and I had been looking for a home for at least eighteen months and admittedly we were picky, but we'd seen nothing that appealed to us. Until one Sunday when we found a newly built home we loved and put in an offer. It was accepted—with one 'potential complication:' another buyer had made an offer with a continency—and had seventy-two-hours to remove it; seventy hours later he did; we were out of luck.

Then Jerry Alaimo, the builder, called; he had one more lot in the area—on Andiron Lane. He was willing to build the same house, for the same price—if we wanted it. We did and moved in sometime in August 1985, just before the kids started school at Mother of Sorrows grammar school. Alaimo Builders had such a solid reputation for building a quality home that, at one point, they had more work than he could handle—so Jerry raised his prices. And attracted *even more* work. "If he's that expensive," buyers reasoned, "he must be great. We had better get in line."

On the first day in our new home, Emily, Jennifer, and I roamed around in nearby open land. Emily, who was almost five years old caught poison ivy; that night, Jennifer, who was eleven, came down with her first period. "In three years, you and the girls will not be living in this house," I told Jeanne, "because, by that time, I think you will have killed each other."

But the kids settled down and at school, they mostly settled in—although Emily, who had very short hair at the time, was irate when a school janitor saw her crying in the hallways and advised, "come on, be a man, my son." Jeanne and I were elected to the School Board; I started a communications committee; and a couple of times a year, I taught creative writing to the eighth-grade class.

I enjoyed it so much, I decided to teach also to a fifth-grade class in a public school. In that school, one day, I couldn't get one of the kids to pay attention to anything I was talking about. After class, I mentioned that to the teacher. "He's having a rough day," she said about the little boy in question. "This morning he met his father for the first time." Shauna, my niece who was a public-school teacher, told me that more than half of the kids in her class had at least one parent in prison.

In our home on Andiron Lane, we learned a lot about the added expenses in building a new house. My sister Pat's husband Ted regraded our lot at least three times, adding ten more truckloads of topsoil. He used "re-grind"—highly-compacted blacktop that had been scraped off highways under construction—to put in our driveway. Our landscape contractor, "Wild Bill"—we called him that because he "made it all up as he went along"—who put in our patio, walkways and screened-in gazebo never filed drawings for permits. And so, later when we moved out, I did the "engineering drawings" myself, with a ruler, graph paper, and several wild guesses. They looked official and the town approved everything so the house could be sold.

Meanwhile, Kodak sent me to the Newhouse School at Syracuse University to get a master's degree in communications to prepare me to play a greater role in the company's future. As Phil Samper, a senior manager for whom I wrote at the time, said: "Gibbons, you need to be focused."

I chose to focus on advertising. At Kodak, I felt that the public relations side of communications was in very good hands; Dave Metz was in charge, and he was a giant in his profession. But in the advertising arena, I thought that Kodak had given away what it once owned—the emotional aspects of the brand—and I wanted to help them get them back. Knowing most of those working on advertising back then, my question was not, "why is Kodak advertising so bad?" but rather, "how can it be as good as it is?"

And so, once a week, I drove from Rochester to Syracuse—about ninety miles—went to class, stayed overnight, went to another class, and then drove back to Rochester to work at my job for three days a week. Although I started with day classes, I soon found that the instructors with the most practical experience taught at night and I gravitated towards those classes, including one I took from the head of the marketing department. One night, as he and I were walking out of class together, he said, "I really like the work you are doing. I especially like your writing." I thanked him, but I said, "I find your opinion irrelevant. I'm not doing this for you; I'm doing this for me." I'm not sure anyone told him that before.

I did well in my classes and was carrying a straight-A average into my final course in communications law. I loved my professor's philosophy: "if you work for a company with its own legal staff," he said, "their goal is to keep you so far away from doing anything that's even questionably illegal that their jobs become easy. My goal is to get you so close to the line that they shudder when they see you coming."

He was a terrific teacher who seemed to have memorized every case—ever—in communications law and so he expected no surprises when he gave us an assignment: we would each write on a case of our choosing; we'd describe our case in a one-page synopsis—and then, with his approval, we'd expand it into a full paper.

I'd just been working with the Walt Disney company, so I knew a lot about that organization, and I described a case where their attempt to put overly commercial messages on public television had landed them in court. The case was heard by the courts in California who had found for the plaintiff; there was a possibility it might make its way onto the docket of the Supreme Court for its upcoming session.

When my professor passed back the synopsis to each of the other students, he approved the various cases they had chosen. He held mine until last. "This is an intriguing case," he said, holding my paper, "but I can't find it. I've spent the weekend online and going through law texts and it's not in there. Where did you find it?" I told him the truth: I made it up.

He disagreed. "You didn't make this up," he said, "because so many facts are correct. "The facts are real," I agreed, "but I wrapped some fiction around them—and hid the seams. Writers know how to do that." He was apoplectic. He assigned me another case to write—and, for my final grade, he gave me a B—but that was OK because in that class, we both learned something.

During my second year at Newhouse, my advisor, Professor Jack Scollay, suggested that I write a thesis, rather than take the comprehensive exam. "You are one of the few students," he told me, "who I believe can write one-hundred-and-twenty-five-pages and make them interesting," he said. He gave me several theses to read for inspiration; I found them turgid and impossible to read. I decided mine would be fun.

My topic was "leadership advertising" and I used a technique I've often used since: I asked the same questions of several ad managers from top companies—United Airlines, Apple, Levi Strauss, Proctor and Gamble, McDonalds, among them—and from their agencies. I cut their answers together to create a "round-table discussion" on what I called *The Six Senses: Talk About the Client-Agency Relationship In The Creation Of Leadership Advertising.* It took me several weeks to conduct interviews and then another week and a half to write it. The Newhouse School liked my work well enough to use it for the next five years as an example of how a thesis should be written.

When I graduated, Dave Metz made me the Director of Special Communications Projects. My first project was to create a communication program to support the company's environmental efforts.

As a large chemical company, Kodak faced several environmental issues and to better understand them, I gathered a dozen of Kodak's top experts and asked them to explain to me the company's environmental goals. They were impatient: they said, "everybody knows what Kodak is trying to do—you need to tell us how to communicate it." I suggested that if "everybody knew," I must be the lone person who did not. But I assured them, if they told me, I'd write everything down so I'd never forget. I grabbed a marking pen and walked up to a white board. "What's the first goal?" I asked.

Bad news. There was lots of silence. It turned out, they didn't know the first goal—or any of them. Nobody had ever asked them before. It took several hours of discussion before I had written down—and we had agreed on—nine goals. But what was most gratifying was that those goals—and the continued progress towards them—formed the basis for Kodak's environmental communications for long into the future.

I had one other special project: to convince Kodak employees that the company had a future. Rounds of downsizing had begun; the future of Kodak was very much on everyone's minds. I had put together a plan to communicate that future and was presenting it to then-Kodak CEO Kay Whitmore when he stopped me. "What," he asked, "would make the program fail?" My answer: "if employees think this is just talk—if they don't see the proof of what we're describing." He asked me to come back with a proposal to make the vision real. He suggested a budget not to exceed five hundred thousand dollars.

When we left the room, Dave cut that budget. "Keep it under three hundred thousand," Dave said. I told Dave that I had no idea what the proposal would cost—because I had no idea what the proposal *would be*.

With the help of some smart and creative people, we figured it out: Kodak would take over the local War Memorial, the largest space in Rochester. In it, we would build "Kodak Imaging World"—a showcase of technology the world hadn't seen from Kodak but was under development in our research labs. I'd seen some it and it was exciting stuff. When I briefed Dave on the plan before I took it to Kay, I said, "this is a big idea, and it will cost big money. I think it will cost more than two million dollars."

Dave came unglued. "Gibbons," he said, "you don't listen. That's four times the amount Kay proposed." "Yeah," I said. "Big ideas cost money. Do you want to hear this one?" He did. Reluctantly. When I finished, he said, "that's a big idea. Let's take it to Kay."

We did—and he loved it. The problem was, to bring it off, I had to convince every business unit manager—and we had seventeen at that time—to let us show work still under development. And they wouldn't agree to that; it could affect current sales—and their current bonus. I shouldn't have been surprised. As a previous Kodak CEO, Gerry Zornow, once told me: "if you want to get something done, ask the person at the top—or the person at the bottom. The people in the middle have no interest in helping you; they want to help themselves." The idea died; and that's a shame because much of "Kodak Imaging World" would have been based on digital technology.

Nearly ten years before, Kodak's director of market intelligence had told the company that digital would begin to impact its business by the early 90's—and that the company had the basis for the capability they needed to compete. Kodak invented the digital camera—and made the first ones offered under the Apple brand. But digital didn't offer the profitability of film and the company dabbled—and soon lost interest.

At home that summer, we decided to put in a swimming pool—with a concrete deck for pool chairs where we could relax while the kids went in swimming. We talked to a pool company; they agreed that our plans were doable, and we signed the contract. I was in Dallas on a business trip when they began installation—and Jeanne called me and put the foreman on the line. "We can't put in the deck," he said; "the soil won't support it; the concrete will crack."

I told him we had to have a deck. "Suppose you were doing this at your house," I suggested. "What would you do to keep the deck from cracking?" "Oh," he said, "if it were my house, I'd use cardboard tubes, fill them with cement and bury them in the dirt, like pillars—and then build the deck on top of those pillars. They'd never crack." I asked him if he had tubes and cement and could do that for us? "If that's what you want me to do," he said. I did. He did.

The deck didn't crack, but Kodak was beginning to. The company kept reorganizing for an ever-smaller footprint; in communications, Dave put a financial wiz named Gary Clark and me in charge of defining our organization for the future—with numerical targets to hit. People shuddered when they saw us coming because it meant that jobs were going. At school, teachers were asking children to pray for their classmates' parents. It was a dark and confusing time.

In the early 1990s, Kodak sent me to Brussels Belgium, to attend a multi-week course for the company's senior managers—or those who were being groomed to be. I found the classes tedious. In one session on leadership, I told the teacher that I had no idea what he was talking about. "Perhaps," he suggested, "you are not cut out to be a leader. . . ." Definitely not in a traditional way. I wanted to lead by doing, by being the key contributor, by showing others how it was done. Like Dave Metz often did. But then, suddenly, on August 3, 1992, Dave retired—and soon after, Kay Whitmore also left the company. The Board had lost confidence in Kay and asked him to leave quietly over the next several months. But Kay was always an honest man: "if I've been fired," he said, "let's say that." He became an elder in the Mormon church.

With Dave and Kay gone, I felt rudderless; I was without my mentors and moved into a company organization working for a manager I'd didn't respect doing a job where I had no real responsibility. He proposed moving Kodak's major US marketing unit to Washington DC—so, it was suggested, his wife would be closer to her horses in Virginia—but that made no sense and never happened.

Meanwhile, I scrambled around for Kodak projects to keep me busy. I provided oversight for the winter Olympics in Albertville, France where Kodak was a sponsor; there, I spent an evening with Brian Boitano who was not only a gold medal skater, but also a superior human being. And I worked with some of the world's finest photographers who were capturing the games on Kodak film. When one of the female photographers complained to me about quality problems with processing, I decided to take up the matter with the Frenchman who was running the film center for Kodak. He seemed unconcerned. "Perhaps," he suggested, "she is just an excitable woman." But just as he said that, there was a loud "BANG!" and all the lights in the center went out. Out of the darkness, I heard him say, "or, perhaps not."

Back in the states, for most of a year, I managed a relationship with the American Advertising Federation where Kodak sponsored a competition among one hundred and fifty colleges where students created ads to encourage their fellow students to become more photographically active using Kodak cameras and films. The students did some brilliant work; one intriguing headline: "*Kodak. Because Your Memory Sucks.*" "It's directionally right," one of the judges said, "but it's not something Kodak could say."

That reminded me of a story told about Kodak's founder, George Eastman, who was often away on hunting trips to Africa. When he returned from one, he found that Kodak advertising had noticeably improved, and he mentioned that to his copywriter, Lewis B. Jones. "When you are here, Mr. Eastman, I write our ads for you," Jones told him in reply. "But when you are away, I write them for the customer."

As my colleague who worked on the Apple advertising account once told me, "The worst ad is what the CEO wants to say; the best ad is what the customer needs to hear."

None of the student work was never used.

At home, there was also a bit of turmoil. We spent one Christmas Eve with firemen and EMTs at our house when my brother bit his tongue and passed out from the sight of his blood. And in 1991, there was a massive ice storm that left us without power for several days; the kids thought it was fun for the first day— when we roasted marshmallows in the fireplace at night; they wanted heat and light when they woke up in the morning.

At Kodak, I felt like I was moving without a sense of direction and struggling without a sense of accomplishment. A few years before, Dave Metz told me, Kay Whitmore had said, "There may be only two people who are more concerned about this company than they are about their own careers—Bob Gibbons and Bob LaPerle." I did love Kodak. I'd spent almost twenty-five years in a great Kodak career; I wanted to stay with the company, but what was I going to do now?

# 39

## CALIFORNIA TO THE RESCUE

**B**IG CHANGES WERE UNDERWAY—FOR KODAK AND FOR ME. When Dave Metz retired, Mike Benard—someone I'd hired to replace me at one point—took his place. People asked me if I was disappointed that I didn't get the job. Not for a nano-second. Not under those conditions. Kay Whitmore had been fired, and the Board brought in outside leadership who may have had proven success, but—I would always contend—didn't understand the uniqueness of the Kodak brand. Phil Samper had both qualities: He was tough, but smart and decisive, and he knew the Kodak legacy. At a lunch with Colby Chandler I enjoyed in 2018, Colby told me, "The fate of the company may have been different if Phil had been chosen." If Phil Samper had been leading the company, I would have fought for Metz's job; corporate headquarters would have been an exciting place to work; Kodak would have taken a different path forward. Instead, Mike's immediate task was to continue to reduce Dave's 625-person staff to about fifty people, and his continuing assignment was to pretend that Kodak was healthy. I couldn't have handled either job.

But I think Mike respected my abilities because he asked me if I had interest in becoming the company's chief marketing officer, handling all major sponsorships with an oversight on advertising. I did, but my career had been spent in a corporate staff unit; I believed I needed more business experience to do that job with credibility—and we worked out a plan for me to get that. I'd move into a position as director of worldwide communications for a Kodak unit called Entertainment Imaging, which managed the company's business in movie film. I'd stay there for two years, then I'd be given the company's top marketing job.

The job I was taking was in California, so Kodak sent Jeanne and me out to look for a house. We found one at the very top of our price range—more than double what we'd paid for our home in Rochester—in a place called Thousand Oaks. It was forty miles, on congested California freeways, from where I worked in Hollywood. I'd need to leave the house by six o'clock in the morning to get to work on time. We had told our realtor to help us find a home with high resale value: we expected to be there for only two years.

Kodak handled the move. They hired Mayflower who packed everything we owned into two hundred and thirty boxes, all of them labeled, many of them labeled wrong. We had two cars and they planned to doble-deck them in the moving van. "Have you ever seen cars loaded in a van?" the driver asked me before he loaded ours. I said I had not. "It goes a lot easier," he said, "if you don't watch."

Once the van was loaded, the driver told us he'd leave Rochester on a Sunday night and arrive at our California home—twenty-five hundred miles away—on Wednesday morning. Jeanne and I and Emily—the other kids came separately after they finished summer jobs—flew out and were in the hotel when, early Wednesday, the driver called. He was at our house, waiting for someone to come out and fix his flat tire. One of the inside tires—the truck had eighteen—had been punctured and needed to be replaced.

Our house was at the top of a hill and when we arrived, he had the fully loaded truck jacked up with two guys underneath it, changing the tire. Once again, I felt I shouldn't look. But I did watch the strongest kid I had ever seen, take Jeanne's oak triple dresser, stand it on end, and—by himself—carry it up to the second floor.

When the movers left, we found ourselves surrounded by two hundred and thirty boxes—and a zillion ants. Jeanne went into the dining room and cried;

Emily wanted to move back to Rochester. But we had the house professionally fumigated and the ants went away. For me, a bigger concern was the aftershocks we felt from the very recent, 6.7 Northridge earthquake. I'd never felt one before; it seemed like the laws of nature had been repealed and we began earthquake-proofing the house.

I was at a party in Hollywood soon after we moved, when the head of advertising for the *Hollywood Reporter* asked me if we'd found a place to live. I told her that we did; we were living in Thousand Oaks. "Why would you want to live there?" she asked. I told her it was a nice community and we'd found a house we liked that we could afford. "Oh," she said, "you're trying to live within your means. That's an interesting concept." Most people I met in Hollywood were living at the edge of their imagination. In fact, I soon decided that, while there may not be too much money in California, there clearly is too much hope. People are hoping for things that just won't happen. And if the state has a motto, it must be this: What's in it for me—*personally?*

Thousand Oaks was the home of a large number of retired airline pilots and former FBI agents: the air was very clear, and the community was very safe. A week or so after we'd moved in, I took Emily to a Disney recording session at Capitol Records in Hollywood; at night, Jeanne and I sat around our pool where we could swim year-round; several other Kodak people lived nearby, and we began getting together for Friday night meals.

In mid-August, about two weeks after we were in our new home, Kodak's chief marketing officer unexpectedly resigned. My future job was available, but it was far too soon to bring me back to fill it. As the company looked around for the right candidate, they decided to restructure the job—and to fill it from outside the company. I was no longer a candidate, but that was fine; I figured we would just wait and see where my career took us.

We were forty-five minutes from Santa Barbara, about a half hour from the ocean. In the beginning, when we thought we'd only live in California for two years, we tried to see everything—from the ocean to the missions, from the sights of Hollywood to the museums in Pasadena—and every Christmas Eve we held a party that people told us they looked forward to. But maybe best of all, Kodak soon introduced a buy-down program to help everyone who moved from Rochester to pay their mortgage. Still, California was expensive.

With Emily in high school and the other kids away in college, Jeanne decided to go back to work. My boss's wife worked at a local company, Consolidated Electrical Distributors (CED), and helped Jeanne get a job as a clerk in loss prevention there; they handled accident claims—sometimes for such employee actions as driving a fork-lift off a loading dock. Jeanne ended up working for CED for fourteen years.

In sophomore year, Tim had a week-long break from school and came home in October to relax, but two days later, a couple of this Notre Dame friends called. They'd flown to Los Angeles on a whim and asked if they could stay with us. When they were ready to leave, they asked Tim to drop them off at the taping of a game show, instead of taking them to the airport. He did and, carrying their bags, they went into "The Price is Right" —where they won $21,000—including $16,000.00 in prizes and $5,000.00 in cash. And then they flew back to South Bend. Tim was sad he hadn't gone with them, but I told him: "This is California. That stuff happens."

At Kodak I went from having ninety people working for me in Rochester to sharing a secretary. I went from a window office to a small cubicle near the copier. I went from working with lots of people who knew me well to working with about fifty people who didn't know me at all, some of whom wondered why I was there. To me, it felt like a promotion—with different responsibility. As one of the most seasoned sales reps put it succinctly: "I figure that most things go wrong because people don't communicate well. You're the head of communications; that means that most problems are your fault."

There were other challenges. One morning, someone delivered a box to our receptionist. "There is a bomb inside," he said. "If you move, it will detonate." We evacuated the building, called the bomb squad—and it turned out to be a hoax. But the receptionist was so shaken, he quit, and we never saw him again. On another day, I looked out to see our building and shipping dock surrounded by pickets from the Screen Actors Guild. When I asked what was going on, the lead picketer told me, "Your company is unfair to unions."

"Or, maybe," I suggested, "you have that backwards because every truck you prevent from entering our property is here to pick up film for a union project. You could be shutting down union movies."

"We'll be leaving soon," he said. And they did.

It was one more indication that a move from Rochester to Hollywood was not a seamless transition; I needed a mentor to teach me how business in California was done—and I found a great one in Don Adams. The trunk of his company car was always filled with Kodak products; his friends were never without free Kodak cameras and film. When someone needed a favor, Don knew whom to ask; he was the one who introduced me to Johnny Grant, the mayor of Hollywood—and they both got along well because, like Johnny, Don was a character.

Don had been working at Kodak in Hollywood for more than twenty-five years before I arrived, and he always had a sense of upbeat fun. His voice impressions of Jimmy Stewart, Humphrey Bogart, Jack Benny, and John Wayne, among others were frequent—and he often lapsed into a Spanish accent to say, with a sweeping gesture across the streets of Hollywood, "once my family owned all this land before the stinking gringos stole it from us." I assumed he spoke fluent Spanish because at a party for a colleague going home to Spain, Don said, "in honor of my friend's heritage, tonight I will make my further remarks in Spanish." And I believed he did, although when I later asked Rodrigo what Don had said about him, Rodrigo said, "I have no idea; whatever language Don was speaking, it wasn't Spanish."

But when I was new to Hollywood, Don took me around and introduced me. As Bud Stone, who ran Deluxe Labs back then told me, "in Hollywood, it's not who you know that's important; it's *who introduced you* to who you know."

The industry had great respect for Kodak—and Kodak people. The division was led by Joerg Agin, who was well known to customers and well loved by his people. He fully understood the business and had a youthful enthusiasm for exploring new opportunities he called "white spaces." The office was managed by Fred Franzwa, a man of great initiative and integrity. And Kodak had been honored by the Motion Picture Academy with nine Oscars for scientific and technical excellence and service to the motion picture industry. Except for studios, that's more than any other company.

My Hollywood job came with its own set of perks—dinners with cinematographers, invitations to movie premieres and recording sessions. At a *First Knight* party, I was wandering around with Richard Gere and Sean Connery; as a sponsor of his Shoah Foundation, Steven Spielberg invited a few of us to dinner with him and his wife. And maybe most glamorous, Jeanne and I went to the Academy Awards several times. That was fun; when we arrived by limo on Hollywood Boulevard, the paparazzi stuck their cameras in the car and asked, "Are you anybody?" When we told them we were not, they moved on. The most interesting part was hanging around on the red carpet as the stars arrived. One year, we stood next to Sharon Stone talking endlessly on her cell phone.

I had a free pass for our family to all Disney parks—and one for Jeanne and me to see movies for free in theatres. We saw concerts and other events from Kodak's front row balcony seats at the Kodak Theatre—and watched Bette Midler, Garth Brooks, and the LA Lakers from Kodak's private box at the Staples Center. But despite all that, I was never particularly star struck. I viewed stars as normal people and when Mel Gibson came up to our table to talk to a cinematographer I was sitting with, they just talked of routine things. I ignored them.

As the new millennium approached, a company named Trizechahn proposed building an upscale shopping and dining complex in the heart of Hollywood. Its centerpiece would be a thirty-six hundred seat theatre that would be the future home of the Academy Awards, so the Motion Picture Academy could "bring the Oscars back to Hollywood where they began" —right across the street in the Roosevelt Hotel ballroom in 1927, the same year that Kodak came to Hollywood.

The Academy had said they would not let the theatre be "sponsored" by any company, but my Kodak boss, Dick Aschman, questioned that decision. He thought Kodak should sponsor it—and asked me to help make that happen. I called John Pavlik, then director of communications at the Academy (Don Adams had introduced us previously) and we arranged a lunch for the key Academy people—and ours. In California, it's illegal, I think, to have a discussion without food and, often, a beverage.

The Academy agreed to consider our sponsorship because they saw at least two points of connectivity: Kodak founder, George Eastman, was one of only two honorary members of the Academy, ever. And, every Oscar winner for Best Picture, ever, had been shot on Kodak film. The Academy said they'd take it up with their Board of Directors. A couple of weeks later, John called me with the verdict: their board agreed that the new facility would be called "The George Eastman Theatre."

"We aren't interested in calling it the George Eastman Theatre," I told John. "Kodak is our brand. We want to brand this the Kodak Theatre." John said their board had to vote again; they did and beginning in 2002—and for ten years afterwards—the Academy Awards were broadcast "live, from the Kodak Theatre in Hollywood."

As a liaison to the builder, Trizechahn, I was able to work with Christine Sullivan, their attentive rep who always made good things happen for us, and who has gone on to become a co-author of children's books.

When the theater opened, I was the Kodak spokesperson dealing with the press and that gave me the opportunity to prove the value of what Dave Metz had once taught me: "Before the press asks its questions, have three or four key messages you want to communicate. And then find a way to make them the answers to their questions." One of my messages was that our sponsorship connected three great brands—Kodak, the Academy, and Hollywood—responsible for the movies.

From one reporter, the first question I was asked was: "What did Kodak pay for the sponsorship?"

Since Kodak didn't give out that information, I said, "We don't look at this in terms of money; we look at this in terms of value. And the value is—this sponsorship connects the three great brands responsible for the popularity of the movies." That sound byte ended up on the news.

The Kodak Theatre was planned to be able to show film, but even before it opened, digital technology had come to the movies. It started with special effects; but movies were still shot on film, and they were shown on film, sometimes under appalling conditions. In helping studios certify theatres for premieres, Kodak reps found one with a screen that had been mounted inside out, so the non-reflective surface was facing the audience; and at another site, they found no screen at all—

the wall had just been painted white.

The future of film in theatres first came into serious question at Showest, a major industry convention in 1999. There, two companies—Hughes/JVC and Texas Instruments—showed digital projectors for the first time. The industry invited Bob Mayson, head of film origination for Kodak in Hollywood, to "defend film." But in the speech I wrote for him, what I really did was "challenge digital" to meet's film's standards. Film, I suggested, endured because it met the creative, operational, technical, and financial needs of the industry. When digital was proved superior by *all* those measures, I suggested, digital would replace film. The standards that the speech laid out were later adopted by an industry-wide consortium as the requirements for the new technology.

At that stage, digital looked good—and the *Hollywood Reporter* suggested "the noise everyone heard afterwards was the sound of Kodak executives jumping off buildings." Actually, the noise was from discussions on how Kodak might help overcome some of digital's shortcomings so we could participate in the business. As a first step, the company formed a small business team—Kodak Digital Cinema—and asked me to manage their communications. I eagerly accepted the job; I thought digital was our future.

To get experience in theatres, we hired Sean Lohan from the exhibition industry (he was the first Kodak employee who really understood how theaters managed their business); and we developed pre-show systems—networks using small digital projectors to replace the slide projectors used to show advertising before the movies. With digital, much more was possible—although some people at Kodak accused us of killing their slide projector business—and within a short period of time, we had more than two thousand systems installed and were the world leader in digital preshow systems.

Eventually, we began distributing digital movies—*Mission Impossible* was the first—and offering in-theatre servers and networks to help exhibitors show their movies and manage their business. For about the last ten years of my Kodak career, I worked in Kodak Digital Cinema, and it was both an exhilarating and an exasperating time. We never had either enough money or support to do what we needed to do, but we were a small team that believed we were inventing

Kodak's future in the entertainment business.

Along the way, Sean Lohan taught me a lot about theatres and how cinema owners think about costs and new products. From Drena Rogers I learned how to sell and work with customers. In Hollywood and Rochester, we had great teams, including Bob Mayson, Don Lane, Andrew Saidi, Jim Sullivan, Chris Simpson Tom Glanville, Denis Kelly, John Arena, Brian Kercher, and others. At one point, I hired a small agency—The Lippin Group, led by Dick Lippin who also handled communications for the Disney family—to help us get the attention of the media.

I knew we were playing above our weight when the president of our division—film and digital reported to him—asked me to stop communications because some film reps were complaining that we were hurting their business. When I ignored him, he took away all my budget—and I had to tell Dick Lippin we had no money to pay for his services. "The decision to stop is wrong," Dick said, "and I can't let that happen. We'll work for free as long as you need us." And they did.

But it wasn't enough. In theatres, digital projection had become universally accepted; if Kodak wanted to stay in the game, it was time for major investments— and the company was hurting. Six months after I celebrated my fortieth anniversary with Kodak, I was at an industry convention when my boss Gary Einhaus called; how quickly—he asked—could I put together a communications plan to announce that Kodak was leaving the digital cinema business? As I wrote that, I knew that after almost forty-one years, I'd be leaving Kodak.

It felt like the right time to be going. The company that had invented the film movie business in the past—and had much of the technology needed to re-invent its digital future—had given up its seat at the table. I didn't want to be around when Kodak ended up on the menu.

My Kodak days would soon be over, but my love of movies would never end.

# 40

# A STAR ON
# HOLLYWOOD BOULEVARD

ORKING IN HOLLYWOOD FOR SIXTEEN YEARS HELPED ME find my comfort place: in an aisle seat, in a dark theatre, waiting for the movie to begin. Growing up, I'd seen some of the more popular Disney movies and, when the kids were young, I took them to the theatre to see ones I thought they'd enjoy. Jeanne and I would also spend an occasional night out in the theatre, but along the way, I missed far more movies than I saw.

That changed when we moved to California. I became an avid movie-goer—for several reasons: I was now dealing directly with the cinematographers who shot movies and I wanted to be able to talk intelligently with them about their work; Kodak sent me to a number of film festivals (Sundance, Cannes, and Avignon, among others) where I fell in love with smaller movies that told better stories; and—perhaps best of all—the president of the largest theatre chain in our area gave me a pass to see all movies in his theatres for free.

We also went to several film premieres for movies large and small, but the most impressive was an event held in a soundstage for the restoration of Steven Spielberg's *E. T. the Extra-Terrestrial.* In the front of the massive room, the studio had rigged up a huge screen on which the movie was projected. But as the film started, the screen was elevated to reveal John Williams conducting an orchestra underneath—to create a live soundtrack. And after the movie finished, Jeanne, Jennifer, Emily, and I went to small party with the movie's cast and crew. It was a magical Saturday afternoon.

I always tell others—if they have a problem in the theatre with sound levels, air conditioning, picture focus, or anything else—speak to the manager. I want theaters to survive. I put my advice to the test one afternoon when I was the only one waiting to see a movie in a small independent multiplex. When the previews started, the image was too dark, so I asked one of the ushers to turn up the bulb. He said they were having bulb problems; he offered to give me a ticket to another movie on another screen. I told him I didn't want to see another movie; I said that when they sell tickets to movies they can't show properly, they do damage to their brand, and they disappoint people who want to love their theater. I was calm but insistent—and that got the attention of the manager. She cancelled a different movie—they hadn't sold any tickets yet—on another screen and moved my movie to that screen so I could see it there. And I was the only one watching it. But customer service like that earns my loyalty. It's where I plan to see lots of future movies.

When some of my colleagues realized I was seeing a lot of movies—sometimes more than a hundred a year—they began to ask my opinion, and I started writing movie reviews. My goal especially was to encourage others to see some of the smaller, independent movies that had spent all their money on a good story and cast—and had nothing left for advertising purposes. In addition to sending the reviews to friends, I became the movie reviewer for five small California newspapers and for a Los Angeles film blog.

Except for horror movies, I found I loved a good movie in any genre—although I was most attracted to smart writing and fresh storytelling, and most offended by lazy and crude humor that wasn't essential to the plot. I've also come to believe that the movies we most enjoy are not only about what's up there on the screen, but also what's going on in our life at the time. If you want confirmation of that, see a movie again that you especially loved in your youth. It may be as enjoyable—but I'd be willing to bet it's a "different movie" —not because it changed, but because you did.

Through the years, my all-time favorite movie has remained *Butch Cassidy and the Sundance Kid*. Even with all the movies I'd seen since, I hadn't forgotten that one—and so in Hollywood, I was thrilled to meet, and spend time with, its cinematographer, Conrad Hall.

His talent was well respected—he'd won Oscars for *Butch Cassidy, American Beauty,* and *Road to Perdition*—but I found his honesty refreshing. When I'd ask what he was shooting, "I'm working on something now," he would say, "that's a piece of garbage." Or "I'm working with a really talented young man named Sam Raimi and he's really got it together." In 1996, when I went to the first CamerImage—a cinematography festival in Poland—they honored Conrad Hall and I had T-shirts made with his picture and a quote from him. "My job," he frequently said, "is to abuse Kodak film."

In mid-December 2002, when a friend told me that Connie was very sick and "might not make it," an idea jumped into my head: What if Kodak could give him a special gift—a star on Hollywood Boulevard? Only one or two cinematographers had ever received that honor—and it was clearly way out of my area of Kodak responsibility to do that because he shot film and I was no longer part of the film team. But I didn't think anyone else in the company knew how to do it, and I wasn't sure I'd be successful. So, I told no one; I asked no one's permission. I just contacted Johnny Grant.

Johnny Grant was the unofficial "Mayor of Hollywood;" he was the one who originally developed the idea of having stars on the sidewalk and he presided over a small Board who decided who got the new ones. I'd been introduced to him by Don Adams and had met him for breakfast on several occasions at the Hollywood Roosevelt Hotel where he lived—and I called him with my idea.

Johnny said that all the stars for the coming year had already been decided, but if I could write him a note, enclose a biography of Conrad Hall, and give him a few days, he would see what he could do. I wrote the note, got a copy of his biography, and messengered it over to Johnny on that Tuesday in mid-December. I told him of the respect that other cinematographers had for Conrad's talent, of the millions of worldwide moviegoers who had enjoyed his work, of the credit he brought to Hollywood, and of his severely declining health.

The next day, Johnny called a special meeting of the Board to consider our request. He called me back on Thursday to tell me the Board had granted our proposal; Conrad Hall would get a star a few months later the next year. I told the manager for our film business what I'd done; he said he'd tell Connie the news when he went up to see him in his hospital room the next day. He did. A few weeks later, on January 6, 2003, Conrad Hall died.

One of the very last things that Conrad Hall heard after a lifetime of great work was that he was going to be honored in a most public way for what he accomplished. I like to hope that the news eased his way into the unknown. I like to think that what I was able to do will forever remain a part of Hollywood.

The star was presented posthumously four months later, on May 1, 2003 with a great crowd in attendance. In a cruel twist of fate, because I was not on Kodak's film team, I wasn't on the list to be able to meet with Conrad's family at the ceremony. I had to stand back with the passers-by—while Kodak people who had nothing to do with getting the star stepped forward to express their condolences and share their memories with Hall's family. Through the years, Hollywood has broken a lot of hearts and that day, it broke mine.

In those days, it cost $15,000.00 for a star—the Hollywood Chamber of Commerce used star ceremonies as fund-raisers—and of course Kodak paid for Conrad Hall. But when the Kodak Theatre was about to open, I had another idea: I called Johnny again and asked if the George Eastman star—he had one on a side street—could be moved in front of the theatre? Johnny explained that "we don't move stars. If we did, you could just imagine how many would want their stars moved, sometimes more than once."

But then Johnny had another idea, something he "had been thinking about."

Despite all his work with the stars—he explained—he had never had a star of his own on Hollywood Boulevard. If Kodak would like to sponsor a star for him, also, in front of the Kodak Theatre, well then, maybe George Eastman could have a second star, like other artists along Hollywood Boulevard, right next to his. If Kodak could handle something like that—$30,000 would be the total cost, he said—well then, maybe George would have the star where we wanted it, after all.

In Hollywood, that's the way things were done. We paid the money and got the stars.

You could visit those stars today—even though, as Kodak went through its financial struggles, the company gave up sponsorship of the theatre and, while some people still call it, "The Kodak," it's now officially the Dolby Theatre. Kodak is essentially gone from Hollywood—and Johnny Grant has also passed away. During his career, he had been a newsman and a disc jockey, he had appeared in a number of films and had joined Bob Hope as a USO ambassador on his tours; since 1980, his full-time job had been the "Mayor of Hollywood." It was an honorary position, but he was a kind of "an elf" who was loved by many.

Johnny Grant died on January 9, 2008. He was eighty-four years old. He was cremated and his ashes were scattered under the "Hollywood" sign above the boulevard where his star still shines.

Every night, I drove past that sign and left Hollywood's "Walk of Fame" to come home to a very different walk. There, a little rescue dog named Sophie waited for me to take her out on the streets of Thousand Oaks.

# 41

# WALKING THE NOODLE

WHO KNEW THAT A LITTLE DOG COULD MAKE such a difference? She was a rescue dog that someone found wandering the streets of Las Vegas, back when Jennifer was living there and had an operation that left her homebound. Emily, who was living with us in California, thought that Jennifer needed to be out walking—and that a dog would encourage her to do that. Together, they went to the animal shelter and, in the last building, found a furry white puppy, maybe seven or eight months old. When they walked by her cage, she flipped on her back, put her paws in the air, and looked them in their eyes. "I've been waiting for you," she said. "It was her signature move," Jennifer came to recognize. She'd use it often.

When someone else in the shelter started to show interest in this little fluffy dog, Emily and Jennifer decided to adopt her. At a cost of $165.00, she was, as Jennifer would say, "one of the more expensive dogs." And always would be; we tried to give her the best possible care.

She was small, eight or ten pounds, and some sort of Jack Russell Terrier mix—maybe with poodle, maybe with chihuahua, maybe even with some Maltese—because she had soft fur. We'd eventually decide her breed was Kardashian because her attitude was "please hold all your attention until it's for me." They named her Sophie and although she was supposed to stay in Las Vegas with Jennifer, she attached herself to Emily—who brought her home to live with us. She'd live with Emily sporadically during her Coast Guard years, but it was easier for everyone if Sophie lived eventually full-time with us—and she seemed to be OK with that.

She had been neutered, was housebroken, but she had one physical problem: on her right eye, she had a kind of pink bubble, as if something had popped out. It's called "cherry eye" and it would take us two operations to get it corrected. And when the medication wore off, she immediately showed "Jack Russell jumping energy." Sofas, chairs, people's laps. Even a three-foot high child gate that was blocking her path. If Sophie wanted to be up or down, she simply went for it, without any sense of caution or fear. I started calling her "Noodle" because she behaved like one. Eventually, it became a term of endearment; I've given nicknames to all our kids and grandkids—and Noodle was hers. Sophie didn't like men—she barked when she met me—and I didn't want a dog—but she wasn't just any dog, she was Sophie. When I called the vet, I identified myself as "Sophie's protector." I identified her as my teacher.

From the beginning, she was a little dog who just seemed to accept what came along, to deal with it, and to get on with her life. Only slightly behind eating—her vet called her a highly food-motivated dog—was her love of walking, and so I began taking her, sometimes as often as three times a day. She was an erratic walker—often distracted by something that caught her eye on the other side of the street, sometimes stopping to eat rabbit poop or lick bird droppings or watch ants on a sidewalk. But just since I've retired, I figured that Noodle and I have traveled well over four thousand miles—one walk at a time.

She believed that walks were a commitment I'd made in return for her agreeing to live with us; she expected me to honor that promise and I did—regardless of what else I had going on, or even how I felt. A deal was a deal.

And Noodle always knew when it was time to go. Morning, noon, or mid-afternoon—she'd wake up, stretch, give a phony sneeze, or clear her throat, and stand there looking at me with her dark eyes suggesting: "It's time for a walk, isn't it?" And we went—every day, except in the rain. She hated water in all its forms: rain, baths, swimming pools, or the ocean. She'd turn around and come back in the house—unless she *really* had to go.

Then, around ten o'clock every night—when I'd be sitting and reading—she'd come over, yawn, and give me a look that said, "It's about time to pee once more before bed, don't you think?" Jeanne or I took her out, she went, got her final treat, and headed for bed. She expected me to go to sleep also. In her little mind, there was a right time for everything.

I sometimes called her "Tonto," my faithful Indian companion. Or "ragamuffin" when she looked like she needed a bath. Or "gluestick" because she was small, white, and stuck by my side. Or "lazy bones" when it was warm, and she laid down in a cool patch of grass. Some days, I called her "boots" or "dark eyes" or other names as we walked along; mostly I called her Sophie or Noodle—and she taught me what she thought I needed to know.

*Deal with problems when they're small.* When Sophie got a burr in her paw or mulch stuck to her fur, she stopped, looked up at me, and waited until I found the problem—and took care of it. Sophie carried no burdens long term.

*Don't avoid things, just because they're difficult.* We live at the bottom of a steep hill; I tried to avoid walking up it; she wanted to tackle it immediately. It got easier every time we did it; we eventually walked all the hills in the neighborhood.

*When you're happy, show it.* When I put her harness on in the morning, Noodle was all wiggles and raw energy. In the afternoon, she often leaped straight up as I opened the door. She loved to walk and wanted me to know how important it was that I provided that special treat.

*Let people know they're important.* When our neighbor, Tom, was telling me a sad story about his dog passing away, Sophie spent a few extra minutes looking at him and letting him pet her; she even let him ruffle her fur; she knew he was having a difficult day.

*Don't let little things slow you down.* When Noodle had operations on her hind paws, she had to have her leg wrapped, so she had to hobble to get anywhere.

Guess who didn't think that having one paw out of commission was really any excuse for missing a walk.

*Don't be afraid to change your mind.* I picked the general direction, but when we came to a corner, I let her choose which way to go—and no two sequential days were alike. She liked to see what had changed overnight—and discover what she could learn if she were standing someplace else.

*Greet everyone in the friendliest possible way.* She believed everyone was waiting for her to come by; she figured that if she looked interested in them, wagged her tail, and acted friendly to them, they would be also. When she wandered up to Julie, Alyssa's mom, I said: "she believes everyone loves her." "Of course," Julie said, "because if they didn't, you'd have to wonder about them."

By the fall of 2021, Sophie had passed her seventeenth birthday—and she began to seriously show her age; despite the fact that she liked to think she was a puppy—and some days tried to act like one—her progression was downward. She had already survived a serious bout of pancreatitis, a urinary infection, and Giardia, which is parasites in her feces; she had several surgeries to repair torn cruciate ligaments with fishing line, an operation to remove stones from her bladder, and one day she had eight teeth pulled including a back molar with three deep roots where the pulp was showing. She whimpered all the way home in the car, but when we put her down, she jumped up on the couch and sat looking at us as if to say: *So that's over; let's walk.*

Although Noodle's medical record—from just our eight years in Oceanside—was one hundred and seventy pages long, as Emily one said, "Sophie is the little dog that could." But finally, we recognized that she really couldn't—and that our plan to keep her forever wasn't best for her. She was mostly blind and seemed in pain from eye problems; she didn't recognize a treat unless we put it in her mouth—and panicked if it fell out because she couldn't smell it nearby. On her walks, she sometimes stopped, confused about where she was; there were times she couldn't stand up. She was urinating in the house daily. We tried to ignore all that—until we also couldn't.

We discussed the situation with Sophie's beloved vet, Dr. Kathy Burnell, who had so often helped Noodle deal with her medical problems and Dr. Burnell told us: "You know how much I adore Sophie and want the best for her. You and your family have given Sophie an incredible life. Allowing her to leave with dignity and before further decline are also gifts for Sophie."

In the end, we were giving her gabapentin for the pain—and feeding her eggs and cheese and other people food that wasn't good for her, but we knew she loved. We knew we were close to having to say good-bye and since dogs live in the moment, we wanted her last moments to be happy.

We gave her the gift of euthanasia on October 19, 2021 when she passed away peacefully with Jeanne and I and her vet petting her and telling her how much she was loved. Before she went to bed the night before, I had a long conversation with her and thanked her for choosing Emily and Jennifer so long ago. I told her all she meant to us over the years—and how we'd remember her always as a part of our family.

But at 10:45 on that Tuesday October morning, after she had given Sophie her final injection, her vet put her stethoscope to Sophie's chest and looked up with tears in her eyes. "Her heart has stopped," she said. That little heart that carried Noodle through so many operations and had beat so enthusiastically when she saw someone she loved, was beating no more. All the pain she pretended she didn't have had gone away.

Before we left the room, I kissed her soft head and thanked her again for all she taught me; and as we walked out, we saw her vet cover her gently with the blanket she was laying on, like a mother covers her child who has gone to sleep. What jumped into my head was a quote from my kindergarten teacher, "May God bless her real good" for all she did to make everyone happy. When I was out walking by myself a few weeks later, a man I'd never met came up to me. "My dog Larry and I are so sad about your loss of Sophie," he said. *That little dog*, I thought; *she knew everybody.*

She was a good dog. She was the one who helped give structure to my days after I had retired from Kodak.

# 42

# KODAK IN MY REAR-VIEW MIRROR

WHEN I FIRST WALKED THROUGH THE DOORS to Kodak Office on that June morning in 1969, who would have thought that the 10,341 work-days that would follow could be so much fun?

It was a long time, a good time, a proud time. I came within a month of spending forty-one years with an amazing company—and having an experience that was rewarding in so many ways. I wish I could do it all again.

When I finally left, not only was I leaving Kodak, but Kodak was also leaving the motion picture business. Movies were increasingly created and distributed digitally—and the company had much of the technology to lead the way. They had developed the digital management system that enabled theatre systems—ticketing, pre-show, feature presentation, monitoring and reporting—to be inter-connected in ways that made great sense for the future. Kodak was also in the final stages of developing a laser projector that would bring new levels of illumination and sharpness to cinema screens. They had a growing relationship with exhibitors they could have built on.

The industry had sent a strong signal that they liked to deal with Kodak, they trusted us to have their best interests at heart. But at Kodak, we lacked the heart and commitment to make it happen. When the industry got serious about going all-digital, Kodak decided to go in a different direction. Film would still be around, but it was only a matter of time before Kodak's enduring legacy in the movies would come to an end. The company that George Eastman brought to Hollywood to help it tell its stories for almost a century was now fading to black.

Joerg Agin, who had managed our film business in Hollywood so wisely and well for so long, came into my office one morning, closed the door, and said, "Bobby [he always called me Bobby], I'm going to retire because I think we need to begin to transition to digital. That will take a long time—longer than I can give—and I think the person who is there at the end needs to be there at the beginning. And that person won't be me." If it had been him—and if the company had listened to him—the results might have been very different

As Kodak prepared its exit strategy, I wrote this:

## When Kodak Leaves the Cinema

In every aspect of life, there are those few who contribute more than could be expected, who raise the stakes for everyone. In the entertainmet industry, Kodak has always been one of those very few.

After Thomas Edison invented the movie projector, he asked George Eastman to supply the film. "How wide should the film be?" Eastman asked. Edison held his thumb and index finger about an inch apart—and the 35mm format was born. In the early days, when Walt Disney couldn't afford his film, Eastman gave it to him on consignment. "That young man has talent," Eastman reportedly said.

Kodak has shown an enduring respect for the movies and for those who make them, for helping those with talent and imagination and ability to capture those moments in ways that speak so clearly about who we are, what we imagine, how we live, and how we can shape a future to help change lives.

Kodak has made complex systems and technology better, easier to use, and more effective. Kodak has built relationships and friendships; the most-celebrated cinematographers in the world have long "shot on Kodak"; every cinematographer aspires to.

For the first seventy-five years, every Oscar-winning Best Picture was proudly made on Kodak film. Kodak has been a part of, or involved in, or the creator of, virtually every major innovation—the 35mm format, color, sound, and others—that made it possible for artists to tell their stories more naturally, more convincingly, under more challenging conditions. Using just light and a lens.

How sad then that the future of the cinema won't have Kodak in it. How unfortunate that Kodak isn't helping with the transition to that tomorrow, the evolution to digital technology, the re-invention of a business to which the company brought art and science, talent and technology—and set free the human imagination.

What could Kodak have contributed to that future? Resources, of course, and a restless quest for quality; an energy to drive standards higher, to cause everyone to play harder, to expect more, to create a future cinema that would be truly worthy of its past.

Now, the entertainment business is moving on without Kodak. And everyone, including Kodak, is poorer for it.

And the industry has a poor memory. In 2014, the Academy of Motion Picture Arts and Sciences gave a special Oscar to the film laboratories that supported the motion picture business for so long. Kodak was never even mentioned in the tribute. When I moved to Hollywood in 1994, Kodak had more than thirty thousand employees making film; within a few years after my retirement, they had fewer than three hundred.

But on February 1, 2010, my last day in my office on the third floor of Kodak's then-headquarters at the corner of Santa Monica Blvd and Las Palmas Avenue in Hollywood, before I logged out for the last time, I wrote a good-by letter to Kodak people. My note said this:

*When I leave for the last time today, I leave with gratitude that this wonderful company once chose me to help tell its stories. Through the years, I've had more fun that I could have ever imagined and was able to work with so many people I respected and learned from; I've had so many jobs that were the right job for me, did so many interesting things along the way.*

*So much of what Jeanne and I and our children have is because of what Kodak enabled me to do. Given that I'm concluding my career in the movie world, it's perhaps appropriate that, in some ways, my career feels like a movie, an unfolding story with lots of special moments. No movie can go on forever, so this feels like the right time to bring mine to an end.*

*When the lights come on and the credits roll, it will feel strangely different, because you can't work with a company for forty years without also falling in love with that company and its people. So, I know I will miss you; not all of you, of course, but you know who you are.*

*I don't yet know what I will be doing; I suspect that it will somehow involve writing; it's something Kodak trusted me to do a lot of and it's something I've found that I love. But what I'll write—and for whom—are still unknown. Until I figure that out, my life will be just an 'untitled sequel' in what has been a great franchise.*

*Thanks for being a part of my story.*

*—Bob Gibbons*
*Kodak: 1969–2010*

Even as I left, the company continued to shrink its way to irrelevance. It went into and came out of bankruptcy; where once it had 149,00 employees around the world, it now had fewer than five thousand. Cuts had been made everywhere; at least half of the two-hundred-and-twelve buildings at Kodak Park had been imploded—and the whole complex had been converted to a business park occupied by other companies.

What happened? My over-simplified answer: Kodak lost the handle on their brand. The company brought in managers who thought Kodak was about technology; they didn't realize the company was really about trust. People trusted

the most important moments of their lives to Kodak—in x-rays, business documents, and presentations—and professional pictures and amateur snapshots, and,
of course, in movies. And Kodak took that trust seriously. Always. Kodak was a
respected brand, an approachable brand, a friendly brand, a high-quality brand.
If it was important, it was worth paying a bit extra for Kodak because Kodak put
extra care into the products they made.

When Kodak started advertising "Cheap Ink" or servicing their products er-
ratically, or shipping products that too often failed right out of the box, the Kodak
brand became like an inflatable lifeboat that's launched with a number of very
small leaks. For a while, no one notices; eventually, everyone drowns. "Don't tell
me what you sell," Frank Zaffino, a Kodak senior manager told me one day, "tell
me about the relationship you have with your customers. Because that's the foundation for your business." When Kodak lost that, nothing else much mattered.

And so, on a mid-January day in 2010, I came into my office for the last time,
packed my few remaining things in cardboard boxes and carried them to the car.
I turned in my pass and logged out of my computer. That—and my office—
would be reassigned. I pulled out of the parking garage, watched the gate close
slowly behind me. I no longer had a pass to get back in. For the first time in almost forty-one years, I was no longer "Bob Gibbons from Kodak."

And we no longer had to live in the greater Los Angeles area. We could live
where we wanted to; but where was that?

# 43

# SEVEN MILES FROM THE OCEAN

WHEN I RETIRED, OUR PLAN WAS TO LIVE IN CALIFORNIA (two out of our three kids, and all our grandkid, live here) without a mortgage—and the way we hoped to do that was to "sell high" and "buy low."

That's difficult, if not impossible, in the same general area, so we began looking outside of the Thousand Oaks area where we lived. When Emily was going to the University of San Diego, and we drove her back and forth, I had found that when I got south of LAX, my heart-rate went down, so we began looking in that general area—north of San Diego. We sold our Thousand Oaks home in two days for the full asking price—almost double what we paid for it—and ended up buying a newly-built house in Oceanside.

Someone gave us a rule of thumb: in southern California, the summer temperature rises one degree for every mile from the ocean. We live seven miles from the beach; the weather is very nice all year around.

If we had built in a town like ours in the Midwest, we'd live on a street named for a tree or a president—or maybe one with just a number, like First or Second or Third. And there wouldn't be a street with the same name somewhere else in town. But here, we live on Sagewood Drive and less than a half-mile away is another Sagewood Drive—and they're not connected. We live between College Blvd. and Melrose Drive and, a few miles away, there's another College Blvd. and Melrose Drive—and they're entirely different streets. The roads here, I often tell people, were named by morons and idiots.

New houses need a lot more work—we discovered that in the first house we built back in Rochester—but in California, we've found that competence is not always a part of the job. Our landscape contractor told us it would take three-weeks to put in our lawn, shrubs, and walkways. His crew started the week after Thanksgiving—and weren't finished until sometime after the next Easter. The person we hired to seal our tile grout showed up without any equipment—or even a battery for his phone—and asked if I had any he could borrow. When we left our house painter alone for a few hours while we ran errands, we came home to find him asleep in our bed.

When San Diego Gas and Electric Company showed up to turn on the meter and the gas—as required before we moved in—they asked if I had a ladder they could borrow because their company doesn't furnish them. And then, in turning on the gas, they caused a leak, which they apparently didn't smell—and left. When we called them back to return and fix it, the dispatcher said, "when you call with a problem, always say that you hear a hissing sound. That makes us very nervous. We send someone out immediately."

When we needed some additional electrical work done, we hired Jay, who came on the recommendation of Eric, the construction foreman for our builder. "Jay's our attic rat," Eric said, "and a bit of a character." That was an understatement.

Jay lived with his dogs in a "tack shed" (where gear for horses is kept) on a farm. He was supposed to come over on a Saturday but didn't because he "didn't feel like it." When he did show up, he looked at the job—and told us what to buy. He had no money to buy anything himself, so he waited while I went to Home Depot. But he was good, fast, and had an uncanny ability to find studs behind walls. He'd just tap, listen, and poke his drill through the wallboard—and he was right every time. I asked him how he did that. It turns out, he was a demolitions expert in the Navy. "You get over in Iran," he said, "and you need to find those IEDs—those bombs they hide in the walls—you either learn how to get really good, really fast, or you learn how to be really dead."

When we found that our hard water was ruining our dishwasher, we decided to buy a soft water system—and got an estimate from Costco to install one for $4,500. That seemed expensive, so I checked with Ted, our neighbor, who "knows where to buy." Ted asked, "Why don't you buy your system directly from Costco's supplier? I know them. I'll give you their number." When I did, they told me, "we'll install one of the units we put on the floor of Costco. It's never been used but we can't sell it as new." The cost, fully installed, was $1,600.

Every once in a while, we find someone really competent—like Scott, who stepped in when our previous landscaper couldn't solve our problems. Scott is so talented and diligent that he's also since become a friend. And as I told my dentist, "Sometimes, I expect to see a pool or a pond in here because I think you walk on water. And not just shallow water." So there are people who know what they're doing, but so much else is "California crapsmanship."

I've gotten involved with our homeowners' association—initially to discourage them from raising our monthly dues—and it keeps me active in the community and helps me to know my neighbors. In the eight years we've been there, some houses are already on their second owner—and at least one person has passed away. One neighbor may meet the definition of "psychotic schizophrenic;" she tore out her sprinkler control box because she was sure people were listening to her through her in-ground lawn watering system. But according to online estimates, our house is already worth nearly twice what we paid for it. If we did move, we'd like to be in a community with a pool—and have a flat lot with a view—but we're not sure where we'd like to go—or if we could afford it—so we're staying here for now.

The house is a little big for Jeanne and me, but it's great when we have a lot of company. When all the kids come home at Christmas time, there is room for all of them to sleep and when we put up an extra table in the living-dining room, we can feed everyone—including our kids, their kids, and even our nephew Chris and Gretchen and their kids, who often join us.

In the front of the house, I have an office with a window that looks across the street to a forever wild area so there's enough peace and privacy here. The San Diego area is a nice place to live. Medical care is first-rate. The zoo and the wild animal park are both world class, and we have a membership in each, which gives us unlimited personal passes. Balboa Park has several interesting museums, which are free to county residents one day a month. The airport is smaller, warmer, and much easier to use than LAX. The ocean is just seven miles away, and stores, restaurants, and movie theaters are nearby..

Of course, there's a downside (or three) to the state: Wildfires are a frightening reality during dry seasons, earthquakes are always a threat, and the cost of water, gas, and other essentials make California an expensive place to live, but so far, so good. This is the fourth home we've purchased—two in Rochester and two in California—and while it may or may not be our last, it's a nice place to live while being retired and not looking for work.

# 44

# NOT LOOKING FOR WORK

J EANNE SAYS: "YOU ALWAYS SEEM HAPPIER WHEN YOU'RE WRITING." I agree. Early on, I discovered there's only one way to get better at writing—write a lot and throw the bad stuff away. Whatever my job at Kodak, I tried to write every day—during work, and also sometimes after.

When I was writing movies as a member of Kodak's motion picture group, other managers would ask mine to let me write their projects—sales meetings, scripts for business presentations, or copy for brochures. He often refused; I was too busy, he said. So, I suggested that those managers hire a local agency—who would, in turn, hire me. I had arrangements with several; I'd freelance after hours on the project—and my boss would never know.

We had young children at the time; they were prone to ear infections and Kodak's medical plan didn't cover everything. The extra money helped. And so, I wrote a variety of scripts—including a movie on punch press safety, without ever seeing a punch press. One year, I took off three days from Kodak to write an entire sales meeting for an elevator company; and with the money, we paid cash for new Chevrolet Malibu station wagon.

I worked a lot with a local agency called Imagesmith where we once bid on producing a large presentation for a local television station. When I turned in my estimate, the station manager said, "I can get this work done much cheaper." I agreed. "In fact," I told him, "if you want the names of cheaper writers to call, I can give them to you. But just remember, you're paying them to learn on the job. I've done this; I know how to do it." He decided to pay me.

Freelance work was sporadic, but it paid well. I decided to charge fifty dollars for each "fully-approved minute" of script—and I estimated it would take me two hours of writing the various drafts to produce that. All changes were included in my price—so if I got everything right on the first draft, I could make some money; if it took me several drafts, I could get some experience.

At one point, the largest advertising agency in Rochester, Rumrill-Hoyt, offered to hire me. They asked me to send them my resume. I said I didn't have one and had no plans to write one. I said, "A resume will prove little about my ability to write what you need—because you won't be hiring me to write resumes. You'll want me to write ads or brochures or press releases or presentations. Why don't you just send me an assignment and I'll write it for you for free. Then, you can judge that." They said they couldn't consider me without a resume—and that was that.

For the nation's bicentennial in Rochester, the area across from Kodak Office where I worked was being developed as a pedestrian area along the banks of the Genesee River. I suggested a nightly slide show on Rochester's history—to be projected across the river and onto the stone cliffs on the other side. Kodak agreed to pay for the show, and I wrote it. For images, we used giant "lantern slides" with an arc projector mounted on the west bank of the river.

One time, when Mary Moore was my secretary at Kodak, I told her: "I think that God must have a soft spot in his heart for children, idiots, and scriptwriters." "Bob," Mary said, "you're being redundant."

When I moved to Hollywood, I began writing movie reviews, so it was probably only a matter of time before I was asked to write the screenplay for a movie. That happened when Lorette Bayle—one of our Kodak sales representatives and an experienced documentary director who wanted to get into narrative films—asked me to look at a script she had written. She had the rights to produce a short movie based on a beloved children's book called *The Bake Shop Ghost,* but the book's author had to approve the script before Lorette shot anything. She had asked two different screenwriters to write a script; both scripts were rejected. So Lorette had tried writing one herself and she wanted my opinion before she sent it to the book's author, Jacqueline Ogburn.

I read the script and had a lot of questions, so many that Lorette asked me if I would take a shot at rewriting it. When I told Jeanne about it, she said, "Oh, you have to do it." I trust her judgment; plus, I've come to realize that whenever a female member of my family suggests that I do something, I'm almost always better off if I agree. I asked Lorette to see the book and when I read it, I realized the problem: there was a hole in the story that needed to be filled in for the movie to work: why did the main character stay in the bake shop when others had left? The book never answered that question: I thought I knew.

So I set about writing the script with three goals: to answer the question; to add more humor to the telling; and to provide more special moments of human emotion along the way. Lorette and Jackie Ogburn loved the script. "I knew I had problems, but I didn't need to solve them for the book. You solved them for the movie," Jackie told me during the shoot. I was very happy with the finished movie; it's a short movie—about seventeen minutes—and stars the late—and wonderful— Kathryn Joosten. *The Bake Shop Ghost* has been shown at several film festivals— where it was often chosen "audience favorite." At some of them, I introduced the movie and answered questions from the crowd. The movie is on YouTube.

When I retired, I figured that I would see where my writing would take me. I was not looking for work when, two months after I left Kodak, Eric Rodli called. I had worked for him when he was a senior manager at Kodak; now he'd been hired to start a new 3D theatrical business for Panavision, a major camera system supplier in Hollywood. The company had developed an innovative projection system—it worked with film and digital and on a white or silver screen— they wanted to introduce at an upcoming industry convention and Eric asked me to "figure out what communications materials we need—and what you'd charge to write them."

When I called him back with my answers, he said: "Wow, your prices are pretty expensive." So, I offered him a different deal: "How about if I write every-thing for free? If you don't think it's exactly what you need, we'll throw it away and you'll owe me nothing. But, if you do agree it's what you need, then you pay my going rate." Eric said he'd "feel bad," if I did all that work, and it was thrown away. I said, *I'd* feel bad if he tried to introduce the new system without having those materials to market it. "And frankly," I said, "I'm at an age where I'd rather have you feel bad."

We agreed. I did the work; he paid me. Panavision introduced the system—and I worked as the head of marketing and communications for Eric and with a small team of people to help seat Panavision's new system in the marketplace. Our team included Sean Lohan and Drena Rogers—both former members of the Kodak Digital Cinema team with whom I loved working. Sean was steady, solid, well-known and highly respected in the industry; he opened doors for us that would have been closed to anyone else. And Drena, as head of sales, was the prototypical enthusiast. When she was explaining something to me, I was often so quiet, she'd ask: "Do you understand?" "You're an extrovert," I told her; "ex-troverts explain things to each other. I'm an introvert; introverts explain them to themselves." Sometimes that took me longer than others.

Over the next fifteen months, I wrote more than one hundred documents—including ads and customer letters, press releases and presentations, marketing strategies and business plans, explanations of our technology and interviews with several members of management. The last thing I wrote was the strategy for Pan-avision to exit the business. They recognized they couldn't be the market leader and so they decided to leave.

I wasn't looking for work when another former Kodak colleague, Tim Knapp found me, and I began freelancing for an archival film scanning and restoration company called Reflex Technologies. Their business was based on a unique film scanner that had been designed and built by a filmmaker in Alaska who used, among other parts, the moonroof from a Cadillac Escalade. It was financed by a member of the Honda family.

Tim Knapp introduced me around and Travis Honda invited me to his home in Las Vegas where he lived near Celine Dion and owned a car service using vintage cars. When he described his business plan to me, I suggested it made no sense. Fortunately, he trusted Tim to know the industry—and when they relocated their business to the Los Angeles area, I began working with them on a freelance basis, writing all their advertising and other materials for major industry conventions.

When Tim decided to finally leave the company, my work for them also stopped. And that was that; until Bob Sunshine, the publisher of *Film Journal*, one of the two leading publications in the exhibition industry, asked me at an industry convention: "How would you like to write for us?" I told him I'd like to write for anyone who agreed to pay me. He promised they'd do that.

Every month, for the next eighteen months, I wrote one—and sometimes two—feature length articles for *Film Journal*. Most were based on me talking to several executives in the industry and putting their points of view together in a series of roundtable discussions on key topics—seating, ticketing, audience demographics, and others—using the technique I'd originally used to write my master's thesis. But I also wrote on the history of the cinema, Canadian film pioneers, and the return of theatres to Saudi Arabia. And they always paid me.

And then, around the time *Film Journal* was sold to its rival publication *Box Office* and that reduced their need for freelancers, Doug Pileri called. Doug and I had worked together at Kodak, before he went on to other companies, including Thompson/RCA and IBM. He'd call me from time to time and I'd do a bit of writing for him—as a friend. A speech I wrote—and he delivered—called "How to Outwit the Future" put him on the cover of *CIO magazine* and so, when he got a new job in Washington, he called to ask if I could help him out of a communications dilemma.

He had been hired as the Executive Vice President of Freedom Partners; a political organization being funded by the Koch Brothers. Doug's job was to introduce business metrics by which political achievements could be measured— and he was caught in a quandary with one of their groups called *Generation Opportunity* which dealt with millennials. GenOpp wanted his approval to e-publish an article with the headline: "Our generation is fucked." Doug told them no. They told him, "That's the way our generation talks," Doug was apoplectic; "How do I answer *that*?" he asked me.

I said I'd do a bit of noodling around and call him back. "On their website," I said on my return call, "is a blog with the headline, 'There's great hope for our generation.' So, you need to ask them, which is the real situation *they believe* our generation finds itself in? What's their point of view? What does the GenOpp brand stand for?"

When Doug suggested they didn't know, he asked if I could help. "Sure," I said, "but not for free." Sometime before, a friend and business coach Randy Block, whom I'd first met in high school, explained to me about charging for information. Randy said, "in the Internet world, information is free. If people don't get it from you, they'll get it from someone else. But there is a difference between providing information—and helping them to use information. For example, I have a lot of free information on my LinkedIn page; but if you want me to teach you how to apply it, that's where money comes in."

When Doug and I agreed on a contract, I began flying back and forth to Washington to teach branding to *Generation Opportunity* and to other members of the Freedom Partners network, including *Libre, Cause of Action,* and others. I described a brand as much more than a mark or symbol, a logo, or a tagline. I told them that the branding process is all about applying *clarity, connectivity*, and *consistency* in all thinking, working and communications. It becomes your GPS, I said, and as you begin to use it, it should begin to make small—but visible and eventually measurable—differences in what you do, what others see and say, and the results you achieve—everywhere.

I told lots of personal stories of my experience with the brands I worked with. I had them laughing and copying things off the screen. Afterwards, the president of *Generation Opportunity* told me, "even people who usually refuse to come to meetings said they enjoy coming to yours. And they all said they learned something." For my initial assignment, I asked each member—on an individual basis—to write an obituary for their organization—what was it trying to do, who were its allies, what were its proudest achievements, and so forth?

The differences I found were fundamental. "Consider," I told them in a subsequent meeting, "listening to a marching band in which only a few of the musicians are playing from the same sheet of music. Imagine what you'd hear . . ."

I ended up writing more than fifty different presentations to explain the nuances of branding and the fundamentals of communications to guide each organization through a process of understanding their brand and using it effectively. I also tried to teach them what I knew about other aspects of communications and marketing—how to maximize presence at a trade show, how to participate on a panel most effectively, how to evaluate sponsorships, how to structure a communications organization, and other topics.

After every session, I set aside an hour in an empty office where I'd answer any question on any topic where I had expertise. One young woman who was always quiet, but who seemed very bright, came in to ask me how to set up partnerships with other organizations and I helped her work out a plan to do that. "You changed her career—and maybe her life," her manager told me.

Although that assignment ended in 2016 when Freedom Partners slimmed down and let most of its central staff—including Doug Pileri and me—go, I enjoyed the teaching part of the experience so well, I thought I might like to do more. But maybe not. For one thing—I like to use humor that's not always understood.

Many years before in my Kodak career, I was teaching in the company's newly built Marketing Education Center, several miles from its downtown headquarters. They invited me to teach presentation writing to Kodak customers—students who came there to learn how to better use Kodak slides and slide projectors to give impact to their speeches. In one of my courses, I referred to MEC as "Kodak's rural home for the slow." Unfortunately, the manager of MEC was in the audience that day and I didn't teach many courses after that.

Plus, as Jeanne told me more than once, "You have no patience with people who don't understand things quickly. You might get very frustrated trying to be a teacher." She's probably right.

Probably what I really like is preparing the lessons—the writing part of the job.

From time to time, I get calls from younger people who've worked with me in the past and may have some work for me in the future. I always express enthusiasm—as Doug once said, "you're an orthogonal thinker, but you're an honest person. If you can help someone solve their communications problem, you will; but if you can't, you'll tell them that right up front." But my optimism always comes with a note of caution: "I've been away from the industry so long," I tell them, "that I may not understand the nuances of what your audience needs to hear."

Although I'd be the first to admit I don't understand or use social media, but in 2015, *LA Film Reviews*, an on-line blog, bought and posted hundreds of my short-form movie reviews; and in 2017, I suddenly became a very active writer for another blog. The Class of '69 blog was started by John Hickey, a classmate at Notre Dame, who realized—at that time—that our fiftieth reunion was fast approaching. We had a large class—more than fifteen hundred students—and he thought we'd be more likely to attend our reunion—and have more fun during it—if we knew each other a bit better.

John had a mailing list of about nine hundred members of the class; he sent each of us a few questions for a "take home interview" to tell him about our life since graduation. I was one of those who responded—and that started a continuing relationship with John. To date, I've posted more than fifty stories—ranging from some of my adventures on campus, to interviews with classmates who are doctors working during the pandemic; and from a mock interview with Martin Sheen as President Jed Bartlet from the *West Wing*, to an ongoing curriculum for the Socially Distant Learning Academy, a school that teaches such vital online skills as "How to Boil Water in Twelve Steps" and "How to Discuss a Book You've Never Read."

In 2019, in collaboration with John and two other classmates, Dave Sim and Gary Campana, I wrote a book commemorating the lives of our classmates; when that was well received, John, Dave, and I wrote another. Copies of both books were purchased by classmates, are in Notre Dame archives, and in the Library of Congress. "The class of 1969," alumni director Dolly Duffy said, "is the best documented class in Notre Dame history." Both books gave me the opportunity to tell stories—and I love doing that.

Once, in my Kodak days, I worked with a man named Don Nibbelink. Don was arguably one of the best storytellers and when he retired, I asked if he might come back to Kodak and teach 'speaker coaching?' At the time, I felt that too many great company speeches had at least one thing in common with great meals: they turned to crap in the end. Don considered my offer and then turned it down. "In my retirement," he said, "I've decided that I'm only going to do things that are fun. And I'm not sure that would be."

I agree with that philosophy; for me, it's fun to write. That's why I'm always happiest when I have some writing to look forward to doing every day; I especially love writing that solves a business problem, or tells a story, or enables me to take a different approach to a subject different from what I wrote about the day before.

But meanwhile, I'm not looking for work.

# 45

# STORIES FROM THE AIR

'VE NEVER HAD A FULL-TIME JOB that didn't require me to fly—yet I've always been nervous in the air. Through countless flights around the United States, to Japan and Europe, I've found that I like a window seat (so I can see what's going on outside) up over the wings (where things seem most stable), a storm-free route with clouds off in a distance, and a pilot who talks to us who've come along for the ride. But I want to be reassured, not further frightened.

We were flying into Munich one night when the pilot came over the intercom. We were on Lufthansa, so he may have been doing his best to translate German to English, but this is what he said. "The Munich airport is telling us that they are experiencing heavy ice and snow. This is not good. But this is good enough for us."

And then there was the time I was flying into Washington, D.C., on a little commuter airplane that was really bouncing all over the sky. The pilot came on and said: "Tower is telling us there is a worse storm ahead and they wanted us to go around it . . . but we talked them out of that."

Kodak sent me to Japan to prepare a speech for our CEO to list the company on the Tokyo Exchange and I was coming out of Tokyo on a United night flight back to Seattle when we hit a typhoon off the coast of Russia. I was flying business class and had an empty seat next to me so one of the stewards came over and sat down. "Do you remember," he asked me, "reading about the flight out of Japan where one of the engines caught fire?" I said that I did. "Well," he said, "if you go back in coach and look out, you can still see the scorch marks on the side of the fuselage." "This plane?" I asked. "This aircraft," he said.

There were other times, especially flying into Denver—or on a very rainy night coming into Atlanta—when I've been tempted to ask the pilot: "Did you land this thing—or were we shot down?"

I took my first flight on a bright sunny Friday, April 8, 1966 when Jim Panehal's father drove Jim, Tom O'Brien and me to the Cleveland airport to fly to St. Petersburg, Florida. I was a Notre Dame freshman and Tom had invited Jim and me to stay with his family for Easter vacation. Flying was fun in those days; it was easy to get on board, there was more room between the seats, it was an upscale way of travelling. Two bags always flew free; sometimes three or four were no problem. There were no weight limits on bags or checkpoints for passengers. Most people dressed up when they flew. And when you were meeting someone who was flying in, you went right up to the gate, and sometimes even out on the tarmac, to greet them.

Most airlines had "student stand-by" tickets that didn't guarantee a seat—although one was generally available—but were half the cost of a regular ticket. Roundtrip from Rochester to Notre Dame—at standby rates—was sixty-six dollars, twice the cost of a train.

Early in sophomore year, I flew up to a dance at Marygrove College in Detroit. On the flight back to Notre Dame on that Sunday night, we had just gotten airborne, and I was dozing off when there was a loud "bang," the lights went off, and the plane went into a dive. The pilot got everything under control—and never explained what happened–but I decided it may have been caused by me falling asleep. Later, I also found that turbulence was often caused by me ordering a drink on an airplane.

My first business flight was for Kodak; early in the morning of April 27, 1972,

Richard Young and I flew from Rochester to Mobile, Alabama to make a movie for and about *America's Junior Miss*. My last business flight was in May 2015 when I flew home from Washington, DC after concluding my assignment with Freedom Partners. My longest flight was from Rochester to Tokyo Japan; my most uncomfortable one was from Topeka Kansas to Ramstein Germany, sitting in the web seating of a C-141 Starlifter with no room to move and no window to look out of. Thereafter, I'd always insist on having a window seat.

That insistence was put to the test one day in Heathrow airport in London when I was randomly selected to "step out of line so we can hand-search your luggage." When I complied, the agent told me, "as a reward, we've given you a free upgrade to first class flying back across the Atlantic." I thanked her and then said, "as long as it's a widow seat." She said, they only had an aisle available. "In that case," I said, "I'd like my coach seat back." She wasn't sure if she could do that; no one had ever wanted that before. But she found she could—and I flew home coach class—in a window seat.

I was flying first class into Los Angeles one day when the late comedian Milton Berle was on the plane. At one point, he got up and went to toilet, which was right behind the cockpit. While he was in there, we hit a bit of turbulence; as he came out, he turned to all of us and said in a loud voice: "Well, I tried to help, but the pilot said he didn't need it."

Heading off to a Kodak marketing meeting in Europe, I flew out of New York City to Rome on Air Italia—on a flight filled with lots of older Italian women. As they were settling in before the plane took off, they must have taken off their shoes to get more comfortable. Because as the plane lifted into the air, there was a horrible rumbling sound as all their shoes came tumbling down the aisles.

Las Vegas airport can be a crowded place for private aircraft; each needs to leave promptly at its scheduled time. We discovered that one day sitting on the Kodak jet out on the runway, ready to take off, with the cabin fully pressurized— when our pilot came back to tell us, "Another aircraft saw something hanging from our nose cone. We need to take a very quick look so we don't lose our place in line. We're just going to pop the doors . . ." Whoa Nellie—as they say.

Letting out all that pressure suddenly did awful things to our ears.

I hate flying on crowded planes, but I was on one, sitting in the last row, heading out of Chicago for Los Angeles with one open middle seat next to me. . . when a burly guy came walking down the aisle and I knew where he was going to end up. I also don't talk much on planes—and I knew he'd want to. "Hi," he said. "What business are you in?" I told him I worked for Kodak and was working with Disney Imagineers on EPCOT. "You and I are in the same business," he said. "We're entertainers."

As the flight got underway, he told me he was a singer and songwriter, and he was headed west with his raw tapes to mix in Los Angeles. He had those tracks on tapes he had with him in his bag, right there under the seat. *Would I like to listen to them?* He had an extra pair of headphones. And so I did—and had the most fascinating conversation. We talked about music, about adding new instruments, about changing the feel of a song. He was good, smart, and talented. I talked from a listener's point of view; I love music, don't fully understand how it's created but have some ideas. I wish I'd recognize him if I saw him again; I wish I even knew his name. Maybe he's famous today. Maybe some ideas I suggested made a difference in his music. I doubt it. But it was one of my most favorite flights.

When Kodak hired actor Lorne Greene to portray George Washington in a bicentennial movie I wrote for Kodak, Richard Young and I flew Pilgrim Airways to meet Lorne at his summer home on Long Island. Pilgrim flew de Havillands, old World War II aircraft that looked like something out of the 1939 movie, *Casablanca*. The plane held eighteen people, there was no stewardess; "*Welcome to Pilgrim Airways,*" the pilot said as we taxied down the runway and lifted off into the sky. "*We hope you enjoy the ride.*" There was no door between the passenger compartment and the cockpit, so I could watch what was going on. As we traveled between the clouds up over Long Island Sound, the co-pilot seemed to be looking at an Auto Club map while the pilot was smoking a cigarette . . . and flicking the ashes out an open window.

Richard and I were in New Orleans to film Allen Emsminger of the National Park Service for the *Mississippi River* film when he suggested we go flying over the bayous of southern Louisiana. We went to the airport and got into a four-seater with pilot Buck Rogers who taxied us out to the end of the runways, talked to the tower, and then shut down all communications. "Those people drive me nuts," he said. We flew over the marshy lands with houses—shacks, really—built on stilts, accessible only by boat. "Looks dangerous," I said. "People living here think it's more dangerous crossing city streets," Allen said. "Let's have some fun." And with that, Buck put the plane into a series of dives as we chased alligators through the water.

The best airline I've ever flown back from Europe was Scandinavian Airlines. In 1988, I flew SAS out of Stuttgart for New York City. When I checked in, the woman at the SAS desk probably noticed my briefcase and asked: "Are you traveling for business?" I said I was. "What will you be doing during the flight?" she wanted to know. I told her I had some reports to write on some meetings I had in Germany. "It will be easier for you to do that if you are sitting someplace quiet," she said. "I will move your window seat to a quieter part of the airplane."

She did and we took off. When we got up over Greenland, the pilot came on the intercom. "It's a beautiful clear day down below," he said, "let's go down and have a look." With that, he took the plane down and began narrating a tour of Greenland. He pointed out some of the features of the island, showed us where the Allies had their bases in World War II. Then he took the plane up and westward over the ocean.

But that was an anomaly. Flying is too often a hassle today.

Yet, sometimes, when the air is smooth, the day is sunny, and we're above mountaintops poking through the clouds, or we're coming into a city at night that looks like a giant circuit board stretched out in the distance, or I'm up over some country in Europe looking down on fields that seem to have been manicured, I recognize that I'm enjoying a perspective that simply wasn't available just three or four generations ago. . .and I realize this is one more wonderful experience I've been able to have along the way.

# 46

# KNOWING WHEN TO LEAVE

'VE LONG BELIEVED THAT KNOWING WHEN TO LEAVE is one of the great secrets of a happy life. I'm fortunate that I didn't have an early check-out, but when I do, I want to go quickly, painlessly, silently, without suffering on my part or on the part of others. I hope it's in the night after I've spent a day making people happy with something I did for them—and I hope it's at a time when I'm feeling good about what's going on.

But before that happens—and while I still have command of the keyboard, I have a few concluding thoughts to share—some by way of summary, others because they really didn't fit anywhere else.

One thing that may be obvious to those who know me: I don't have a bucket list. I've largely gone where I wanted to go, done what I wanted to do, said what I wanted to say. If no one is standing by when I exit for the final time, I'll be OK with that. There are no amends I want to make. I'm hoping that those I love, know how I feel about them; I know how they feel about me. I can't imagine my life without Jeanne and the kids—and those others who've made a difference along the way.

Who would have thought that a boy from Rochester would have adventures like I've had? I've been in forty-seven of the fifty states—including Alaska and Hawaii—and in Japan and multiple counties in Europe. I've seen castles and sat with CEOs. I've flown in a corporate jet to a secret meeting in Texas; in a small airplane, I've chased alligators in the swamps south of New Orleans. And in walks around the neighborhood, I've learned a lot from a small curious dog

I've been underground at Disneyland—and worked with Disney Imagineers to bring Figment to life. I've spent an evening talking with Bob Newhart, been to the Oscars and the EMMY awards several times, sat with movie stars at premieres, followed cowboys on a cattle drive in Wyoming, won a short story writing contest and wrote a movie that played in film festivals across the world.

And—most extraordinary of all—in a hospital in Rochester NY, I watched the miracle of our three children being born. Of all the titles I've had, the one I'm proudest of—is "dad." "Grandpa" runs a close second.

There are some things I've never done that many people would consider normal. I've never ridden a horse (although I did sit on one, petrified, when I was young); I never got up on water skies (although I tried very hard one Sunday afternoon); I never drove a motorcycle by myself (although I rode on the back of a small one for almost sixty miles). I never owned a boat or a cottage; I never drove a truck; I don't know how to create an Excel spreadsheet or do any home repairs that involve plumbing or electricity.

But I don't think I've missed out on anything important; in fact, I think I have been fortunate far beyond what I could ever have hoped to achieve—and met some remarkable people who helped me become who I became along the way. Besides my family, I can't imagine Army days without Patrick O'Dell; I couldn't have had a better first girlfriend than Paula Klos; wouldn't have found my talent without Richard Young; but there were so many others who contributed to my life in ways great and small. I trust they know they're in my heart, even if I don't name their names.

Although I've had good friends, I'm also happy being alone, comfortable being by myself; I like to sit and think—and I try to read and write a bit every day. I find that reading primes my writing pump—and I alternate between reading fiction and non-fiction—mostly between murder mysteries and biographies. I've never read most of the classics—and have no intention to. One of my favorite activities is scouting used bookstores, although I will only buy books in very good condition. I would never harm children, small animals, or books. Most years I read more than a book a week, depending what else is going on. I try to keep track of what's being published. But I don't keep books I've read. When I finish, I give them away—most often to the library.

But since my drumming days, I've always loved music, mostly music of the fifties and sixties, and I have a few hundred CDs of music of that era—after getting rid of hundreds more. I dumped my favorite songs into my computer. And, at one point, I made a Playlist of My Life—ninety-three songs that are special to me, music that brings back memories of what was going on in my life at the time. When I put them in chronological order, I found that only about a third were from my youth, but they include instrumentals and vocals; the list starts with Artie Shaw's "Begin the Beguine" and (so far) concludes with "Folsom Prison Blues" by Tommy Emmanuel. I keep the list in my computer; I'd like to get the list up to a hundred songs.

I'm an introvert; others sometimes find me shy. The first time I gave a speech, I said, "In just a few moments, there's going to be a horrible smell in this room and it's going to be coming from the seat of my pants," but when that didn't happen, I found I enjoyed public speaking—especially if I'd written the script. I looked for opportunities to do more of it.

I've never liked games or contests. If I had a choice between working out in a gym or having a root canal, it would be a difficult decision. I mostly hate very large gatherings—although I enjoy dinners with family and a few friends. I like people, but I don't need to be with them always. I told my boss once that I didn't attend office parties because I didn't want everyone I worked with to get the wrong idea that I liked to be around them any more than I had to.

I can't work if there is noise in the background. My home office is far away from the family room. In all the hotel rooms I've stayed in, I could count on one hand the number of times I've turned on a television set. I really like the quiet.

Email makes it easy to stay in touch with friends around the world—most of mine are here in the states, but also in Canada, Europe and Australia—and I do.

I have a couple hundred on the list to whom I send movie reviews—and that's enabled me to connect with old friends I thought I'd lost forever. But I'm not on social media because I don't need to know everything going on in their lives—and I'm sure they don't want to know what's going on I mine.

But in addition to my *can'ts* and *won'ts*, I also have several *needs* and *wants* and *likes*. Here's what's important:

*Common sense*, I suppose, is number one. If something doesn't make common sense, I find other explanations worthless. In a Department of Motor Vehicles office in Rochester, the clerk asked me the gross weight of my car when I was reregistering my vehicle. I told her, mine was a reregistration—and that the information she needed was already in her computer; she insisted I tell her the weight. "I'm OK with a little stupidity," I said, "but gross stupidity drives me crazy." I found that stupidity makes me crazy everywhere, not just at the DMV.

*Creativity* is important. I try to look at things from a different point of view—and am attracted to others who do also. A good friend—and very talented photographer—Ric Sorgel told me once that, after taking several courses, he concluded that the most creative person is a five-year-old kid. "At that age, you don't know what's not possible and you aren't yet copying anyone else," Ric said. "And I think of you, Bob, as a five-year-old."

I value a *willingness to appear dumb*. "My talent," I tell people, "is portable ignorance. I take it everywhere. I use it to ask questions others are afraid to ask and listen carefully to the answers. It's the best way I've found to learn." Sometimes when I ask people to explain things that others may consider obvious, I find that no one understands them clearly after all—they were just afraid to ask.

I love *simplicity*. When I interviewed John Ankeny, the communications manager for Levi Strauss, I asked him to write his main job responsibility on a matchbook cover. John wrote: *I'm the protector of our brand*. "If you have an idea that will make us millions but compromise our brand, I'll throw you out of here," he said.

I value *respect*. I want to be respected for what I know and trusted for what I can do. I had worked closely and often with Phil Samper, a member of Kodak's Office of the CEO, when he got a new staff assistant, Ron, who told me: "you'll no longer deal with Phil, you'll deal through me." "I need direct access," I told Ron, "and if you prevent that, there could be disconnects that make me look bad. But if those happen, I will make you look like an absolute idiot." I continued to deal directly with Phil, but I kept Ron informed. Respect works both ways.

I love *humor.* I don't tell jokes; I try to find something gently humorous based on a shared experience—or point of view. If I can get others to laugh, I can get them on my side—and reassure them I'm on theirs. I once asked Bob Newhart if he used 'blue humor.' "I don't," he said, "because that's too easy. I think I'm better than that." Adding a four-letter word doesn't automatically add humor.

I like to tell *stories with a purpose.* When I was talking to marketing students at San Diego State University, I told them about the night I was in Walmart with my sister who wanted to buy a digital camera. She wanted to know the differences among those made by Canon and those made by Sony, Nikon, even Samsung.

We waited until the head of the camera department had time to help us— but when we asked him the most basic questions, the only thing I knew for sure was: *He didn't know the first thing about cameras.*

You may tell me: Well, Walmart doesn't pay as well as other companies. But I don't buy that. People who equate the effort they'll expend to the pay they receive are using the wrong measure. Money is among the worst measures of success. Energy and enthusiasm and personal initiative are the keys to every job. You either have those qualities—I told the marketing students—or you don't. People with them attract more customers—and better future jobs.

I like people with the *right values.* Times change; everything evolves, but Sam, the piano player in the 1939 movie, *Casablanca,* got it exactly right when he sang, "the fundamental things apply as time goes by . . ." and those fundamental things are values. When I had the opportunity to promote people at Kodak, I looked for those with the right values. Skills can be learned; when times got tough and difficult decisions had to be made, I wanted to be working with those who shared my values.

*Religion* also remains important to me. Growing up without a dad around, I found praying to be a comforting conversation with a God I depended on to help me sort things out—and he has. I value St. Joseph and the Holy Spirit as mentors, and I find Sunday mass and holy communion to be nourishing. But I've come to recognize that having faith is a bit like having talent; both are sometimes hard to explain. You either have them or you don't, but if you do, it's good to practice them.

I don't have many role models, but one man I highly respect is Father Theodore Hesburgh, who was President of the University of Notre Dame for thirty-five years, including the four years I was there. He passed away in 2015, after a life spent bringing great change to his university, his country, and his world. In his autobiography, *God, County, Notre Dame*, he wrote: "When I have said or done something, it's over; I put my worries aside. I say my prayers and I go to sleep."

In some ways, I've tried to follow that advice: do the best I can—and move on. And, as a result, I've been able to enjoy the happiest life I could never imagine. I've seen and done so many wonderful things since those days growing up on Oriole Street. But sometimes I wonder if my favorite stories are waiting to begin tomorrow.

## About the Author

Born the eldest of four children, Bob Gibbons grew up in Rochester, New York. After graduating from the University of Notre Dame with a degree in Modern Languages, he joined Eastman Kodak Company before being drafted into the military. As an army journalist, he was stationed at Fort Riley, Kansas, and Fort Bragg, North Carolina, winning three CONARC Copy Desk Awards, the highest recognition given for army journalism.

Returning to Kodak, he began a forty-year career during which he held a variety of leadership positions—mostly involving writing—in Rochester and Hollywood. Kodak sent him to the Newhouse School at Syracuse University to earn an M.S. in Advertising.

In retirement, Bob has provided communications for Panavision 3D Systems, Reflex Technologies, and *Film Journal,* as well as brand coaching for Freedom Partners. He wrote the screenplay for *The Bake Shop Ghost*, co-authored two books for Notre Dame, and regularly writes movie reviews and a humorous curriculum for the fictional Socially Distant Learning Academy on the Notre Dame Class of 69 blog.

Bob and his wife Jeanne live in Oceanside, California. They are parents to three children and grandparents to five.

Every day, he tries to spend some time writing.

CPSIA information can be obtained
at www.ICGtesting.com
Printed in the USA
BVHW041511120722
641927BV00010BA/486